BULL'S-EYES
and
MISFIRES

*50 People Whose Obscure Efforts Shaped
the American Civil War*

CLINT JOHNSON

Rutledge Hill Press™
Nashville, Tennessee

A Division of Thomas Nelson Publisher, Inc.
www.ThomasNelson.com

Published by Rutledge Hill Press, a Division of Thomas Nelson, Inc., P.O. Box 141000, Nashville, Tennessee, 37214.

Photos on pages 3, 48 & 176 courtesy of the U.S. Army Military History Institute.
Photos on pages 8, 18, 23, 28, 33, 38, 43, 53, 59, 64, 85, 91, 97, 102, 108, 119, 125, 130, 137, 172, 181, 187, 211, 225, 234, 245 & 254 courtesy of the Massachussetts Commandery Military Order of the Loyal Legion and U.S. Army Military History Institute.
Photo on page 13 courtesy of the Maryland Historical Society.
Photos on pages 70, 114, 143, 148, 153, 157, 162, 192, 197, 201 & 250 courtesy of the Virginia Historical Society.
Photo on page 75 courtesy of the Civil War Library and Museum.
Photo on page 80 courtesy of the National Archives.
Photos on pages 167, 206, 216 & 240 courtesy of the Museum of the Confederacy.
Photo on page 220 courtesy of private collection: C. Twiggs Myers.
Photo on page 229 courtesy of the Naval Historical Center.

Library of Congress Cataloging-in-Publication Data

Johnson, Clint, 1953-
  Bull's-eyes and misfires : 50 obscure people whose efforts shaped the American Civil War / Clint Johnson.
    p. cm.
  Includes bibliographical references (p.) and index.
  ISBN 1-55853-961-1
  1. United States—History—Civil War, 1861-1865—Anecdotes. 2. United States—History—Civil War, 1861-1865—Biography—Anecdotes. I. Title.
E655 .J673 2002
973.7'092'2—dc21   2002009976

Printed in the United States of America

02 03 04 05 06—5 4 3 2 1

CONTENTS

This book is dedicated to all my ancestors who fought in the War, whose varied experiences continue to drive my interest. There was the Florida sergeant who lost an arm at Fredericksburg, the Georgia lieutenant who spent two years in a prison camp at Johnson's Island, Ohio, the Georgia militia general who tried to stop Sherman at Griswoldville, the Alabama captain who fell mortally wounded at Chickamauga, and the Georgia cavalryman whose pension application reads: "addle-brained by the war."

They defended their homes, which was all the War was about to them.

ACKNOWLEDGMENTS

I WANT TO THANK ROD GRAGG, AUTHOR OF BOOKS SUCH as *Covered With Glory—The 26ᵗʰ North Carolina Infantry at the Battle of Gettysburg, Confederate Goliath, The Confederate Reader,* and other books. Rod helped me refine the idea of obscure people who had an impact on the War, and did some critiquing on the early draft.

I want to thank Larry Stone, founder of Rutledge Hill Press, for seeing the value in this idea. One of the problems Civil War writers face is looking for something that hasn't already been written. Larry recognized that this idea of focusing on these little known personalities had not yet been done.

I also want to thank Geoff Stone, my editor at Rutledge Hill, for refining the manuscript. Thank you Bryan Curtis for making everyone aware of this wonderful book and to the sales team for getting it in the bookstores.

Thanks goes to the staff at Forsyth County Public Library in Winston-Salem, North Carolina, for constantly sending away for inter-library loan books – volumes that were sometimes 100 years old – that I scoured looking for details on the lives of these people.

Thanks, too, to Jay Graybeal of the United States Military History Institute, Stephanie Jacobe of the Virginia Historical Society, Heather Milne of the Museum of the Confederacy, Megan Lynch of the Maryland Historical Society, and the staff of the U.S. Naval Institute for finding the bulk of the photos for this book. Special thanks also go to Russell K. Brown of Augusta, Georgia, for help finding a photo of

Marion Myers, and to C. Twiggs Myers of Sheffield, Massachusetts, for giving his permission to use that photo of his ancestor.

Finally, I have to thank my wife, Barbara, for putting up with Civil War reenacting, Civil War travel, and Civil War burials. If I go first, I have asked Barbara to scatter my ashes at the crest of Snodgrass Hill at the Chickamauga National Battlefield in northern Georgia.

Yes, I am sure scattering the ashes of a southerner in a National Military Park must be against some federal regulation, but we southerners don't always do what northerners ask us to do. I am hoping my Wisconsin-born southern-transplant wife respects my wishes despite some Yankee rule.

The reason I want to end up at Chickamauga is I had a great-great grandfather, Capt. Richard Newton Moore, who fell mortally wounded leading his company of Hilliard's Legion from Alabama up Snodgrass Hill. His regiment suffered 73 percent killed and wounded. If he couldn't make it to the top, I want one of his descendants to do it.

INTRODUCTION

HISTORIANS OF THE WAR BETWEEN THE STATES (AS southerners call it) or the American Civil War (as northerners call it) love to think about alternative history.

"What if Stonewall Jackson had been at Gettysburg? He would have taken Culp's Hill that first day," say southerners. They may be right. Jackson was aggressive, had advocated invading the North since April 1861, and likely would have seen the value of taking that high ground.

Most southerners do not ask the next question: "What would have happened had the Confederates gained the high ground?" The answer to that question can be intriguing. One answer could have been that Union Gen. George Meade might have thought about simply surrounding that high ground, and bringing in more and more militia units to seal Robert E. Lee's army off from escape.

How long would Lee's entire army have lasted on that high ground before their food and water ran out? If Meade would have had unlimited supplies of both food and water and could have taken his time about bringing in militia units from around the North, could Lee's army have been starved into submission without firing another shot after July 1?

"What if Grant had started his career in the East?" is the question northerners like to ask themselves. They imagine a bold Grant climbing up the ranks in the East, capturing Lincoln's attention much sooner and pushing aside lesser lights like Burnside in December 1862 and Hooker in March 1863.

Northerners do not ask the next question: "What if Grant had led his men into slaughter like he did at Cold Harbor early in the war in full view of Lincoln?" It seems doubtful that a demanding Lincoln would have tolerated Grant's lies about the losses at Cold Harbor early in the war. That could be proven by how quickly Burnside was sacked after the disaster at Fredericksburg in December 1862. Ironically, Grant committed the same errors less than two years later and enjoyed Lincoln's full support.

That is what is entertaining about asking these alternative history questions. There are no right or wrong answers because the alternative history never happened. Any theory is as good as any other theory on what might have happened.

What *Bull's-Eyes and Misfires* does is take a look at alternative history by focusing on fifty obscure figures who did or didn't do something that could have—but didn't—change history. These people may very well have been pivotal figures in shaping the outcome of the War. While it's impossible to know when speculating on "what ifs," it is likely that if any of these people changed something about the choices they made—the War might have turned out differently.

Yes, that does sound complicated, but once you read about these people, the point of the book will become clear. I purposely did not focus on famous people because the contributions of the famous have already been told. I wanted to find rarely written-about personalities who had some sort of impact on the war.

Some of their contributions are obvious. It is hard to ignore Confederate Col. George Rains who manufactured three million pounds of gunpowder, more than enough to have kept the South supplied for three years. Some people require some thought. Elizabeth Keckley never claimed to be a war hero, but she most definitely performed a valuable war service by doing her best to keep Mary Todd Lincoln sane and out of the thoughts of President Abraham Lincoln.

I had trouble labeling some of these people "bull's-eyes" and "misfires." Some of them made only one mistake in otherwise spectacular careers that got them the "misfire" label. Some of them had particularly poor careers, but they slipped up and performed something amazing that got them a "bull's-eye" label. You may disagree with the labels, but

I think you will agree that all of these twenty-five Confederate and twenty-five Union characters are fascinating.

If you have other characters you would like to nominate for "bull's-eye" or "misfire" status, please let me know by contacting me through my Web site: www.clintjohnsonbooks.com. If I don't meet you at book signings at bookstores, you will find the opportunity at this Web site to buy personalized, autographed books from me by mail. Since 1996 I've written six books focusing on the War with a particular focus on how to find well-known and obscure Civil War sites.

UNION

Maj. William F. Barry

(1818–1879)

WHEN MISTAKEN IDENTITY COST A VICTORY

✳ MISFIRE ✳

HAD MAJ. WILLIAM F. BARRY HAD BETTER EYESIGHT AND judgment at the battle of Bull Run on July 21, 1861, there would not have been a Second Bull Run one year later. In fact, there probably would not have been a second major battle of the war.

Had Barry taken a good hard look at what was right in front of his eyes, he might have ended the war with that one great victory the Union had been hoping Bull Run would be. But Barry missed the obvious. While he later went on to a decent career, Barry's performance at Bull Run has to be counted as the Union's first major misfire.

Barry did well at West Point, finishing in the top third of his class of 1838. He was assigned to the artillery. Handling cannon agreed with

Barry over the next twenty-two years of military service. He was so good that he was named to a three-person team chosen to write a new comprehensive manual on field artillery tactics. The book came out in 1860, just in time to be used by both Union and Confederate forces.

Because of his twenty-two-year seniority, Barry was chosen to command all of the artillery in Gen. Irvin McDowell's Army of Northeastern Virginia, then forming in Washington, D.C., in July 1861, in anticipation of capturing the railroad junction at Manassas. Barry must have been confident. He commanded more than thirty cannon, thought to be more than enough to drive the Rebel rabble from the field.

As fifteen thousand Federals splashed across Bull Run, they were met by increasing numbers of Confederates. The fighting slowly shifted from Sudley Ford to Matthews Hill then on to Henry House Hill. Gen. McDowell ordered Barry to send two cannon batteries ahead of the infantry to clear the Confederates off the hill.

The two batteries had too big of a job. In fact, more Confederate infantry, among them Gen. Thomas J. Jackson's First Virginia Brigade, began to arrive on Henry House Hill. At about 2:00 P.M. the batteries moved their guns from a nearby hill to a part of Henry House Hill on Jackson's left. Now the two sides began an artillery duel with each other.

McDowell, who had personally ordered the guns closer, now realized he had put his eight cannon in danger. He had rushed the guns forward so fast that there was no Federal infantry support to protect them from a Confederate infantry charge. In effect, the Federal cannon were now on the frontlines of the battle and the Federal infantry was far behind them, the opposite of how most battles developed.

Looking behind him and seeing no Federal infantry support coming his way and looking in front of him and seeing plenty of Confederate infantry filing onto the field, one battery commander, Capt. Charles Griffin, decided to move his battery. He limbered two cannon and boldly moved further south, even closer to the Confederates, and further away from any hope of Union infantry support. Now he was lined up perpendicularly with Jackson's line. He was in perfect position to deliver enfilading fire, meaning he would be firing down the line and sure to hit many Confederates with his rounds.

Griffin was excited because the Confederates did not seem to be paying much attention to him. They were still busy firing at the other battery. Griffin realized that if he could unlimber and aim his pieces, he
would be able to get off several devastating rounds, maybe even kill that
Confederate general who seemed to be standing like a stone wall as he
directed his troops.

As Griffin was preparing to fire down the Confederate line, he
noticed a blue clad regiment coming at his position from the right. As
they were coming from the south and all of the other Federal troops
were on the north side of the battlefield, Griffin decided that the regiment must be Confederate. He had to take care of this direct threat first.
Once he smashed this advancing column with a few rounds of canister,
he would then shift back to that other line of Confederates who still
seemed oblivious to his presence.

Just then Major Barry, the commander of all the Federal artillery,
rode up from the rear ranks. Barry saw Griffin was aiming his guns at
the blue-clad soldiers.

"Don't fire there. Those are your battery support!" he shouted.

Griffin was incredulous. The men were coming from the woods on
the Confederate side of the line. Dressed in blue or not, they had to be
Confederates.

"They are Confederates as certain as the world!" Griffin returned.

Barry would not be moved.

"I know they are your battery support. Do not fire on them!" Barry
demanded.

Griffin, a captain, obeyed orders from a major. He watched as the
blue-clad regiment continued marching forward until it got to within
point-blank range. The regiment lowered their muskets and fired into
his battery.

In his official after-action report Captain Griffin did not accuse
Major Barry by name but wrote that he had shifted his battery and had
fired two rounds "when it was charged by the enemy's infantry from the
woods on the right of our position. This infantry was mistaken for our
own forces, an officer on the field having stated that it was a regiment
sent by Colonel Heintzelman to support the battery. In this charge of

the enemy every cannoner was cut down and a large number of horses killed, leaving the battery (which was without support except in name) perfectly helpless."

The blue-clad soldiers who had fired into Griffin's battery were actually the Thirty-third Virginia, part of Jackson's First Virginia Brigade who were still wearing their prewar militia uniforms.

Barry's mistake was easily understood. He had asked McDowell for infantry to support his batteries and McDowell had promised to rush some regiments forward. Barry was expecting those supports to be in blue, though blue was not yet the standard color for the Union army. The supporting Federal unit that was on its way to help the artillery from the north was dressed in red. They were the Eleventh New York Volunteers, a Zouave unit made up of New York City firemen who dressed in red shirts and white turbans. The Zouaves had been chased off the field by Confederate Gen. J. E. B. Stuart's cavalry before they ever arrived to support Griffin.

What is unexplained is how Barry could have mistaken a unit coming from the south as Federals when all of the other Federal units were on the north side of the battlefield. The only explanation that seems plausible is that the troops Barry saw were in blue and he simply lost his sense of direction when his eyes and brain assured him the troops were Federals.

Now noticing Griffin's battery and seeing how one regiment of his brigade had already captured the guns, Jackson ordered a full-scale charge on the remaining Federals. Within minutes the Federals were rushing back toward Washington in total disorganization.

On the retreat back to Washington, Griffin stopped to water his horse. Up rode Barry to water his horse. Griffin asked his commanding officer if he still believed the blue-clad regiment was his support. It was an insolent remark that normally could have gotten Griffin court-martialed, but Barry did not say a word.

Barry's after-action report reads differently from Griffin's. In Griffin's report, the Confederate infantry fired first into the battery and then the New York Fire Zouaves arrived to be chased off by Stuart's cavalry. In Barry's report, the Zouaves were driven off, and then the Confederates attacked the battery. Nowhere in Barry's report does he mention that he ordered Griffin not to fire. Nowhere does he mention that the Confederates were dressed in blue uniforms. Barry made no acknowledgment in his official report that he had caused Griffin's battery to be overrun and its gunners and horses killed, wounded, and captured.

Barry's career did not suffer because of his mistake. In fact, he was promoted to general not long after Bull Run. He eventually transferred west to serve under General William T. Sherman who found him to be a master of artillery. The irritated Griffin also made general.

Had Barry not mistaken the Thirty-third Virginia for a Federal unit, Griffin's guns would have first blown away Jackson's support and then fired down the remainder of Jackson's line. Jackson himself was no more than a couple of hundred yards away from Griffin's cannon that were loaded with canister that could throw lead minié balls for six hundred yards. Had Barry not made his mistake, Stonewall Jackson might not have survived his first major battle. The Confederacy might not have survived its first major battle.

Gen. Don Carlos Buell

(1818–1898)

LINCOLN'S WESTERN THEATER IRRITANT

✴ MISFIRE ✴

GEN. DON CARLOS BUELL WAS A PROFESSIONAL SOLDIER who figured prominently in two incidents in one year, one that would result in the opening of the war and the other in a battle that would make U. S. Grant a national hero.

Buell, however, would never become a hero himself because he refused to play the political games Washington politicians demanded of generals. Instead, the politicians, starting with President Lincoln, ruined Buell's reputation and ended his career. The Lincoln administration could tolerate bad generals, but it would not tolerate disobedient ones.

Despite his early success on the battlefield, including riding to the rescue of Grant and his army, Buell succumbed to an inability to read the often quirky, nonlinear minds of politicians. It was Buell's straight arrow belief in separating soldiering from politicking that doomed his career in the war and forever labeled him a misfire.

A poor student, Buell graduated near the bottom of his West Point class of 1841, although he turned out to be an excellent soldier. By 1860 he was a lieutenant colonel, one of the highest ranking officers in the tiny prewar army.

In early December 1860 Buell was sent on a secret mission to Charleston, South Carolina, to assess the mood of the citizens in that city. Buell's instructions were so secret that his orders were not even written out. The orders he gave orally to the federal commander in Charleston, Maj. Robert Anderson, were contradictory: not to do anything to antagonize the citizens of Charleston but be prepared to do anything to maintain the presence of the United States government in Charleston.

Buell learned that Charleston's citizens were ready to take over Fort Moultrie on Sullivan's Island and Castle Pinckney and Fort Sumter in Charleston Harbor. Just before Buell left for Washington, he told Anderson that the United States expected him to defend the forts. He should be ready to move to Fort Sumter as it would be much easier to defend in the middle of the harbor than the low-walled Fort Moultrie on the mainland.

What Buell had just done was set the stage for the standoff that would launch the war.

On December 26 Anderson took Buell's advice and moved his garrison to Fort Sumter. He would remain there until April 14, 1861, when he would surrender the fort after a bombardment that began on April 12.

Appointed brigadier general in May, Buell was given command of the Department of the Ohio, headquartered in Kentucky. From there he helped hatch a plan to use the Cumberland and Tennessee Rivers to attack the western Confederacy. By February 1862 U. S. Grant had captured two key Confederate forts on the rivers, Forts Henry and Donelson. By the end of the month, Buell had captured Nashville, the first Confederate capital to fall to the Union.

Now the toasts of the Union for their victories, Buell and Grant set their sights on Corinth, Mississippi, a major railhead southwest of Nashville. In preparation for the campaign, Grant began to mass his forces at Pittsburg Landing on the Tennessee River near a little church called Shiloh. Buell would march his Army of the Ohio from Nashville to meet Grant on the river. Together they would attack Corinth.

Grant was so confident that he barely paid attention to security for his army though the Confederates were massing a defensive army at Corinth, barely a day's march away. He was so confident he violated one of the basic rules of warfare: Do not put your army's back to a river. If the Confederates were to attack, there would be no place for his men to go but into the water.

If Grant had not noticed his precarious position, Confederate Gen. Albert Sidney Johnston, commander of the forty-four-thousand-man Army of Mississippi, surely had. Learning that Buell was moving from Nashville with twenty-five thousand men, Johnston decided on a bold strategy: Hit and defeat Grant before Buell could arrive. He would then lie in wait for Buell's unsuspecting army.

The Confederate attack at Shiloh on April 6 was a complete surprise but poorly executed by both inexperienced commanders and soldiers. The battle took all day and slowed as darkness fell. Johnston was mortally wounded. His second in command, Gen. P. G. T. Beauregard, decided to hold off further attacks until the next morning, figuring Buell was still miles away.

What Beauregard did not know was that Buell had arrived. Noting that the riverbank was choked with the frightened remnants of Grant's army, Buell asked Grant a dumb question. "What plans have you made for retreat?"

Grant replied, "I have not despaired of whipping them, General."

As Buell's men bulled their way through the shattered remnants of Grant's army to set up a defense, they remembered how Grant's army had been called heroes for capturing the Cumberland River forts, while their own capture of Nashville had been ignored. Now, here they were saving Grant's reputation. They savored that status.

As the first of Buell's men filed into place, the Confederates launched an attack around 6:00 P.M. Had they done it an hour earlier, Buell's men would not have been in place. The half-hearted attack against a now-solid Union front was repulsed.

The next morning Grant attacked at dawn, just as the Confederates had done the previous day. Beauregard, who had no intelligence telling him that Buell's twenty-five thousand men had arrived during the night, was as surprised as Grant had been on April 6. The Confederates fell back to Corinth. Shiloh would be a Union victory, a Grant victory.

Grant, embarrassed that he had been surprised by the Confederates, downplayed Buell's contributions in his postwar memoirs, saying that Buell's arrival on the evening of April 6 had no direct outcome on the last Confederate charge of that day. He did acknowledge that Buell's army moving across the Tennessee that night nearly doubled his forces for the attack that would be made on April 7.

Buell continued in the western theater for the rest of 1862. It was Buell who countered Braxton Bragg's invasion of Kentucky at the battle of Perryville in October; but he did not follow President Lincoln's demands to pursue and destroy Bragg's forces.

Irritating Lincoln was not a good idea on Buell's part. The president was already angry that Buell's old friend McClellan had not pursued Lee back into Virginia after Antietam. Now Buell was not chasing Bragg. Lincoln fired both Buell and McClellan.

Needing an explanation as to why a war hero had been fired, the Lincoln administration launched a whispering campaign against Buell. Stories were circulated that Buell, who was married to a Southern woman from a slave-holding family, was really a Southern sympathizer who was intentionally slow to come to Grant's aid at Shiloh and then allowed Bragg to escape.

A furious Buell demanded a formal trial. He got it and was cleared of charges of mismanagement of his army. That did not mean that Washington wanted him back in the army. His wife's family still held slaves and that did not look right when the federal government had just issued the Emancipation Proclamation.

Buell did not help his case when he insisted that he was fighting to reunite the Union, not to free the slaves in the rebelling states, as the proclamation said.

When Buell refused to endorse the war as an effort to end slavery, the Lincoln administration refused to send him any orders.

Not even Grant, the hero of the day, could change Lincoln's mind. Lincoln ignored Grant's request to reinstate Buell to command. Grant wrote after the war that Buell was a man who was incapable of being disloyal to the Union.

By June 1864 Buell was out of the army, and he spent the rest of his life managing a coal mine and iron works in Kentucky.

Buell never understood why he had been fired. He was the first Union officer to conclude that the Federal forces would have to move from Fort Moultrie to Fort Sumter. He had contributed to the successful campaign against the Confederates in Tennessee. He had captured Nashville, the first Confederate capital to fall. He had saved Grant's army at Shiloh. He had defeated Bragg in the field at Perryville.

What more did the Washington politicians want? What Buell never figured out was that the Lincoln administration wanted a yes-man who would do its bidding without question. When he refused to do that, Buell became a liability.

Buell has always left questions in his wake. What if he had been a day later in arriving at Shiloh? Could Grant have successfully reorganized his frightened army without Buell's fresh, steady twenty-five thousand men? If Grant had been pushed into the Tennessee River would Buell have been able to put up a fight? Had Buell lost that fight, would the Confederates have moved down the river to try to retake New Orleans?

No one will ever answer those questions. Buell did arrive on the night of April 6 and he did help Grant win Shiloh on April 7. Within six months of helping to establish Grant as a national hero, Buell was out of a job.

Anna Ella Carroll

(1815–1894)

A WOMAN RARELY GIFTED
BUT MAYBE NOT A MILITARY GENIUS

✷ MISFIRE ✷

HEARING THE NAME OF ANNA ELLA CARROLL DID NOT strike terror in the hearts of President Abraham Lincoln and his cabinet members. She wasn't Stonewall Jackson, but being told Carroll was waiting outside their offices certainly roused feelings of exasperation and irritation.

How often Carroll actually met Lincoln is unclear. What is clear about her place in Civil War history is that in late 1861 she developed a strategy to split the Confederacy into two pieces. She then spent thirty years claiming sole credit and trying to get two hundred thousand dollars for the idea.

One of two things happened: Either generals U. S. Grant and Don

Carlos Buell stole her strategy and took credit for it themselves or Carroll stumbled onto the very same strategy they were already developing, which careful reading of history's timelines seems to prove.

One thing is certain. The strategy worked. The South split into two pieces a few months after Carroll presented her idea to a Lincoln cabinet member. That crack widened each month until the Confederacy literally fell apart.

Even if Carroll was a brilliant, unofficial member of Lincoln's cabinet, as she liked to describe herself, she let her real and imagined access to the men in power in Washington go to her head. When the Union army and navy cooperated, just as she had suggested, she allowed her head to swell so much that it almost exploded. She was a misfire.

Born the daughter of a former Maryland governor, Carroll was fascinated by politics. Her career writing political pamphlets grew into campaigning for President Millard Fillmore. Working in national politics seventy years before women would get the right to vote, Carroll counted among her acquaintances the future Secretary of State William Seward and the former Secretary of War Jefferson Davis.

In 1861 Carroll was a forty-five-year-old, never-married, female political writer whose pamphlets and letters to the editors of major newspapers garnered attention and replies from national political leaders.

She had not supported Lincoln in the 1860 presidential election, but when he won she jumped on the bandwagon. In August 1861 she published an attention-grabbing pamphlet called "Reply to Breckinridge," attacking point by point a speech former Vice President John C. Breckinridge had made early in 1861 questioning Lincoln's powers to make war on the South without approval of Congress. Lincoln liked the tone of the pamphlet so much that the administration reprinted and distributed copies around Capitol Hill.

Carroll interpreted that endorsement as personal approval from the Lincoln administration. She wrangled an oral contract with a gullible assistant secretary of war in Lincoln's cabinet to write pamphlets for the War Department.

Carroll soon went beyond the role of pamphleteer and into the realm of military strategist.

Early in the war Lincoln's strategy in the West involved moving Union troops and ships down the Mississippi River from Illinois all the way to New Orleans, effectively cutting Louisiana, Texas, and Arkansas off from the rest of the South. Countering that strategy, the South began fortifying river towns like Vicksburg, Mississippi, and building forts above and below New Orleans. After some sharp fighting along the river, Northern generals recognized that an immediate move down the Mississippi would not work. They needed alternatives.

While Lincoln and his generals were mulling their options, Carroll went to St. Louis to gauge Union support in Missouri. She met a woman at her hotel whose husband was a skilled riverboat pilot. Carroll arranged a meeting to ask him if there was another way of getting at the heart of the Confederacy other than going down the Mississippi. Using maps showing the locations of cities and rivers and questioning the pilot about details such as the depths and locations of sandbars, she focused on the Cumberland River, which flowed past Nashville, Tennessee's capital, and the Tennessee River, which ran right through Tennessee, into Alabama, and skirted Mississippi. The South would still be split, just not along the Mississippi.

She immediately wrote several letters to the Lincoln administration detailing her idea. In late November she laid out her strategy to that assistant secretary of war. Her details were precise, even pointing out that both rivers flowed north so crippled gunboats could use the current to float toward their bases, while the Mississippi River flowed south, away from safety.

Carroll's plan to invade the Confederate West was everything military leaders want in strategy. It was backed by research, it was workable, and it was practical.

Unfortunately for civilian Carroll and her place in Civil War history, virtually every detail of her strategy had already been thought of by the generals in the field. At least they said they had already developed a similar plan. In September 1861 two months before Carroll submitted her plan, Gen. U. S. Grant was already sending gunboats up the rivers to check the strengths of Fort Henry on the Tennessee and Fort Donelson on the Cumberland. In response the Confederates were beefing up forces in both forts anticipating an impending attack.

What Carroll perceived as a paralyzed, confused military structure in November 1861 waiting for one great idea on how to act was apparently a military structure waiting for supplies and approval to mount a major land and river offensive. Since the generals' plans were secret, Carroll had no idea she had come up with the strategy already in place for at least two months.

After the February 1862 attacks on Forts Donelson and Henry resulted in their capture, Carroll began to claim public credit for the capture of the two forts.

According to Carroll, Lincoln told her in confidence that he could not publicly give her credit.

"The officers would be thrown off their epaulets if they knew they were acting on the plan of a civilian, and good God, if they knew it was a woman, the whole army would disband!" she quoted Lincoln as saying to her in a private meeting.

When the war ended, Carroll clung tenaciously to her belief that she had originated the Tennessee–Cumberland River strategy and that she was owed money for that strategy.

Starting in 1870 Carroll became more insistent and more outrageous in her demands that the country pay her for both the invasion plan and for the pamphlets she had written for the War Department. Her last demand was for $250,000 plus a pension.

In 1877 Congress finally said she had already been paid about $2,000 for her pamphlets and that true patriots do not ask for money for plans that saved the Union. That was that, in the eyes of Congress, but the congressmen had never met anyone as tenacious as Anna Carroll.

The Women's Suffrage Association took up Carroll's cause in 1877, creating the legend of the unrecognized female member of Lincoln's cabinet. After four years of lobbying, by 1881 another movement gained momentum to force Congress to recognize Carroll's claims. Former Union Gen. Edward S. Bragg, chair of the Senate Committee on Military Affairs, declared her to be the author of "The Tennessee Plan that gave mastery of the conflict to the national arms" and a person who was due "the thanks of the nation."

Thrown into confusion with the assassination of President James A.

Garfield in the summer of 1881, Congress never got around to acting on Bragg's suggestion. It was the closest Carroll ever came to getting compensation.

As Carroll grew older, her stories grew more fanciful. She told an interviewer that she met President Grant after the war and "he was like a child with eyes as bright as stars" as she described how she had come up with the plan he would use to capture Forts Henry and Donelson. "I am convinced that he had no conception that it was this that brought us victory," she said.

Carroll died in February 1894 at age seventy-nine without ever receiving the compensation she believed she deserved. Her tombstone reads: "A Woman Rarely Gifted—An Able and Accomplished Writer." There is no mention of the Tennessee–Cumberland River plan.

Anna Carroll went to her grave believing her Tennessee–Cumberland River plan preserved the Union by splitting the Confederacy. The only problem with Carroll's plan was that it was also simple—so simple that even male Union generals thought of it first.

Sec. of Treasury Salmon P. Chase
(1808–1873)

THE MAN WHO PLOTTED
A COUP AGAINST LINCOLN

✳ MISFIRE ✳

SALMON PORTLAND CHASE OF OHIO WANTED TO BE president of the United States. He wanted the presidency so bad that he considered undermining the ability of the incumbent president, Abraham Lincoln, to win electoral votes. What Chase considered was using a Union army to stage a virtual coup against a sitting president.

Speculating what would have happened had Chase's coup been successful is intriguing. Would a Union army that loved Lincoln have rebelled against a new president and staged its own coup to install whom they wanted? How would the nation's civilians have reacted to that? How would Chase have conducted the war differently from Lincoln?

In the end Chase's ham-handed attempts to grab power were discovered by Lincoln who easily brushed him aside. Chase was a misfire.

Born in New Hampshire with an insatiable appetite for power and influence, the lifeblood of politicians, Chase moved to Cincinnati, Ohio, to establish his political reputation and hone his legal skills. In the 1830s he was one of the few lawyers who would defend runaway slaves. By the early 1840s he was the nation's leading advocate for slowing the growth of slavery in the emerging territories and then, over time, eliminating it in the South.

In 1849 Chase was elected to the U.S. Senate where he continued to promote his antislavery agenda. He later returned to Ohio and ran successfully for governor.

Chase thought about running for president in 1856 for the Republican Party that he helped create, but Ohio Republicans felt he was too antislavery and too nationally focused in his political ambitions. They refused to back him. The nomination went to John C. Frémont.

Stung by the rejection of his own state party to his national political ambitions, Chase again ran for governor. At the same time he kept in the national news by holding true to his antislavery principles. He believed abolitionism would make him the logical choice for the Republican presidential nomination in 1860.

Chase had not counted on his antislavery sentiments being viewed as radical by other northern politicians. Once again, he was denied the candidacy in favor of someone he had dismissed as competition early on— Abraham Lincoln. While Chase was vocal in his antislavery rhetoric, Lincoln craftily played both sides. Lincoln assured southerners slavery was fine where it already existed, while telling northerners that "a house divided against itself cannot stand."

Chase, who felt he had been outfoxed, nevertheless campaigned for Lincoln. His loyalty was rewarded with a cabinet post as U.S. treasury secretary. Lincoln knew Chase still hungered for the presidency. He also figured he could keep his eye on Chase better if he was in the cabinet.

Several months after killing a Chase-backed plan to free slaves in captured sections of South Carolina, Lincoln suggested freeing the slaves in the rebelling states if those states were not back in the Union by January 1, 1863. Chase warmly seconded the emancipation proposal, believing Lincoln was finally endorsing his ideas. Chase believed a grateful nation would one day recognize that freeing the slaves was really his idea and thus would reward him the presidency once they knew the truth.

Chase did not always please Lincoln. He embarrassed himself in the administration when he enthusiastically backed fellow Ohioans like Irvin McDowell, George McClellan, and William Rosecrans for generalships. None proved up to the task of defeating the Confederates.

As the war dragged on through the summer and fall of 1863, the nation began to question Lincoln's leadership. Chase had always believed he could do a better job, so he began a covert campaign to gauge his political friends' support for his declaring for the Presidency again, just as he had done in 1860.

Throughout the rest of 1863, Chase corresponded with political operatives, starting with the lowest form of bureaucrats, the tax collectors, and working his way up to include governors. Some assured Chase that they would back him against Lincoln though they did not want to go public until nomination time.

It was late in 1863 when Chase hatched a convoluted plan to steal the next election. As the Union army captured portions of Southern states, such as coastal South Carolina, western Tennessee, and New Orleans, Federal tax commissioners moved in to foreclose on property. The properties, owned by Southerners who were not paying any Federal property taxes, were being resold at public auction for their tax value, usually to carpetbagging friends of the commissioners. Chase, boss of the commissioners in his role as treasury secretary, began to see the lowly bureaucrats for what they were becoming—king makers in the occupied Southern states.

Even Lincoln himself unknowingly played into Chase's hands by ramming through a proclamation that said if at least 10 percent of a Southern state's population would take a loyalty oath, he would recreate a new state government and readmit the state into the Union. This was a continuation of a policy that had already led to puppet governments set up in Tennessee and Louisiana. Lincoln seemed to have a firm grip on those states, but there were still plenty of Southern states that could fall under Chase's influence.

All Chase needed was a newly conquered Confederate state in which to test the effectiveness of his scheme.

That chance came in January 1864 when Gen. Quincy Gillmore readied an expedition under Gen. Truman Seymour to Jacksonville, Florida, with the idea that the force would move west toward Tallahassee. Lincoln, who was cooking up his own plan to bring Florida back into the Union, sent Gillmore a letter urging him to cooperate in setting up a reconstruction government in the state. It is unclear if Gillmore was already under Chase's influence, but he seemed surprised to find Lincoln so interested in his upcoming invasion of Florida. Gillmore was very uncomfortable when Lincoln sent his personal secretary, John Hay, along on the expedition.

If Chase thought he was duping Lincoln over who was really in control of the Florida invasion, he was sadly mistaken. Hay quickly figured out that Chase had insiders in Florida and kept Lincoln fully informed.

It was not long after starting the invasion of Florida's interior that General Seymour realized that he, Gillmore, and Chase had been misled by Chase's operatives about Florida's willingness to return to the Union.

"Florida will not cast its lot [with the Union] until more important successes elsewhere are assured," Seymour wrote in a letter to Gillmore.

The plan to bring Florida back into the Union in February 1864 blew up in Lincoln and Chase's faces when Seymour's five-thousand-man force was soundly defeated at the battle of Olustee on February 19. Seymour's force suffered more than one-third casualties, among the worst defeats suffered by any Union army during the entire war.

Had the Federals won the battle and marched on to Tallahassee and captured it, Chase would have expected his tax commissioners to start secretly gathering support for him to take over its electoral votes for that November's election. But Hay knew about Chase's secret plans and would have moved against his operatives for malfeasance in office.

Chase never had to answer to Lincoln. At about the same time Chase was hatching his Florida plot, his friends were writing a pamphlet called "The Pomeroy Circular," which advocated his nomination over Lincoln.

When that circular was leaked to several newspapers, Chase was embarrassed to see himself portrayed as opportunistic.

In June 1864 Chase got into a minor spat with Lincoln over patronage in the Treasury Department. Chase offered his resignation as he had on several previous occasions. Chase always believed Lincoln truly needed him in the cabinet so the threat of resignation had always been hollow. To Chase's shock, Lincoln accepted his resignation.

Lincoln left Chase without a job for a few months in retaliation for the Florida foolishness. Then he appointed Chase chief justice of the United States. As chief justice he said the Union could not ever be broken so the Confederate states had never really seceded. Yet some historians wonder if Chase also secretly told President Andrew Johnson to drop all charges against Confederates like Jefferson Davis and Robert E. Lee so the constitutionality of secession would not be tried in public.

Chase never gave up his dream of becoming president. In 1868 he even allowed some speculation that he might run as a Democrat against U. S. Grant running as a Republican. He did not modify his bedrock stance that all men, black men included, should have the right to vote. That stance angered the Democratic Party and the draft Chase movement never materialized.

Chase died in 1873, never having realized his goal of even running for president.

How would President Chase have prosecuted the war? He probably would have stuck with Lincoln's choice of U. S. Grant to head the Union army. Grant was from Ohio. If there was anything Chase was loyal to, it was a home state boy. After the war, Chase may have been even harsher on the South in terms of the occupation. He would have likely pressed immediately for black suffrage.

One Union politician summed up why so many other politicians did not like Salmon Chase and never supported his drive for higher office.

"Chase is a good man, but his theology is unsound. He thinks there is a fourth person in the Trinity," said Ohio Senator Benjamin Wade.

Asst. Naval Sec. Gustavus Fox

(1821–1883)

THE BUREAUCRAT
WHO WON THE NAVAL WAR

✯ BULL'S-EYE ✯

FIGHTING MEN OFTEN COMPLAIN THAT THE BUREAUCRATS behind the lines have no concept of war, and strategy is often based on politics rather than sound military theory.

That was not true in the U.S. Navy during the 1860s when Gustavus Fox was appointed assistant secretary of the navy to help Naval Secretary Gideon Welles. Thanks to Fox's familiarity with the real heavy seas that sailors encounter, and Welles's ability to negotiate the imaginary heavy seas of politics flowing around Washington, D.C., the U.S. Navy enjoyed virtually unhindered support at the same time the Lincoln administration was micromanaging the land war for the U.S. Army. Under Welles's and

Fox's guidance, the U.S. Navy grew from 23 ships in 1861 to 641 ships, more than enough to control the South's coastline.

From his first contribution to the U.S. naval effort as a knowledgeable civilian to his last day in office, Fox saw his duty clearly: Win the war on the ocean. He had no designs on the job of his boss. He made no demands to be paid for any of his ideas. He plotted no schemes to grow rich on the letting of naval contracts. Fox was just what he appeared to be: a bureaucrat who knew what he was doing. He was a bull's-eye.

Graduating from the U.S. Naval Academy in 1845, Fox fought in the Mexican War from aboard ship and then sailed the world's oceans for the next eighteen years. Love forced him ashore when his fiancée demanded that he give up his career. He went from deep-water sailor to a salesman for a woolen mill.

The threat of war brought Fox to national prominence, though not as a naval officer.

In early 1861 Fort Sumter in Charleston's harbor and Fort Pickens in Pensacola's harbor were surrounded by Secessionists demanding that the U.S. government turn the forts over to the seceded state governments. It was only a matter of time before the garrisons would run out of food and be forced to give themselves up, whether or not the Secessionists fired on them.

Fox knew the waters around Fort Sumter well after his participation in a U.S. Navy coastal survey. Without being asked or ordered, as he was a civilian, Fox drew up a plan to resupply the garrison and presented it to President James Buchanan. Fox's plan called for fast, shallow-draft boats to run food, men, and ammunition into Fort Sumter under cover of darkness. If Confederate shore batteries fired on the supply ships, supporting Federal warships would attack those batteries. It was a plan that would either force the Union to attack the Confederate shore batteries or force the Confederacy to capture Fort Sumter before the Union support would arrive.

President Buchanan shrank away from such an aggressive plan, believing that it would lead to war. Fox waited until President Abraham Lincoln took office on March 4, 1861, then he tried for an appointment by going through his wife, who was sister to the wife of Lincoln's new postmaster general. Fox, a Democrat who had not voted for Lincoln, made an immediate impression on the president, who liked the plan's boldness.

Most of Lincoln's cabinet feared that the plan would ignite war but Lincoln approved it on March 12, just a week after his inauguration. He sent Fox to Charleston where he met with Fort Sumter's commander. The commander explained he would have to surrender within three weeks as he was running out of food for his men.

Fox urged Lincoln to act immediately and sailed on April 10 with a hastily assembled force of warships, troops, food, and ammunition. The mission was so quickly thrown together that one of the warships Fox was counting on to help him at Fort Sumter was also assigned by the president for a separate relief mission to Fort Pickens. Lincoln had promised the same ship to two different secret missions he was separately organizing with two different cabinet members. Fox was irritated, but the mission was already under way and there was nothing he could do.

When Confederate peace negotiators in Washington learned about the Fox mission, they telegraphed word to South Carolina's governor. Anxious to take control of the fort before reinforcements reached it, the Confederates demanded its immediate surrender. When refused, a bombardment was commenced on April 12, 1861. Fox arrived off Charleston Harbor later that morning. He watched helplessly as the shells crashed into the fort. Two days later, instead of using Fox's ships to save Fort Sumter, they were used to transport the surrendered garrison back to New York.

Impressed with his ability to get things done, Lincoln then appointed Fox assistant naval secretary. Fox, never a professional politician or a career bureaucrat, was a man of action who did things rather than hold a meeting to talk about doing things. He acted quickly, such as leasing shallow-draft ferries, common in cities that had unbridged harbors like New York. These ferries were modified to river patrol boat use in the South.

Fox was the first to realize that a successful blockade would be one that controlled the South's river mouths and sounds. It was he who planned the first major Union success of the war, invasion of North

Carolina's Outer Banks in August 1861, which closed hundreds of miles of shoreline, rivers, and creeks that could have sheltered blockade-runners. In November of 1861 he planned the capture of Port Royal Sound, South Carolina, converting it to a coaling station for blockading ships.

Fox's crowning achievement in the war may have been the capture of New Orleans. It was Fox who spotted the name of David Farragut on a list of potential officers who could be tapped to run up the Mississippi River and past two Confederate forts with an invasion fleet. While other naval bureaucrats questioned if a sixty-year-old still had the ability to fight, Fox insisted that a fighting man was a fighting man and Farragut would do the job he was asked to do. Fox's faith in Farragut proved to be correct. Farragut ran past both forts and captured New Orleans on April 25, 1862, one of the early devastating losses for the Confederacy.

Not all of Fox's ideas worked. He tried to close Charleston Harbor by sinking a fleet of old wooden ships loaded with stones in the shipping channel. The ocean current, naturally, carved out a newer, deeper channel around the stones. He was an enthusiastic supporter of ironclads based on the USS *Monitor*, which proved to be unseaworthy as well as vulnerable to Confederate armor-piercing shells. A monitor attack on Confederate-held Fort Sumter in April 1863 proved disastrous, with several monitors being riddled with accurate fire from the Confederates while the ironclads could not hit a stationary target—the fort.

One of Fox's ideas proved to be just plain stupid. Still obsessed with closing the Confederacy's ports, in November 1864 Fox approved a plan to tow a ship loaded with black powder near Fort Fisher, a mile-long sand fort on a beach south of Wilmington, North Carolina, which protected the mouth of the Cape Fear River. The idea was that the concussion of the blast would start a wave of sound and wind, maybe even a tidal wave, which would blow down or wash away the thick sand walls of the fort.

A grasp of oceanography and physics was not Fox's strong suit. The only thing the explosion of the ship did was to wake up the sleeping garrison inside Fort Fisher. Fort Fisher would fall, but it would be accomplished at great cost to a Union army landing force, not by a bomb-created sound wave.

Fox remained in his position as assistant secretary of the navy for the entire war, content to handle the nuts and bolts of naval proceedings while Welles handled the public face of the Navy Department. While several of Lincoln's cabinet members maneuvered around his back trying to feather their own political nests, Welles and Fox kept focused on their jobs, defeating the Confederacy. After the war Fox could have stayed in the cabinet or even run for high office, but he kept his promise to his wife and returned to selling wool.

Gen. William Buel Franklin

(1823–1903)

MISREAD ORDERS COST
A BATTLE AND A CAREER

✷ MISFIRE ✷

CIVIL WAR–ERA ORDERS WERE WRITTEN IN FLOWERY, formal style, so filled with qualifiers that one wonders if the generals of the day understood what was being asked of them.

They often did not. Gen. William Buel Franklin found his military career quickly sidetracked after he misinterpreted one order and did not seek clarification before carrying out what he thought he was supposed to do.

Franklin's failure to figure out confusing orders at Fredericksburg on December 13, 1862, cost him and his boss their jobs and emboldened the Confederacy's belief that it could still win the war. Had Franklin simply asked what his orders meant, Robert E. Lee's army might have been crushed in the snows of December 1862.

Not content to simply bear the wrath of his boss after one lost battle, Franklin tried going over his head to the ultimate boss, the president of the United States. That maneuver ended just like Franklin's part of the battle—poorly. He lost his job and will forever be labeled a misfire.

Franklin was a brilliant boy, gaining admission to the U.S. Military Academy at sixteen and finishing first in his class of 1843. He spent the next eighteen years conducting land surveys and overseeing government construction, including the U.S. Capitol dome.

Though in the army for eighteen years, Franklin had no combat experience when the war opened. That lack of practical field experience would come to haunt him.

Promoted to colonel from his prewar status as captain, Franklin was given a brigade of four regiments at Bull Run. He did fairly well in that battle, so his responsibility was upped. Within months he commanded a division under Gen. George McClellan in the spring 1862 Peninsula campaign. McClellan liked his fellow engineer, so Franklin was soon promoted to major general and given command of the Sixth Corps. Franklin, never before a field commander, was quickly rising in rank and responsibility, not because of what he knew but because of who he knew.

Franklin's inexperience first showed itself at the battle of Crampton's Gap, Maryland, on September 14, 1862. After sweeping aside a tiny force of Confederates guarding the gap over South Mountain, Franklin swung his corps southwest toward Harpers Ferry with the intention of attacking Stonewall Jackson who was besieging the Union garrison. However, instead of marching his little-used corps toward Harpers Ferry at night, Franklin made camp. The next day when Franklin was still far from Harpers Ferry, Jackson took the surrender of more than 12,500 Union soldiers. Had Franklin marched forward the night before, he might have caught Jackson unawares. Lee's army would have been split into two pieces and forced to do battle. Franklin would have been the hero of the nation.

Now cognizant of his mistake at Harpers Ferry, Franklin begged to be part of the Union army's attack at Antietam, but McClellan kept Franklin's men in reserve rather than sending them forward onto Lee's battered army. That failure to crush Lee caused Lincoln to remove McClellan from command. The Army of the Potomac was given to Ambrose Burnside.

When armies change hands, generals loyal to their old commander frequently lose out under the new commander. However, Burnside liked Franklin so he actually gave him more responsibility. Franklin, the bookish engineer whose talents lay in drawing lines on paper, was given direct command of almost half the army, nearly sixty thousand men.

Burnside's plan to defeat Lee at Fredericksburg in December 1862 was to cross the Rappahannock River in two places, downtown and then east of downtown. He believed Lee's forces would have to scatter to cover the broad battlefield and he could defeat the Confederates in parts.

Franklin's job would be to make the east crossing and smash into the forces of Stonewall Jackson, which would force Lee to shift men from the left to come to the defense of his right flank. Once those Confederates were out of their trenches and in motion, Franklin would then swing northwest to come in on Longstreet's right flank, which was facing downtown. Longstreet would then be fighting on two fronts, something he could not sustain for long.

On paper the attack looked sound. When seeing the actual ground, it looked like suicide. The men attacking Longstreet on the right would have to march up a steep cleared hill into defensive positions that were dug into the hill behind a stone wall. Franklin's men on the left appeared to have the easier job, though they too would have to march across large expanses of open ground before they reached the Confederates.

Still, Franklin was up for it. He understood he would be making the main attack and trying to draw the Confederates out of their trenches.

Franklin got his final orders on December 13, written at nearly 6:00 A.M., but inexplicably not delivered until nearly 8:00 A.M., not long before the attack was to start. Franklin was surprised at the orders' wording. He believed from an in-person meeting held the night before that he would make an all-out attack.

Now, minutes before launching that attack, Franklin got what he thought were different orders. Now the orders implied that he should wait for the fog to lift before attacking. Even more puzzling, the orders read that he should take utmost care in protecting the bridges across the Rappahannock in case the Confederate cavalry were to discover them and rush across to the Union side of the river.

The most important part of the orders read: "The general commanding directs that you keep your whole command in position for a rapid movement down the old Richmond road, and you will send out at once a division at least to pass below Smithfield to seize, if possible, the heights near Captain Hamilton's, on this side of the Massaponax, taking care to keep it well supported and its line of retreat open."

By his reading of the orders, Franklin had just been relegated to supporting the major attack. Critically, Franklin did not ride to meet Burnside to clarify what he wanted.

At the designated time of the attack, Franklin committed only a third of the sixty thousand men he had at his disposal. The rest were held in reserve to protect the river pontoons. The attacking twenty thousand did break Jackson's line but were eventually forced back. Both the right and left Union attacks failed, leaving more than 12,500 Union soldiers dead, dying, and wounded on the Rappahannock. The Confederacy suffered only 4,200 casualties, the most lopsided Confederate victory of the war.

Burnside blamed Franklin for ignoring his orders to make the main attack. Franklin countered that he had followed Burnside's orders, which he believed had drastically changed from the previous night.

Immediately after the failed attack, Franklin did something that eventually ended his military career. He wrote Lincoln a letter complaining about Burnside's handling of the campaign. Two subordinate generals under Franklin traveled to Washington and delivered much the same message to their congressmen in person and then to Lincoln.

Lincoln, who expected loyalty from his staff, expected the same from the staff of his generals. He told Burnside of the critical letters and visits. Burnside asked Lincoln to remove the mutinous generals from the army. Lincoln took the lesser measure of having the other generals reassigned, but he totally removed Franklin, whom he blamed for not taking advantage of his strength in numbers. Lincoln also surprised Burnside by removing him. Lincoln was convinced that the Army of the Potomac would quit the field unless it got a new commander.

Months later in testimony before a congressional committee investigating Fredericksburg, Franklin said he interpreted the orders to mean that his all-out attack had been changed to be "an armed observation to ascertain where the enemy was." He later testified: "I put in all of the troops I thought it proper and prudent to put in. I fought the whole strength of my command, as far as I could, and at the same time keep my connection with the river open."

The congressional committee, made up of Republicans who knew Franklin was both a Democrat and a close friend of McClellan, who was now a *persona non grata* in the army, laid the blame for Fredericksburg entirely on Franklin. The congressional report concluded: "The testimony of all the witnesses before your committee proves most conclusively that had the attack been made upon the left with all the force which General Franklin could have used for that purpose, the plan of General Burnside would have been completely successful, and our army would have achieved a brilliant victory."

Franklin was banished to the West for a year. U. S. Grant tried to get his old West Point classmate back into a job when he took over command in the East, but the bureaucrats in Washington would not have him back. One of the brightest men to ever graduate from the U.S. Military Academy never returned to the battlefield.

If Franklin was bitter about his treatment at the hands of his country's political leaders, he never let it get him down. He ran the Colt firearms company after the war and led an otherwise successful life until his death in 1903.

Gen. Quincy Adams Gillmore
(1818–1883)

FROM HERO TO GOAT
AFTER ONE JUDGMENT LAPSE

✳ MISFIRE ✳

QUINCY ADAMS GILLMORE WAS ANOTHER FIRST-IN-HIS-class engineering graduate of West Point (1849) whose career had its ups and downs. Gillmore should be remembered as the brilliant general who destroyed the centuries-old image of masonry forts as impregnable. He could be remembered as the general who besieged Charleston, symbol of secession. He will be remembered as the uncaring white general who ordered a suicidal charge that decimated the most famous of the black regiments formed during the war.

Gillmore's label as misfire is richly deserved, not because he sent so many black troops to their deaths, but because he did not follow his own basic engineering training and instincts before he ordered such a bloody,

33

useless attack. The man who single-handedly made carefully engineered masonry forts obsolete allowed a fort built with wheelbarrows of sand to forever besmirch his military career.

Gillmore was such a good West Point engineering student that soon after graduation he was assigned as an instructor. He would spend much of the next decade completing and repairing the nation's forts.

After the Revolution, the United States launched a national defense initiative to line its coasts with forts built of forged bricks or blocks of stone. With walls several feet thick and heavy cannon covering both the sea and narrow channels through which any invading ships would have to pass, the forts were considered impregnable.

At least that was the theory. No enemy since the British had fired on Fort McHenry in 1812 had ever tested the forts.

Gillmore's first battle action gave him a false sense of accomplishment. In November 1861 he took part in the bombardment and capture of two lightly defended sand forts defending Port Royal Sound, South Carolina. He may have thought this first experience with the vulnerability of sand forts to be typical, but he would learn better in the summer of 1863.

Just three months after taking Port Royal, the Union targeted nearby Savannah, a home port for blockade-runners. Guarding the entrance to the Savannah River was Fort Pulaski. On paper Fort Pulaski was invulnerable, with seven-foot-thick brick walls and a wide moat filled with water. Guns facing the river were presighted so any attacking ships would come quickly under fire by practiced cannoneers. Land attacks would have to be made across a flat approach cleared of any cover for hundreds of yards.

When Robert E. Lee inspected the fort, he saw only one possible way Fort Pulaski could be attacked: a heavy bombardment originating on Tybee Island, some seventeen hundred yards away. But Lee was not worried. He told the fort's commander that artillery shells fired from that distance from the standard smoothbore cannon of the day would not have much velocity left. They would likely bounce right off the fort's walls. Lee was confident Pulaski was a safe place to be.

But Lee's education in building forts was thirty years old. More critically, he had not kept up with the new kinds of cannon being introduced to the battlefield. Younger Federal artillerymen like Robert Parrott were designing rifled cannon that spun conical-shaped shells. That spin greatly increased the muzzle velocity, punching power, and firing distance over the old-style smoothbore cannon with which Lee was familiar.

Gillmore decided there was no better place for a live fire experiment of smoothbore versus rifled cannon than an attack on Fort Pulaski. Just as Lee had predicted, the Union army landed at Tybee Island in February 1862. Gillmore spent the next several weeks installing thirty-seven heavy cannon, ten of which were rifled.

On April 10 Gillmore started his bombardment. The smoothbore cannon shells and balls bounced off the fort's walls, just as he and the Confederates had expected. The rifled cannon rounds, however, burrowed deep into the brick walls before exploding. Within a few hours, the surprised Confederate commander and Gillmore both reached the same conclusion. If the Federals concentrated their fire on the fort's southeastern wall, the wall would crumble, exposing the fort's powder magazine. Faced with no choice other than annihilation, Fort Pulaski's commander surrendered on April 11.

In two days of shelling, Gillmore's experiment with rifled cannon had rendered obsolete the nation's forts, built over fifty years at costs of millions of dollars.

In the summer of 1863, Gillmore was offered the job of capturing or destroying Fort Sumter. The navy had already tried and failed miserably in reducing the fort. Gillmore recognized that if he succeeded in destroying the symbol of secession he would be a national hero.

Gillmore's engineer's eye quickly saw what needed to be done: get as close as possible so he could concentrate his cannon fire. To do that he had to capture Battery Wagner, a sand fort on the north end of Morris Island just fourteen hundred yards from Sumter. Once Gillmore captured Wagner, Fort Sumter would be under his guns and he could shell the bricks into rubble. Once that occurred, Charleston would be easily invaded from the sea. The city would wake up and find the entire Union fleet floating in its harbor. Taking the city itself might even be bloodless.

Gillmore may have confused the puny sand forts of Port Royal he had destroyed just eighteen months earlier with Battery Wagner. He made a big mistake.

Battery Wagner's thirty-foot-tall walls were made of sand, turf, and palmetto logs. At the top of those walls were ten heavy cannon. Surrounding it was a moat fifty feet wide and five feet deep, filled with water constantly fed by the ocean tides. Inside the fort was a bombproof shelter large enough to hold nine hundred men. Though made of sand like those Port Royal forts, Battery Wagner was better designed and better defended by battle-hardened veterans.

Gillmore's common sense failed him when he planned his first attack on Battery Wagner. He waited less than a day after taking the south end of Morris Island before launching a simple frontal assault against Wagner. He ignored the fact that there was only one way to reach the fort, charging up a beach that was no more than one hundred yards wide on which every Confederate musket and cannon would be aimed.

The first attack ended quickly with more than three hundred Federal casualties. Gillmore then tried to reduce the fort's garrison by artillery from his own cannon and navy monitors. More than nine thousand shells were fired into the fort in anticipation that it would be followed by an infantry charge that would mop up any remaining defenders. What Gillmore had not counted on was the simplicity of Battery Wagner. When those rifled cannon shells landed, they burrowed deep, as they were designed to destroy masonry forts. But the sand had less resistance than masonry so when the shells exploded, they were deep underground. Only eight Confederates were killed. Most defenders just got sand in their hair and ringing in their ears from all the heavy shelling. Gillmore had no idea his bombardment had failed. He believed any attack would be a mop-up operation, but Battery Wagner was as strong as it ever was. Gillmore's attacking column of over six thousand troops stretched more than a mile down the one-hundred-yard beach. At the head was the Fifty-fourth Massachusetts, a regiment of free blacks formed in Boston earlier that year. Gillmore was so confident his artillery had virtually destroyed the resistance, he scheduled the attack for late evening on the same day as the bombardment. The danger in that was if the attack took longer than expected, the Federal column would be hampered by darkness.

As the Fifth-fourth Massachusetts rushed toward the moat, the Confederates rose up onto the walls and sent a rain of musket fire down on the surprised black soldiers. As night fell, the blacks fought valiantly and some reached the top of the walls. But Battery Wagner's defenders had every upper hand. More than half of the Fifth-fourth Massachusetts were killed or wounded before the attack was recalled. All told, the Federals suffered more than fifteen hundred casualties compared to just over two hundred for the Confederates.

Gillmore would never take Battery Wagner by force. After besieging it for two months, the Federals woke up one day to find the fort abandoned. The Confederates simply left in the middle of the night. Embarrassed that his engineering skills and generalship had been defeated by a handful of Confederates inside a fort built by dumping wheelbarrows of sand, Gillmore launched a massive campaign to reduce Fort Sumter to rubble and to terrorize the citizens of Charleston. Operating against a brick fort he understood, Gillmore soon reduced Fort Sumter from the three-story fort that it was before the war to one story. At the same time Gillmore sent shells whistling into downtown Charleston knowing that the city itself had no military targets. He knew he was targeting civilians.

Gillmore was promoted to major general for his success in reducing Fort Sumter, but he actually never succeeded in making either the fort or the city surrender. Both stayed in Confederate hands until the very end of the war.

After the war Gillmore continued his military engineering career by rebuilding some of the same forts that he had blown down. The building material of choice was reinforced concrete, and the forts were built just one story tall to keep a lower profile. The millions spent in reconstruction was wasted as no U.S. fort was attacked after 1865.

Gillmore had proven forts to be obsolete in 1862, but it took another eighty years before the army accepted the idea.

Julia Dent Grant
(1826–1902)

THE WOMAN WHO
KEPT GRANT SOBER

⋆ BULL'S-EYE ⋆

GEN. ULYSSES S. GRANT DRANK WHISKEY. JUST HOW MUCH and how often he drank has always been open to question. President Lincoln perpetuated the disquieting rumors when he once asked what brand of whiskey Grant drank because he wanted to send barrels of it to his other generals.

In all likelihood Grant probably drank no more than any other man of the 1860s and maybe even less. However, when he was drinking, only one person could get him to stop. That was his wife of more than thirty-seven years, Julia Dent Grant. Her ability to make her husband focus on the task at hand—winning a war—makes her a bull's-eye.

The story of General and Mrs. Grant is a true love story, the binding of two soul mates who devoted themselves to each other at first sight and who remained in love with each other to their dying days. While many men, particularly those in the 1860s, saw their wives as mere appendages to their careers, General Grant saw his wife as the linchpin holding his entire life together. Evidence indicates that when she was not around, Grant would find company in a bottle.

Mrs. Grant would likely deny that sort of influence, as she always maintained that stories about the general's drinking habits were mistaken perceptions of Grant's hereditary problems with debilitating headaches. When strangers would look in on Grant during one of these episodes, they would often see him in a darkened room lying on his back, sometimes talking in a delirious state—the same sort of behavior he might exhibit if he were drunk.

Even if Grant did drink to excess on occasion, he does not appear to have been an everyday drinker or one who would drink until he passed out, as is often presented as the stereotype of an alcoholic. The proof of Grant's true drinking habits might be determined from his two terms as president. It was during Grant's military career when he was accused of drunkenness, not during his eight years as president.

Grant first developed his reputation as a heavy drinker during a two-year period of his life, 1852–1854, when he was stationed at a remote base in California. Julia stayed in Missouri. His letters to Julia from the post describe the loneliness he was feeling being separated from her and his young children.

The official records are silent on what really happened in California, but Grant resigned from the army at that post in 1854. In his memoirs Grant claimed he could not support his family on an army officer's pay, so he resigned to look for a better-paying civilian job. But soldiers stationed at the same base reported that Grant had been offered the chance to resign or face a court-martial over his habitual drinking.

After his 1854 resignation Grant seemed to lose his purpose and drive. When the war started he was a clerk in his father's harness store, probably the lowest status position of any living West Point graduate. Most of his friends from the army were high-ranking officers or leaders in private business. But significantly, as low as he must have felt about his personal career, he was not drinking because he was with his family. When alone, he drank. When Julia and his children were with him, he did not.

What sort of woman had such an effect on such a man as U. S. Grant, future General of the Army and president of the United States?

Julia Dent, born short, plump, and with a "wandering eye" that frequently crossed, made up for her lack of physical beauty by developing a keen sense of humor. When her brother Frederick came home on leave to their home in St. Louis from West Point, he brought along his roommate, Ulysses S. Grant.

From the moment Grant and Julia saw each other, each knew that they had found the one person they would love forever. They wed in 1848 after Grant returned from the Mexican War. Grant's biographers have noted that his own mother rarely showed him affection as a child. As a married man, he seemed to hunger for attention from his wife. The Grant children remembered that even as middle-aged adults, their parents held hands and insisted on sitting next to each other whenever possible.

Julia once described her husband: "He was always perfection, a cheerful, self-reliant, earnest gentleman. His beautiful eyes, windows to his great soul, his mouth, so tender, yet so firm. One must not deem me partial to say that General Grant was the very nicest and handsomest man I ever saw."

When the war started Grant offered his services to the governor of Illinois who promptly appointed him colonel of a regiment of volunteers. If the governor had heard of Grant's drinking reputation, it made little difference now that the United States needed trained officers.

Grant gained early attention from his superiors with an aggressive if eventually unsuccessful attack at Belmont, Missouri. Having proved he could still fight, his superiors forgot the old drinking stories and gave him more responsibility.

Perhaps anticipating a recurrence of his old demons, Grant began writing letters to Julia asking that she visit him in camp. Perhaps recognizing what she had to do to keep those demons at bay, Julia readily accepted. She was in camp so much that one irritated officer on Grant's staff suggested she should pay board.

It was during the planning of the attack on Forts Henry and Donelson that Mrs. Grant personally saw the charge of "drunkenness" again made against her husband by an obnoxious civilian businessman who demanded that Grant use his boats to transport troops at an inflated price. When Grant refused, the man wrote a complaint letter to Washington, charging that the general and his staff were drunks.

Grant sometimes sent for his family too soon. Once Mrs. Grant passed through Holly Springs, Mississippi, just hours before raiding Confederates burned his supply depot. That close call did not seem to bother her or the general. Her appearances at headquarters even became somewhat of a joke. He once told her that he had moved his entire headquarters to Nashville, not to be nearer the enemy or to his own army, but to make it easier for her to visit.

As Grant grew more famous and important to the Union cause, Mrs. Grant began to wonder if her wandering eye and plain looks were embarrassing him. She told her husband she had consulted a surgeon about fixing her eye and had been told it was too late to do anything about it as an adult.

The general drew her to him and said: "Did I not see you and fall in love with you with those same eyes? I like them just the way they are, and now, remember, you are not to interfere with them. They are mine, and let me tell you, Mrs. Grant, you had better not make any experiments, as I might not like you half as well with any other eyes." Mrs. Grant never again worried that a prettier lady would turn her husband's head.

Mrs. Grant could handle herself in a bad situation. Just weeks before the war ended, President Lincoln and his wife came to review the Union troops in a large field east of Richmond. Mrs. Lincoln, showing obvious signs of her coming mental breakdown, flew into a rage when she saw another man's wife riding a horse near Lincoln. As Mrs. Grant tried to calm Mrs. Lincoln, the first lady turned on Mrs. Grant, accusing her of wanting to live in the White House herself.

"I am quite satisfied with my present position," Mrs. Grant calmly replied.

Mrs. Grant would stand by her man for another twenty years until the general's death in 1885 just days after he finished his memoirs as a way of taking care of the financial future of his family. She would wear mourning clothes in his memory for the rest of her life.

It would be more than fifty years after her death that the idea of Mrs. Grant's being the general's buffer against drinking would emerge with the publication of a journal kept by a newspaper reporter named Sylvanus Cadwallader.

Cadwallader claimed that during Grant's siege of Vicksburg he took a riverboat trip down the Mississippi with the general. During the course of that trip Grant found a cache of whiskey and got roaring drunk. According to Cadwallader, it was he who put Grant to bed and threw the whiskey overboard. Patting himself on the back, Cadwallader also said that he pointedly decided not to file a story on the incident, knowing that it would affect Grant's reputation.

In his journal Cadwallader claimed that John Rawlins, one of Grant's aides, was normally charged with keeping the general away from liquor. When Rawlins could not control the general, his wife could.

"Everything seemed absolutely safe when she was present. Her quiet firm control of her husband seemed marvelous. When the army had a period of repose and inaction it was noticed that Mrs. Grant and family invariably visited headquarters for a few weeks when all went merry as a wedding bell," Cadwallader wrote.

While Cadwallader's story of trying to sober up Grant on the riverboat did not come to light until decades after the deaths of everyone involved, there is one fact that may lend at least a shred of truth to his claims. Cadwallader was in the room when Lee surrendered to Grant at Appomattox Court House. Grant hated newspaper reporters and had imprisoned more than one of them who tried to report on his armies' activities.

Did Grant just want someone to record the moment for history? Was he responding to journalistic blackmail? Or was he paying back a favor to Cadwallader for his silence?

What is known is that U. S. and Julia Grant had a storybook romance that lasted nearly forty years. It is clear that they loved each other. It is also clear that her frequent visits to his wartime headquarters played a very real, large role in keeping General Grant focused on the war and not on any loneliness he would have felt without his family near him.

Gen. Alexander Hays

(1819–1864)

RECKLESS BRAVERY WINS ONE BATTLE AND LOSES ONE LIFE

✴ BULL'S-EYE ✴

IMPETUOUSNESS KILLED RED-BEARDED, RED-BLOODED Gen. Alexander Hays.

His fighting spirit and reckless abandon helped seal the Union victory at Gettysburg in July 1863, but his fighting spirit and reckless abandon got him killed at the Wilderness in May 1864. That was the way he wanted to go out in life. Hays was not a man to study a battle plan. He wanted to fight. He was once quoted as saying, "Strategy is a humbug, next thing to cowardice."

Though the same bravery Hays exhibited in July 1863 led to his death in May 1864, his cool, calm actions on Cemetery Ridge gave his men the courage they needed to face and defeat thousands of Confederates who seemed to target them. Hays was a bull's-eye.

Born in Pennsylvania as the son of a U.S. congressman who wrangled an appointment for his less-than-brilliant son, Hays graduated twentieth out of twenty-five cadets in the 1844 West Point class. He fought in several battles during the Mexican War, including one in which his leg was mangled. Surgeons were able to keep the leg rather than amputate it, but the wound's effects lingered and were so painful he resigned from the army in 1848. After failing to find any gold in the California gold rush, he spent the next thirteen years acting as a bridge engineer for a Pennsylvania railroad. That was a curious career choice as Hays had finished at the bottom of his West Point class. The U.S. Army had not thought him smart enough to become an engineer, but he found such a job as a civilian.

When the war broke out Hays rejoined the army and was first given a captain's command of one of the few existing regiments of U.S. Regulars. By fall he had raised his own volunteer regiment, the Sixty-third Pennsylvania.

Hays began to show his lust for battle during the Peninsula campaign in the spring of 1862. During the Seven Days' battles he personally led a bayonet charge in order to break up a Confederate attack on a Union artillery battery. He came out of the fight with blindness in one eye and partial paralysis in an arm.

The colonel proved to be quite a dramatic writer as well as a fighter. In his official report on the Peninsula fight, Hays wrote: "At once the men sprang to their feet, and with leveled bayonets dashed upon the enemy. The conflict was short, but most desperate, especially around the buildings. It was muzzle to muzzle, and the powder actually burned the faces of the opposing men as they contended through the paling fences." Later he wrote in a letter, "In a flash, yelling like incarnate fiends, we were upon them."

That sort of zeal for close-in, personal combat would mark Hays for a shortened war life. Several months later Hays would be wounded again with a shattered leg at Second Bull Run. It is unrecorded if the leg was the same leg first injured in the Mexican War. Again, the surgeons were able to save the leg rather than amputate it.

Though promoted to brigadier for his actions at Second Bull Run, Hays would be frequently absent from frontline duty for the rest of the year while the leg healed. During that time he was put in command of a brigade that had a reputation for being cowards, as they had surrendered to Stonewall Jackson in September 1862. Hays took advantage of a lull in the fighting after the battle of Antietam in the late fall of 1862 to drill the brigade until he could trust them. He then proclaimed them to be fighters waiting for the chance to prove it. He would get his chance in seven months.

Just before the battle of Gettysburg, Hays was judged fully recovered. He and his former coward brigade were added to the Third Division, Second Corps of the Army of the Potomac. Though he was only an untested brigadier after his long recovery, he was made division commander. That might have been unwise in most armies as brigades, units formed of four or more regiments, wanted to know under whom they were fighting. Two of the three brigades forming the Third Division had never seen Hays.

Within a week, the men would come to love him.

Hays later wrote about Gettysburg: "I was fighting for my native state, and before I went in thought of those at home I so dearly love. If Gettysburg was lost all was lost for them, and I only interposed a life that would be otherwise worthless."

Hays did not have much fighting to do on the first and second days of Gettysburg, but that would change on the third day when the fighting would shift to Cemetery Ridge. The brigade's position was to the right or north of what would be called "the Angle," a right turn in the stone wall that was just north of the clump of trees that would become the familiar focal point of the third day assault formally known as the Pettigrew-Pickett-Trimble assault and dubbed Pickett's Charge by Virginia newspaper editors.

Hays's men formed the far right of the Union line on Cemetery Ridge. If any part of his line folded under attack and the Confederates wheeled right, they would be able to deliver enfilading fire down the Union line.

On the afternoon of July 3, 1863, the entire Union line came under heavy Confederate cannon fire at 1:00 P.M. Knowing the psychological

45

effect exploding cannon shells had on men who could not do a thing about it, Hays kept his men busy. He ordered them to roam the ground to find discarded muskets. He then ordered the weapons cleaned, loaded, and stacked. He was accomplishing two goals: focusing his men's minds on something other than the cannonade and preparing them for the Confederate infantry attack he guessed would commence once the cannon fire ended.

Once the Confederates came out of the wood and seemingly lined up directly in front of his position nearly a mile away, Hays did something even more remarkable. He ordered some regiments up and into a drill formation. As they watched the Confederate line march toward them over Hays's shoulder, the general calmly drilled his men in the manual of arms. Once again his purpose was to calm his men and make them focus on loading and firing their muskets.

As the Confederates closed on his line, Hays split off several regiments from the line. He rushed them first north and then west down the Bryan Farm Lane until they were perpendicular with the Confederates. From there they joined with another regiment to pour fire into the Confederate left flank.

Within minutes the Pettigrew-Pickett-Trimble assault crested and then melted away. Hays could not resist doing something to celebrate the victory. He reached over and kissed one of his more-than-surprised aides.

Hays and two aides then grabbed up three Confederate battle flags that had been captured. Hays then grabbed a United States flag. With that flying high and with the three Confederate flags dragging in the dirt behind them, Hays and his aides rode up and down the Union line signifying the victory.

After the battle Northern newspapers focused on the fighting near the Angle where the Union line broke, instead of Hays's part of the line where it did not. That angered Hays and his men who pointed out that the Confederate attack began to fold from the left, thanks to their heavy firing. Had they not held fast while the Union center wavered, the whole Union line might have failed.

Hays continued to command the Third Division for the rest of the year. His next major victory was at Bristoe Station, Virginia, in October when his division was able to surprise attacking Confederates by rising up from behind a steep railroad embankment. The Confederates lost nearly 1,400 men while the Federals lost only 550 with nearly half of them coming in Hays's division.

When the Army of the Potomac was reorganized in March 1864 to consolidate units, Hays lost his division command status and reverted to command of the Second Brigade of the Third Division, the same brigade he had before accepting division command.

It was in the afternoon of May 5, 1864, the first day of the Wilderness, that Hays's reputation for running toward a fight caught up with him. Ordered to relieve the pressure on the Union line, Hays's men pushed forward into the thick undergrowth. As the men pressed forward, Hays came upon his old regiment, the Sixth-third Pennsylvania. As he paused to give them words of encouragement, a Confederate minié ball hit him in the head. He was dead before he hit the ground.

A lieutenant colonel who kept a diary about the men around him wrote of Hays: "A braver man never went into action and the wonder only is that he was not killed before, as he always rode at the head of his men, shouting to them and waving his sword."

Grant said of Hays in his memoirs: "I am not surprised that he met his death at the head of his troops, it was just like him. He was a man who would never follow, but would always lead in battle."

Col. Thomas Wentworth Higginson
(1823–1911)

JOHN BROWN'S CONSPIRATOR
TURNED ARMY COLONEL

★ BULL'S-EYE ★

JOHN BROWN'S NAME AND HIS RAID ON HARPERS FERRY are familiar to most amateur historians, but few people know of the Secret Six. That would please them. The Six were not dubbed "secret" for nothing. The Secret Six were New England abolitionists who bankrolled Brown's mission to start a slave revolt they hoped would spread throughout the South.

Once Brown was captured and their backing discovered, five of the Secret Six denied knowing his plans. Most denied knowing Brown at all, prompting that sixth one to compare the others to the Apostle Peter who denied he knew Jesus Christ after he had been arrested.

When the war began less than two years after Brown's execution, only one of those Harvard-educated elites put on a uniform to fight. That was Thomas Wentworth Higginson. To be fair, only two of the six were young enough to take the field, but only Higginson stayed true to his long-held beliefs all during his career.

Higginson was a Unitarian minister, radical abolitionist, women's rights advocate, author, and the first colonel to lead a black regiment in the war. More than six months before the famous Fifty-fourth Massachusetts Regiment, made up of educated, northern-born blacks, would go into battle, Higginson would command the unfamous First South Carolina Volunteers, made up of recently freed slaves. It was Higginson who would first prove that black Union soldiers were equal in ability to white Union soldiers.

Higginson's dedication to his causes, his willingness to finally fight for them, and his belief that all men deserve freedom make him a bull's-eye.

As a minister before the war, Higginson railed equally against slavery in the South and the low wages offered by factory owners in his own northern hometown. Curiously, he also came down pro-South on one issue: against the high national tariffs New Englanders favored to protect the high prices of goods they manufactured. In 1853 church leaders, who included the factory owners Higginson despised, finally tired of Higginson's beratings and fired him.

In 1854 Higginson participated in the bloody clashes between proslavery Missouri and antislavery Kansas. Here he met John Brown, an abolitionist with a streak of insanity in his family who would become famous in two years for hacking to death five proslavery men in Kansas. The murders of the five men, who were not slave owners, did not bother Pastor Higginson, who wrote that the abolition of slavery was more important than determining if the nation would remain at peace or at war.

When Higginson moved back to New England, Brown approached him with a fantastic plan: financing an armed invasion of the South by dedicated abolitionists who would incite a slave revolt that could spread from Virginia to Texas.

Higginson and five key ministers, school teachers, and wealthy financiers gave Brown money to buy weapons. They described themselves as "stockholders" in Brown's plan. Anxious to see returns on their investment, they grumbled when Brown kept delaying his invasion.

When the raid finally was staged on Harpers Ferry, Virginia, on October 16, 1859, the stockholders were ecstatic—until they heard that Brown and his followers had been quickly captured, along with a cache of letters that named his financiers. Now dubbed the Secret Six by the newspapers, they panicked. Some consulted lawyers. Others fled to Canada to avoid prosecution for treason. Another had himself committed to an insane asylum until the heat died down. Dr. Samuel Howe, married to Julia Ward Howe, future composer of "The Battle Hymn of the Republic," ran out the door shouting to his surprised, pregnant wife that if men came looking for him, she didn't know where he was and he had never met Brown.

Only Higginson made no attempt to hide his involvement. For a while he thought about mounting a rescue mission to free Brown. He offered to speak for Brown before a U.S. Senate committee investigating the raid. Two of the Secret Six were subpoenaed and flatly denied they knew of Brown's plans, but Higginson, the most active conspirator, was never called.

When the war started, Higginson told everyone that while he would like to fight to end slavery, his invalid wife needed him at home. Finally, ashamed to be at home when so many other Massachusetts men were fighting, Higginson changed his mind. He was recruiting his own regiment in August 1862 when he got an invitation he could not refuse.

Union Gen. Rufus Saxton, military commander of the Sea Islands around Beaufort, South Carolina, offered Higginson command of the First South Carolina Volunteers. In March 1862 Saxton's predecessor, Gen. David Hunter, had declared all black slaves in his district free. President Lincoln immediately disavowed Hunter's unauthorized attempt at emancipation, but Hunter never disbanded a regiment of armed blacks he had created at the same time he freed them. That summer they were made legal soldiers by an executive order that vaguely referred to them as militia.

Though Higginson had no military experience, one officer wrote of him: "He was a born commander. He met a slave and made him a man."

Higginson approached his First South Carolina Volunteers with the idea that black men were little different from white men, a radical idea even among abolitionists, who were against slavery but not necessarily for racial equality.

"It needs but a few days to show the absurdity of distrusting the military availability of these people. They have quite as much average comprehension as whites, as much courage, as much previous knowledge of the gun, and above all, a readiness of ear and of imitation, which, for purposes of drill, counterbalances any defect of mental training. To learn the drill, one does not want a set of college professors; one wants a squad of eager, active, pliant, school-boys, and the more childlike these pupils are the better. There is no trouble in the drill; they will surpass whites in that," wrote Higginson in his postwar book *Army Life in a Black Regiment.*

Higginson's book revealed his own prejudices, although he thought of himself as the perfect abolitionist. He called blacks "perpetual children, gay, docile and lovable." When he quoted blacks speaking to him, he imitated a black dialect. He wrote that the word *nigger* was offensive but that his soldiers used it to describe each other. He wrote that the black soldiers described each other with the word around camp and they used it "far more common than with well-bred slaveholders." He noted different skin colors among the slaves freed from Florida from those freed from South Carolina, speculating their ancestors were from different African tribes.

The First South Carolina followed Higginson's orders without question once he explained that blacks followed orders not because white officers gave them, but because officers gave them. In March 1863 Higginson's blacks and a white regiment participated in a joint exercise, the occupation of Jacksonville, Florida. It was the first time black and white troops had been thrown together. To Higginson's relief, there were no clashes between wandering white soldiers and black provost guards whose job it was to guard the city of Jacksonville.

While under Higginson's command, the First South Carolina did not participate in any large battles. Most of the missions consisted of plantation raids in South Carolina, Georgia, and Florida to free other slaves.

Higginson enjoyed the reaction he saw when he freed men from bondage.

"Before the war, how great a thing seemed the rescue of even one man from slavery; and since the war has emancipated all, how little seems the liberation of two hundred!" wrote Higginson, proclaiming that the war had been worth the cost in dead in order to end slavery.

The colonel kept a sense of humor about him. Once on a raid into Florida, a breathless white officer rushed into Higginson's camp reporting the discovery of a large Confederate camp. Higginson's regiment swooped down on the supposed camp only to find a woman hanging sheets out to dry. The white officer had mistaken the hanging sheets for tents. Higginson described the incident as "the Battle of the Clothes Line."

Higginson commanded the First South Carolina barely a year and a half, resigning in May 1864 several months after a cannonball brushed his side, which he claimed affected his health.

After he left, the regiment was redesignated the Thirty-third United States Colored Troops. The taking of the regiment's historic South Carolina identity irritated them and Higginson. The history-making unit would later join with the Fifty-fourth Massachusetts to fight in the last action in South Carolina at Boykin's Mill on April 18, 1865. That created the improbable scenario of the first black slave regiment and the first free black regiment fighting in the last battle in the first state to secede from the Union.

Two sergeants of the First South Carolina Volunteers later served in the South Carolina legislature, a fact Higginson noted with pride. He noted that other veterans of the unit went on to earn good livings after the war.

"The increased self-respect of army life fitted them to do the duties of civil life," he wrote. "We who served with black troops have this peculiar satisfaction that whatever dignity or sacredness the memories of the war may have for others, they have more to us. The peculiar privilege of associating with an outcast race, of training it to defend its rights and to perform its duties, this was our special need. The vacillating policy of the Government sometimes filled other officers with doubt and shame; until the Negro had justice, they were but defending liberty with one hand and crushing it with another. From this inconsistency we were free."

Higginson never gave up campaigning for causes. When he died in 1911, his attention was on integration of public schools and for giving women the right to vote.

Gen. Henry Hunt

(1819–1889)

THE ARTILLERYMAN WHO WON MALVERN HILL AND GETTYSBURG

✴ BULL'S-EYE ✴

THE BEST SOLDIERS ARE OFTEN IGNORED BY HISTORY because they don't know how—or refuse—to play the politicians' games.

Such was the case with Brig. Gen. Henry Jackson Hunt. Thanks in large part to Hunt, the Army of Northern Virginia was virtually crippled at two different battles, and at another battle the Confederates' recognition of Hunt's abilities kept them from counterattacking and destroying a crippled Union army.

It was Hunt's skillful use of artillery in battle after battle that made him a bull's-eye. He was one of the most skillful artillerists in the history of the U.S. Army. Without his careful alignment of guns and his stingy husbanding of ammunition during the war, the Union army might have lost.

Though Hunt contributed greatly to many Union victories, his own commanders and the Washington politicians virtually ignored him. He remained a colonel months after worthless politicians were made brigadier generals. He remained a brigadier the entire war when much less talented men paraded around in major generals' uniforms.

Why was Hunt ignored? First, he was an artilleryman, an expert in aiming cannon in an army commanded by infantry generals who believed battles were won by men standing shoulder to shoulder firing muskets at each other. Second, Hunt was a loyal friend of George McClellan, the general who fell out of favor in the fall of 1862. In a political army headed by a political commander in chief, having the wrong friends meant your contributions to the war effort were suspect.

Hunt excelled in the West Point mathematics and geometry classes, which would prove handy when figuring firing angles, but he regularly chalked up demerits for wearing his hair too long and dressing in a slovenly manner. In his junior year he was only twenty demerits short of being expelled. He finally graduated in 1839.

Awarded two brevets for bravery in the Mexican War, in 1856 he joined a three-man panel in writing a new manual of artillery for the army. The manual would be published just in time to be used by both sides.

Hunt's first major service to the Union was developing the plan to destroy the Harpers Ferry Arsenal should Secessionists attack it. Within hours of learning Virginia had seceded, the man who followed Hunt as commander of the arsenal destroyed fifteen thousand muskets by putting them in a massive fire, as Hunt had conceived.

Major Hunt proved his value as an artillerist at the first major battle, Bull Run, when his four-gun battery covered the retreat of the shattered Union army. After Bull Run he was promoted to colonel.

It was during the Peninsula campaign that Hunt developed his reputation as a stickler for accuracy and economy of fire from his gunners.

"Under no circumstances will it [cannon fire] be so rapid that the effect of each shot and shell can not be noted when the air is clear. . . . There is no excess of ammunition, what we have must be made the most of," Hunt ordered.

Hunt would first save the Union army on June 30, 1862. On the last day of the Seven Days' battles as George McClellan's Union army began to swarm back past his position, Hunt ringed the crown of Malvern Hill with more than one hundred cannon parked hub to hub.

Hunt's old friend Robert E. Lee tried to break the Federal position with his own cannon but Hunt's gunners were so well trained they found the range of every Confederate gun that tried to unlimber.

With his artillery virtually destroyed, Lee ordered his infantry forward. More than five thousand Confederate infantrymen fell before Hunt's guns in one of the few battles fought almost exclusively by Federal cannon against Confederate muskets.

McClellan rewarded Hunt's Malvern Hill performance by putting him in charge of all of the army's artillery, a plan Hunt had been pushing for months.

When Gen. Ambrose Burnside replaced McClellan, Hunt retained his position as artillery chief. However, he must have considered resigning soon afterwards, because he was ordered to fire on Fredericksburg in December 1862. Hunt later wrote that using his artillery to level the town was "barbarous" because the shelling was directed at civilian targets rather than military.

Hunt watched helplessly as the Federal infantry rushed up the steep slope on the south bank toward Marye's Heights. Not a single Federal soldier reached the stone wall. More than 12,500 were killed and wounded. Hunt could not fire on the Confederates out of fear of hitting Federals.

But it was the presence of Hunt's guns on that north bank that kept Lee from pursuing Burnside once the Federal army was beaten back across the river in total defeat. Lee remembered the last time he had faced Hunt's guns when they had the height advantage of Malvern Hill. Hunt had saved the Federal army from disaster just by being who he was and where he was.

After Fredericksburg, Gen. Joseph Hooker replaced Burnside, which was not remarkable considering Burnside's spectacular and bloody defeat. What was remarkable was that Hooker demoted Hunt. All of Hunt's carefully constructed plans on how to use artillery were also dismantled. Instead of the artillery being under one commander, Hunt, Hooker distributed the guns to all of the division commanders. Some of these men were political appointees who had little training in the placement of cannon.

When Stonewall Jackson's flanking movement smashed into Hooker's right flank at Chancellorsville, the Federal guns were scattered all over the thick woods, just as Hooker had ordered. They were useless in stopping the onrushing Confederates.

After the battle Hooker owned up to his mistake in replacing Hunt, who was reinstated. His suggestions that the artillery batteries be grouped into brigades attached to the corps were approved.

Hunt did not let Hooker off the hook when writing his official report on the battle of Chancellorsville: "I doubt if the history of modern armies can exhibit a parallel instance of such palpable crippling of a great arm of the service in the very presence of the enemy."

It was just two months later that Hunt would prove his value yet again to the Union army. The place was Gettysburg.

On the third day of the battle, Hunt saw that the Confederates were massing their cannon on Seminary Ridge and pointing them at Cemetery Ridge. Hunt realized that the Confederates were aiming their guns straight on, rather than from an angle that would give them enfilading fire. If Lee was willing to put his guns in such a disadvantageous position, something else must be up. Hunt ordered his gunners to save their ammunition rather than reply heavily to the expected Confederate cannonade.

Hunt the artillerist was appalled at the ineffectiveness of his foe's fire. Most of the Confederate shells were being fired too high and were clearing the ridge, landing in the rear of the Union lines. The few Confederate guns that were in an enfilading position did not seem to make the most of their advantage. Hunt was most irritated because he knew that some of the Southern gunners had once served under him and had supposedly read his instruction manual.

When Hunt's gunners replied, he cautioned them to treat their fire like target practice, meaning he wanted them to be slow and precise in their aim. After a while, Hunt ordered the Federal cannon to stop firing so they could conserve ammunition for the infantry assault he assumed would be coming.

Though Hunt had not intended it, that simple act of stopping fire influenced the following Confederate actions. Lee interpreted the Federal lessening in fire to mean that their batteries were either destroyed or had run out of ammunition. Observers saw some guns leaving the line, which the Confederates wrongly interpreted to mean that the Federal guns were abandoning Cemetery Ridge.

One Union corps general, Winfield Scott Hancock, overrode Hunt's orders to stop firing. His Union Second Corps guns kept firing at the distant Confederate cannon.

Hunt did not have time to confront Hancock over the dispute. Nearly twelve thousand Confederates surged out of the woods and there was no time to argue.

Time would prove Hancock wrong and Hunt right. By the time the Confederates reached the center of the field, Hancock's gunners were out of ammunition that could reach them. That meant more than a third of the Federal guns could not stop the Confederates until they got within four hundred yards. That was the range of canister, tin cans filled with small musket balls that turned cannon into shotguns. Canister was deadly against infantry, but it was also the ammunition of last resort. It also meant that Hancock's gunners would be in range of Confederate rifle fire before they could reply with their cannon.

As the Confederates crossed the Emmitsburg Road, Hunt finally ordered his artillery to again fire into them. The effect was what he expected. Great gaps opened in the lines of the remaining Confederates. Only in front of Hancock's corps did the Confederates reach the stone wall.

Hunt himself came close to being killed. Five bullets hit and killed his horse as the artillery commander incongruously fired his pistol at the rushing Confederates. He kept shouting, "See them? See them?"

Just as the tide of gray had reached the wall, it receded before round after round of canister fire.

There would be no more instances during the war when Hunt would save the Union army from its commanders. U. S. Grant would eventually appoint Hunt to command all of the siege operations against Petersburg, a job Hunt hated since it again involved targeting civilians. He never was promoted beyond brigadier general, and was reverted to colonel's rank in the peacetime army.

By the early 1880s Hunt was retired and broke. In 1883 a bill was introduced in Congress that would have given Hunt the retired status of a major general, a title many of his lesser known and lesser skilled contemporaries in the infantry had attained.

Republicans, angry at Hunt's mild treatment of former Confederate officers in his Reconstruction postings and remembering his loyalty to McClellan, repeatedly stalled the bill. It finally passed but President Chester A. Arthur refused to sign it.

Hunt died in February 1889. The same Washington politicians who would not grant him a general's pension during his lifetime went all out upon his death with an elaborate funeral and posthumous congratulations for what he had done for the artillery.

It would take the *Army and Navy Journal* to boldly print the truth about the politicians' terrible treatment of a true hero of the war. The newspaper wrote of Hunt: "Had his services and his abilities received their proper recognition he would not have died as a colonel upon the retired list."

Gen. Rufus Ingalls
(1818–1893)

THE COZY QUARTERMASTER
WHO KEPT GRANT SUPPLIED

★ BULL'S-EYE ★

WHEN THE GENERAL IN CHIEF OF THE UNITED STATES Army refuses the warm, comfortable accommodations of a home, choosing instead to spend a damp winter in his tent, there must be a reason. The reason U. S. Grant gave was he did not want to disturb the routine of the chief quartermaster of the Army of the Potomac, Gen. Rufus Ingalls.

The routine Grant preserved was the round-the-clock buildup of supplies coming into City Point, Virginia, starting in the summer of 1864. If keeping the ships rolling in and the supplies rolling out toward Petersburg and Richmond meant cold toes for him and his staff while Ingalls and his pencil pushers remained warm, so be it.

Ingalls never drew a saber or a pistol in battle. He probably never even saw a Confederate face to face. But if keeping an army supplied can be considered strategic, Ingalls was one of the most important generals in the war. He was a bull's-eye.

Ingalls did not show any of his organizational abilities early in his military career. A native of Maine, he placed thirty-second among thirty-nine West Point graduates, nine spots behind his roommate and future boss, Grant. It was while stationed in Washington State that Ingalls developed a reputation for writing detailed reports. This meticulousness would shape Ingalls's Civil War career.

He was involved early in the war, serving as quartermaster for a relief expedition to Fort Pickens in Pensacola, Florida, before Fort Sumter in Charleston was fired upon in April 1861. During the summer of 1862 McClellan named Ingalls quartermaster of the Army of the Potomac. He would hold the post for the rest of the war.

Ingalls literally got a trial by fire in his new position. At the same time he was promoted, McClellan was evacuating his army from Harrison's Landing, Virginia, after failing to win the Seven Days' battles. While quartermasters usually transported supplies to the front, Ingalls's first job was keeping his ample supplies from being captured. Less than two months later his job was complicated when Lee's Army of Northern Virginia also routed Gen. John Pope's Army of Virginia after Second Manassas. Ingalls had to salvage the wreckage of two defeated armies separated by nearly 150 miles.

Not long after straightening out that mess, Ingalls rushed supplies northward as McClellan was given back command of the Army of the Potomac as it chased Lee into Maryland. Finally in November 1862 Ingalls was given a chance to catch his breath and catch up with his inventory. Then President Lincoln sacked his friend McClellan for failing to destroy Lee's army.

The new commander, Gen. Ambrose Burnside, wired Washington asking for scores of pontoon bridges so he could bridge the Rappahannock River at Fredericksburg in December 1862. There was little Ingalls could do to speed the delivery of those bridges as all of them were out of his jurisdiction. The slow Washington bureaucracy ignored

Burnside's demands for haste and delivered the boats long after Lee had arrived on the opposing bank.

As Ingalls's responsibility grew, so did his rank. He was promoted to brigadier general of volunteers May 1863. That summer the army was more than one hundred thousand men and now chasing Lee as he made his way toward Pennsylvania.

Hardly a day went by that Ingalls did not hear from some general in some division that he needed something—immediately. Ingalls's job would have been easier if northern manufacturers had been more cooperative with the war effort, but many were not. One problem Ingalls uncovered was the manufacture of a military cloth that was of such poor quality that he rejected it. That cloth, called "shoddy," has since entered the American language and changed from a noun to an adjective describing any poorly manufactured product.

The job of army quartermaster took on new challenges in the spring of 1864 when Grant took command. Under past commanders the Union army had a predictable habit. Lee would beat the Army of the Potomac in the field and its generals would retreat to refit. Under Grant the Union army would be beaten in the field, but it would then press on after Lee's army. Ingalls's usual methods of resupply suddenly no longer worked. While in the past he had been resupplying the army in the rear, now he had to resupply almost on the front lines.

Ingalls reached the pinnacle of his career when he established the supply depot at City Point, Virginia, a natural port southeast of Petersburg where the smaller Appomattox River joins the much larger James River. From here he would supply two armies, Grant who was besieging Petersburg, and Gen. Ben Butler who was trying to take Richmond in the Bermuda Hundred campaign.

City Point first started taking form in June 1864 on a captured plantation. Within months Ingalls would transform the farm fields into a combination small city and seaport. Eight wharves covering eight acres, with almost two acres under roof, would dominate the waterfront. Three hundred buildings would house his support personnel of ten thousand men. On any given day twenty-five supply ships could be unloaded on the wharves and their supplies loaded on a rail line built from City Point to the front lines. On any given day between 150 and 200 ships would be in the harbor waiting their turn to unload.

Ingalls thought of everything the army needed. One example was a bakery that turned out one hundred thousand loaves of bread a day. Soldiers told stories of hot bread being loaded onto train cars for delivery to the front lines more than twenty miles away. The bread would still be warm when served. City Point had a wagon repair shop to keep Grant's five thousand wagons on the road. A virtual army of blacksmiths and farriers took care of the horseshoe and harness needs of the sixty thousand horses and mules the army employed.

City Point was so massive that it could not escape Southern notice or envy. On August 19, 1864, a Confederate secret agent sneaked a time bomb aboard an ammunition barge. The bomb killed 43 and wounded another 126. Grant himself was showered with body parts and wooden splinters that wounded members of his staff. The chain reaction explosion and massive fire that the agent hoped would spread from ship to ship never occurred.

Not wanting to take any more chances, Ingalls unloaded all ammunition at a special ordnance wharf some distance away from the rest of the wharves.

Grant set his headquarters tent on the front lawn and told his staff he would not remove Ingalls from the house that had been serving as headquarters. Grant's grumbling staff members, envious of the fireplaces and beds of the bean counters inside the house, went along with those orders until the general left for an extended visit to the front lines. As fast as they could, they scrounged lumber and built a series of rough cabins in which to spend the winter of 1864–1865.

Grant was not happy when he returned and found the cabins serving as his headquarters, but he let them stay.

Strangely, Grant never really gave credit to Ingalls for his victory over Lee's army. In Grant's memoirs he writes: "There never was any corps better organized than the quartermaster's corps with the Army of the Potomac in 1864." After writing that line, however, Grant does not mention Ingalls by name except to comment on how the quartermaster put corps badges on the canvas of supply wagons so they could be easily identified. Other men who had much less to do with the Union victory than Ingalls got much more mention in Grant's postwar book. Grant's slight likely had to do with Ingalls's status as behind-the-lines support instead of a frontline soldier.

Ingalls may have been wanting to get in on some of the fighting once it was obvious that the war was winding down. According to Julia Dent Grant's memoirs, Ingalls made a pest of himself by constantly asking Grant why the Confederates had not tried to take City Point. He wanted the chance to defend his base. With Grant at the McLean House when Lee surrendered on April 9, 1865, the quartermaster, who had supplied Grant's army with everything he needed to defeat Lee, humbly asked the Southern general for permission to see his old Confederate friends.

Ingalls stayed in the army for more than forty years, eventually reaching the highest office he wanted, quartermaster general with a permanent staff ranking of brigadier general, the highest rank allowed under law. Barely fifteen months after his last promotion, Ingalls retired. He lived another ten years, dying in 1893.

While the Army of the Potomac and the Army of Virginia (John Pope's army) had seven different commanding generals, there was only one chief quartermaster for both armies. Ingalls was all they had ever needed.

Naval Engineer Benjamin Isherwood
(1822–1915)

THE LANDLUBBER WHO BUILT
THE STEAM NAVY

✸ BULL'S-EYE ✸

BENJAMIN ISHERWOOD DID NOT KNOW MUCH ABOUT
sailing, but he did know steam engines. Because he was not a sailor, he
often clashed with the men who were. The navy men of the 1860s hated
him with a passion, but sailors today who cruise the world protecting the
interests of the United States know that Isherwood was right and those
old salts, their predecessors, were wrong.

Isherwood probably knew a ship's bow from its stern, but his experience in—and interest in—ships did not progress much beyond this
knowledge. It was not the ships themselves that captured Isherwood's
attention, but the steam engines that propelled them through the water.
Americans can be thankful he had this interest, for Isherwood dragged

a reluctant U.S. Navy kicking and screaming into the nineteenth century era of steam power. Without him, the navy never would have developed the power plants their ships needed to catch up to the steam-assisted blockade-runners moving in and out of Southern ports. Isherwood's vision for the navy of his present and the future makes him a bull's-eye.

Isherwood never really had any other interest in life than learning the advantages and limits of steam power. Forced to find employment at age fourteen after first his father and then his stepfather died, Isherwood apprenticed himself as a draftsman in a locomotive repair shop. He never attended any other school to earn the title of "steam engineer" that would define the rest of his career.

In 1842 the U.S. Navy was beginning to experiment with steam-powered vessels. Armed with knowledge that few other men had, Isherwood easily found a position as a first assistant engineer in the U.S. Navy. For the next twenty years Isherwood experimented with steam engines and adjunct means of propulsion, such as testing the efficiency of paddle wheels against screw propellers.

Isherwood's first contribution to the wartime navy came in April 1861 before the war had started. Though Virginia had not yet seceded from the Union, it seemed likely it would follow its sister states. Docked at the Gosport Naval Yard in Norfolk, the navy's largest repair facility, were several ships that were of value to both the Union and the fledgling Confederacy. Among them was the USS *Merrimack*, a forty-gun steam frigate finished in 1854 that had been put into Norfolk to repair its small, inefficient, and inadequate steam engines. Isherwood had not designed those engines.

Ordered to Norfolk to rush repairs on the *Merrimack's* engines, Isherwood took only three days to get them working, far short of the four weeks another engineer had suggested the job would take. Isherwood found a volunteer crew and began to build steam in the *Merrimack's* engines so she could be sailed out before Virginia's Secessionists realized what was happening and captured the ship.

When he made one final check with Gosport's navy commander, Isherwood was stunned when the old, possibly drunk or senile, man said he had not decided if he would let the *Merrimack* leave out of fear that it would antagonize the local populace who still were citizens of the United States. Isherwood tried to persuade the ship's captain to sail anyway, but the captain was leery about ignoring orders from a superior officer. Isherwood thought about taking out the vessel himself but he too feared that a rigid navy could court-martial him.

Isherwood rushed back to Washington to alert his bosses. By the time a replacement commander made it to Norfolk, it was too late to sail the *Merrimack*. She was burned at her moorings to keep her out of the hands of the Confederates, but she was later salvaged and used as the hull of the ironclad CSS *Virginia*. Isherwood got some pleasure from that experience. The *Merrimack's* engines that he found atrociously designed would cause the Confederates much grief when on the *Virginia*.

Luckily for Isherwood, the secretary of the navy knew the loss of the *Merrimack* was not Isherwood's fault. He liked Isherwood's spunk in accomplishing what had been described as a four-week task in three days. The naval secretary nominated Isherwood first as the navy's chief engineer and then later to head the new Bureau of Steam Engineering.

Faced with trying to control nearly two hundred ports and three thousand miles of ocean coastline and rivers deep enough to float blockade-runners, the U.S. Navy had to expand by building ships that were faster than any blockade-runner. To Isherwood that meant only one thing: The days of sailing were over and the era of steam-powered ships had arrived. While Isherwood was never able to standardize an engine design that could be mass produced by the scattered steam boiler and engine manufacturers in the North, he did succeed in designing machinery and engines for forty-six paddle wheelers and seventy-nine screw steamers.

It was while building this steam navy that Isherwood developed a prominent enemy, John Ericsson, the inventor of the USS *Monitor*. Isherwood never understood why Ericsson hated him, but the answer was obvious. Isherwood presented a threat to Ericsson's ego.

When Isherwood designed his own ironclad based on Ericsson's *Monitor*, Ericsson hit the roof. He refused to speak or write to Isherwood, but he did go to numerous congressmen and to the assistant secretary of the navy with charges that Isherwood was trying to steal his designs and run him out of business. To satisfy Ericsson, the navy created an independent "monitor bureau" outside the direct control of Isherwood.

Ironically, it was not Isherwood but someone on Ericsson's own staff of monitor designers who undercut Ericsson's credibility. When the navy asked Ericsson to design a series of monitors that would draw very little water, he turned the job over to another engineer named Alban Stimers. When Stimers's monitors were constructed, they barely floated even when empty of coal and ammunition. Ericsson tried unsuccessfully to blame Isherwood for the monitors' problems, but Isherwood explained to investigators that since the shallow-draft monitors fell under the monitor bureau, which Ericsson had created, they were not his responsibility. Eventually, Stimers took the fall for the poor design and was forced out of the navy.

Not all of Isherwood's ideas worked immediately, but some proved to be visionary. In the spring of 1862 he appropriated the USS *Roanoke*, a sister ship to the *Merrimack*. His idea was to build a true ocean-going ironclad that would not have the low freeboard of the typical monitor that allowed water to wash over and down below decks. He removed the ship's masts and cut the ship down to the gun deck. He covered it with iron and added three turrets. What he had designed was the world's first battleship. Though a good idea, the iron plating and the turrets were too heavy and the ship never went into service on the open ocean.

Isherwood also could be proved dead wrong. He steadfastly said that iron was the best material for building ships. He rejected the new product of steel as little more than a type of iron that had not been proven as a quality material. He thought using steel was a shipbuilding fad.

Even when Isherwood made great accomplishments he found critics. His biggest enemies remained the old seafarers who longed for the days when ships moved exclusively by sail. They saw Isherwood as a landlubber who had ruined their lifelong love of the ocean. Sometimes their criticism was ridiculous. In trying to come up with ever faster blockading ships, Isherwood married his engines with a new hull design to create a prototype that made nearly eighteen knots an hour, making it the fastest ship of its day. The old salts reviewing the ship complained that the ship's engines were so big they reduced the size of their cabins. They even tried to claim that the ship was not really as fast as it appeared, that the wind helped push it to the recorded speed. The ship had no sails so any wind assist was minimal at best.

With the war won in 1865 and no other Confederates to fight, the old salts decided they now had free rein to go after Isherwood's status as chief engineer. Leading the pack was Adm. David Porter, a sailor who had greatly benefited from Isherwood's steam-powered ships. Reading Porter's own accounts, it seems that he attacked Isherwood solely out of boredom now that the Confederates had been defeated.

"I assure you I never get tired of pegging away at Isherwood. After all the efforts made to dislodge him it would be hard if in the end we fail to dislodge him," wrote Porter.

Isherwood never knew when to keep his mouth shut, even when he was correct. He enraged veteran naval officers when he claimed that it was naval engineers—not the fighting men—who played the biggest role in defeating the Confederacy on the sea. Isherwood explained, quite rightly, that the Union had many naval engineers while the South had few, so it was easy for him to rationalize why the Union had won. Rubbing salt into that wound, Isherwood went on to claim that the future navy would have to turn even more power over to naval engineers so they could perfect new hull and engine designs for the fighting men.

Isherwood was continually attacked. He was accused of buying used tools from a New York contractor when new ones purchased from a Philadelphia manufacturer would have been more productive. The most ludicrous charge was that after the war the U.S. Navy was forced to rely only on steam power while the rest of the world's navies used steam and sails. In effect, the old salts were complaining that Isherwood had modernized the navy. Even Ericsson got into the act, claiming Isherwood had lied when he said he had improved upon Ericsson's ventilation system in the original *Monitor*.

The chief engineer's fate was finally sealed when incoming President U. S. Grant gave Isherwood's most powerful enemy, Admiral Porter, command of the Navy in 1869. Porter tried hard to find a valid reason for removing Isherwood. He even asked Isherwood to account for every steam engine built since 1861, hoping the engineer had sold U.S. property to a private shipowner. Finding no graft, Porter had to settle on just firing the man who had developed the ships the Union had used to destroy Confederate ships.

Retirement was never really a lifestyle for Isherwood. Even after being forced out of the navy, Isherwood continued to advocate his vision of a fleet of U.S. ships that would dominate the world's oceans. He seems to have invented the idea and the name of a small, quickly deployed type of ship called a "destroyer."

Remarkably, all that talk of sailing the seven seas fell on deaf ears at the navy. The admirals of the day preferred a fleet that would only be defensive in nature. They did not want to leave sight of their own shores.

In May 1915 Isherwood received a letter from the U.S. Navy that it was honoring his contributions by naming a building at the Naval Academy after him. The building would house the marine engineering and naval construction departments.

One month later Isherwood died at the age of ninety-three.

Elizabeth Keckley

(1820–1907)

THE FIRST LADY'S
SANITY KEEPER

⋆ BULL'S-EYE ⋆

ELIZABETH KECKLEY NEVER SERVED IN THE MILITARY, but she completed a very important mission during the Civil War. She kept President Lincoln focused on his job of winning the war.

Keckley makes few history books because she was black. Polite white Northern society of the 1860s could not imagine a black woman having any major role in history, so she was mostly ignored in her day.

What Keckley did that was so important was to keep First Lady Mary Todd Lincoln on this side of reality and off President Lincoln's back. She never threatened, berated, cursed, or otherwise controlled the fragile Mrs. Lincoln. Instead, Keckley sewed Mrs. Lincoln's dresses, listened to her fears, shared her woes, and offered the first lady something few others in Washington, D.C., were willing to give her—friendship. For doing all those seemingly simple things, which turned out to be complicated when dealing with Mrs. Lincoln, Keckley deserves to be a bull's-eye.

Born near Petersburg, Virginia, Keckley's birth year is unknown but is assumed to be around 1818. At various times in her life she reported her father to be a slave from a nearby plantation and sometimes her white owner. Her son reportedly served in the U.S. Army as a white man, lending credence to some white heritage.

Given as a wedding gift to her owner's daughter, Keckley moved to St. Louis where she developed into a fine dressmaker. She convinced her loyal customers to lend her enough money to buy her and her son's freedom. By 1855 she was a free woman.

In 1860 Keckley moved to Washington and supposedly took as a client Varina Davis, wife of Mississippi Senator Jefferson Davis. Keckley's reminiscences of encounters with her and others cause some historians to question Keckley's truthfulness. According to Keckley, Mrs. Davis told her that she would rather "be kicked around in Washington than go South and be Mrs. President." The timing of that statement seems to be January 1861, which meant Varina Davis would have been making some unlikely assumptions that her husband would be named president of a Confederacy when most of its states had not yet left the Union. Keckley claimed she mailed some finished sewing to Mrs. Davis in June 1861, long after the war was underway.

In time Keckley met with Mrs. Lincoln, who had heard of her dressmaking skills through friends in St. Louis. Delivering Mrs. Lincoln's inaugural gown in record time plus arranging her hair secured Keckley her job as "modiste" or dressmaker. The woman who had been born a slave was now working in the White House of the United States of America.

Keckley might have been one of the first to recognize that Mrs. Lincoln was not stable when she generously described the first lady as a "peculiarly constituted woman." On the night that she delivered the dress, Mrs. Lincoln threatened to remain in her room rather than go to the inaugural ball because Keckley was slightly late in delivering the dress.

As time passed, both President Lincoln and Mrs. Lincoln seemed to accept the presence of Keckley almost as a part of the family. They seemed to talk freely in front of her. According to one encounter, Mrs. Lincoln warned her husband that Salmon Chase, the treasury secretary, was "anything for Chase." When Mrs. Lincoln later warned the president not to have anything to do with Secretary of State William Seward, Lincoln replied, "If I listened to you, I would soon be without a cabinet."

Keckley's first real experience with the fragile nature of Mrs. Lincoln came early in 1862 when her son Willie died of fever. Mrs. Lincoln dissolved into a grief so profound that Lincoln dragged her to a window, pointed to an insane asylum, and threatened to put her in it unless she came out of her depression.

In 1864 as Lincoln was running for reelection, Keckley began to notice more slippage in Mrs. Lincoln. The first lady began buying clothes and hiding the bills from her husband or persuading the shopkeepers that she would steer society business their way if they gave her the goods. She became worried that if Lincoln lost the election, the bills would come due.

"She was almost crazy with anxiety and fear," wrote Keckley, who then quoted Mrs. Lincoln as saying: "The Republican politicians must pay my debts. Hundreds of them are getting immensely rich off the patronage of my husband and it is but fair that they should help me out of my embarrassment."

Keckley was so close to Mrs. Lincoln that she accompanied her on a tour of Richmond not long after it had been captured. Keckley wrote that she sat in the chair of Jefferson Davis as the two women toured the Confederate White House.

Keckley inadvertently foretold Lincoln's assassination when she mentioned to Mrs. Lincoln that it would be easy for someone in a crowd listening to him giving a nighttime speech to take a shot at him.

"Yes, yes, Mr. Lincoln's life is always exposed," Mrs. Lincoln said, as quoted in Keckley's book. "Ah, no one knows what it is to live in constant dread of some fearful tragedy. The president has been warned so often, that I tremble for him on every public occasion. I have a presentiment that he will meet with a sudden and violent end."

On the morning after the president's assassination, Mrs. Lincoln sent for Keckley. She was the only friend Mrs. Lincoln called on to help her deal with the death of her husband.

Keckley recorded that Mrs. Lincoln had completely broken down, "emitting the wails of a broken heart, the unearthly shrieks, the wild tempestuous outbursts of grief from the soul." She also recorded the distraught Mrs. Lincoln said, "The only happy feature of his assassination is that he died in ignorance" of the seventy thousand dollars she owed to merchants.

Keckley recorded that the new president, Andrew Johnson, never tried to call on Mrs. Lincoln and never inquired as to her welfare. After being physically removed from the White House, Mrs. Lincoln insisted that Keckley move to Chicago with her.

"Lizabeth, you are my best and kindest friend," Mrs. Lincoln told her.

That assessment of Keckley by Mrs. Lincoln would change in 1868 with the publication of a book. Keckley pioneered the "tell all" genre with her *Behind the Scenes—Thirty Years a Slave and Four Years in the White House*. It was presented as an autobiography with much of the book dealing with her friendship with Mrs. Lincoln.

The book, which historians consider accurate in some details and embellished in others, gave an insight into the marriage of the sixteenth president of the United States that embarrassed the remaining members of the Lincoln family. Robert Lincoln, the eldest and only surviving son who put his mother into an insane asylum, pressured the publisher to pull Keckley's book from publication. Failing that, he pressured them to do little to promote its existence. He even insisted that the work be promoted as that of a mulatto woman, half black and half white, as if being not racially pure had anything to do with what Keckley saw and heard in the White House. The combination of strategies worked. Few copies of the book were sold in Keckley's lifetime.

The book's publication ended Keckley's friendship with Mrs. Lincoln who would later dismiss Keckley as "that colored historian," a description meant to hurt the former slave who had frequently dropped whatever she was doing to rush to the former first lady's side.

The quashing of the book did not have much immediate effect on

Keckley, who went on to make dresses for the daughters of Andrew Johnson, the seventeenth president. In 1892 she joined the staff of a black college to teach dressmaking, but a stroke within a year forced her to resign. For the next sixteen years she lived in obscurity. She died in 1907 in a home attained for her by the National Association of Destitute Colored Women and Children.

It was not until years after Keckley's death that Lincoln biographers such as Carl Sandburg started using *Behind the Scenes* to explore the relationship between Abraham Lincoln and Mary Todd Lincoln. They found and then told the stories that have become standard in describing the pair's relationship, such as Lincoln's threatening his wife with institutionalization after the death of Willie. No one witnessed that scene but Keckley.

While she may not have known it at the time, Elizabeth Keckley served her nation by being the one true friend Mary Todd Lincoln ever had in the White House. By helping Mrs. Lincoln take care of her children, by nursing them when they were ill, by helping to prepare the body of Willie for burial, by listening to and comforting the tragic figure of the president's wife, Keckley took pressure off of the president of the United States.

Maj. Jonathan Letterman
(1824–1872)

THE LIFESAVER OF THE UNION ARMY

⭐ BULL'S-EYE ⭐

SOMETIMES A SOLDIER'S JOB IS TO SAVE THE LIVES OF other soldiers, even his enemies. That was the way Major Jonathan Letterman looked at warfare and lived his professional military life. Thanks to Letterman's pioneering work 140 years ago at finding, evaluating, treating, then evacuating the wounded, soldiers today are more likely to survive their battlefield engagements.

Letterman, a rare combination of professional soldier and physician, saw the problems of both his chosen professions in an unusually clear manner. Until Letterman came along to test his methods of emergency treatment of the wounded, military men saw casualties as burdens rather than humans who needed care. A wounded man could no longer fight and caring for him took resources away from the main goal of war—killing the enemy. Though frustrated by his superiors during his own service, Letterman's methods eventually became the norm for the military. For changing centuries of military thinking about the wounded, Letterman deserves the title of bull's-eye.

Letterman must have been destined to be a doctor. Born the son of a doctor in Pennsylvania, he attended Jefferson Medical College in his hometown of Philadelphia, then the leading medical school of its day. Instead of opening a private practice, he chose to join the U.S. Army as an assistant surgeon.

One of Letterman's early postings was Fort Meade, Florida, a frontier post in the state's interior where duty was so routine and peaceful he had plenty of time to think about what doctors should do in wartime. Most of his thoughts revolved around how to get men wounded by arrows back to where conditions were more hospitable. Among Letterman's friends at the fort in early 1851 was an equally bored if eccentric lieutenant named Thomas J. Jackson. After earning the nickname "Stonewall" ten years later, Jackson would give Letterman plenty of opportunity to test his medical theories about evacuation and treatment of wounded.

Though assigned early in the war to the Union Army of the Potomac, Letterman would not emerge as a major figure until June 1862. Promoted to major and medical director at the end of Union Gen. George McClellan's disastrous Seven Days' campaign, Letterman was thrust immediately into the chaos that raged at Harrison's Landing on the James River. While McClellan was trying to extract his army, Letterman was trying to evacuate the wounded to hospitals back in Washington. It was a crash course on a huge scale of all of Letterman's small-scale theories of battlefield evacuation.

Determined to avoid chaos in the sure-to-come next battle, Letterman drew what would become his master medical plan for all future battlefield evacuations and treatment of the wounded. Heartily approved by U.S. Surgeon General William Hammond and by McClellan himself, the plans were forwarded to Secretary of War Edwin Stanton who also verbally approved them.

Until Letterman's plan was submitted, removing the wounded from the battlefield was haphazard at best. Regimental commanders relied on regimental band members and men who were considered poor soldiers to be detailed to be stretcher-bearers. But sorry soldiers also were usually sorry stretcher-bearers who were more likely to steal from the dead and dying and run when under fire. The army's standard methods rarely resulted in saving the lives of the wounded.

Letterman's new plan called for the creation of a professional, full-time ambulance corps. The plan called for two trained stretcher-bearers and a driver to be on board each ambulance. Two such ambulances would be assigned to each regiment (ideally one thousand men but often as few as five hundred men). A medical director who would be separate from the military command would command those ambulances. In fact, the drivers and stretcher-bearers would answer only to the medical directors and would not be drawn from the ranks of the soldiers or from the marching bands as had been done in the past. The ambulances would transport the wounded to field hospitals that Letterman eventually decided should be controlled at the division level.

Once Stanton and Maj. Gen. Henry Halleck, Lincoln's main military advisor, read the details of Letterman's plans, they changed their minds and opposed it, even though Stanton had already verbally approved it. The major sticking point was Letterman's suggestion that the ambulance drivers and stretcher-bearers not be fighting men. Stanton commented that the plan would "increase the expenses and immobility of our army without any corresponding advantages."

Even though their bosses expressed disapproval, both McClellan and Letterman continued with the plan to organize the ambulance corps. They believed if they proved its efficiency under combat conditions Stanton would formally approve it.

Letterman's plan was tried under fire at the September 1862 battle of Antietam, less than three months after the disaster at the Seven Days' evacuation. He saw the plan had some kinks. Some of the ambulance drivers were caught stealing from the wounded, and one day after the battle there were still eight thousand wounded on the field.

Antietam's casualties were so numerous Letterman saw that his doctors were overwhelmed. He discovered that doctors under such pressure often made mistakes, so he suggested that only the best three surgeons in each division perform surgeries.

That suggestion ruffled some feathers. Civil War surgeons usually were drawn from the society elite and none of them appreciated an army bureaucrat judging their skills, even if he was a doctor himself.

Though criticized by his own doctors for sometimes questioning their skills, Lettermen defended those same doctors against charges by the soldiers that they were "butchers." Though soldiers frequently survived amputation of arms and legs, the most common surgery performed during the war, battlefield doctors often had only rudimentary knowledge of or concern for hygiene. They would wipe off bloody saws on their bloody aprons before starting to saw on another man's limb, being unaware that they should have been using sterilized tools to keep infection from spreading from one casualty to another.

Though Letterman knew he had some incompetent doctors, he also chafed when he heard criticism of those physicians.

"It is not to be supposed that there are no incompetent surgeons in the army. It is certainly true that there were, but these sweeping denunciations against a class of men who will favorably compare with the military surgeons of any country, because of the incompetence and shortcomings of a few are wrong and do injustice to a body of men who have labored faithfully and well," Letterman wrote after the war.

Letterman's careful plans were torn asunder after the battle of Fredericksburg when his field hospitals were swamped with more than nine thousand wounded returned from Gen. Ambrose Burnside's attack. Against Letterman's counsel to let him treat all of the men before they were evacuated, Burnside ordered all of the wounded removed from the area. Just as Letterman feared, the wounded overwhelmed all means of transportation away from the town. They were loaded onto open railroad cars in the dead of winter and onto troop ships that had no facilities for caring for wounded. Many died before ever seeing a doctor as doctors had stayed behind at the field hospitals.

Though often overwhelmed beyond anyone's ability to serve the wounded, Letterman's Medical Department plans were officially recognized by the War Department. By midwar Letterman had refined his plans. When the Army of the Potomac went into the battle of Gettysburg in 1863, it had 650 medical officers, 1,000 ambulances, and close to 3,000 drivers and stretcher-bearers. By the morning of July 4, just one day after the battle had ended, more than 14,000 Union wounded had been transported to field hospitals.

Letterman's plans could only do so much. No one expected Gettysburg to be the size it was. One study shows there were more than 300 patients for every doctor at the Gettysburg hospitals.

As with many reformers, Letterman made enemies with "the old guard" who often have the ears of the men at the top. Almost without warning in January 1864 Letterman resigned from his post as medical director of the Army of the Potomac. Letterman's resignation came at the same time his boss, Surgeon General Hammond, was forced out of his job. Behind both resignations was Secretary of War Stanton.

Stanton, a nasty, vindictive man, had finally remembered that he had counseled against the acceptance of Letterman's ambulance plan and had been overridden, and the ambulance plan accepted. Though Letterman had saved thousands of Union soldiers, the important thing to the politician Stanton was that a mere doctor had defied him. Now that Hammond was forced out, Letterman would have been next on his list. Letterman resigned before Stanton had the pleasure of firing him.

Letterman died at age forty-eight of chronic intestinal trouble, perhaps stomach cancer, in 1872.

Other than changing from horse-drawn wagons to trucks and helicopters, Letterman's system of rapidly collecting men for transport to emergency hospitals and then on to larger, more permanent hospitals is still in place in the modern military. It was he who first developed the idea of the Mobile Army Surgical Hospital, the M.A.S.H. unit that would one day have its own television show.

Had this man not come along, thousands, perhaps tens of thousands, more men would have died on the Civil War battlefields.

Rear Adm. Hiram Paulding

(1797–1878)

THE OLD SALT
WHO TOOK CHARGE

☆ BULL'S-EYE ☆

AFTER FIFTY YEARS OF SERVICE STARTING IN 1810, HIRAM Paulding could have and should have sat out the Civil War. In fact, federal law required him to retire from the navy at age sixty-two in December of 1861, but that did not keep him from contributing to the war effort.

Two actions Paulding took early in 1861 sealed his place in Civil War history. In April he set fire to the Gosport Naval Yard at Norfolk, Virginia, destroying valuable stores that could have been used by the Confederates. In August he sat on an ironclad review board that approved construction of the USS *Monitor.*

Paulding, one of the highest-ranking naval officers in 1861 and one of the oldest of the nation's "blue-water sailors" could have remained wed to the type of fighting that had held him in good stead for his entire service. Paulding was also a man willing to adapt, willing to change with the times when technology showed promise. For that he was a bull's-eye.

Bored with milking cows on the family farm, the thirteen-year-old Paulding signed on with the U.S. Navy as a midshipman in 1810. Three years later the teenager was proclaimed a national hero after directing gun crews during the battle of Lake Champlain during the War of 1812.

Paulding spent the next fifty years sailing the world's oceans, fighting pirates off North Africa, mutineers in the South Pacific, and American revolutionaries in South America. Some of his voyages lasted as long as four years. Forced into retirement by the Buchanan administration for violating international laws, the sixty-one-year-old commodore was brought back to duty by Lincoln, who needed seasoned men in his new naval department.

Paulding had been in office a month in mid-April 1861 when he was faced with Virginia's threat to secede. At Norfolk was Gosport Naval Yard, the largest naval repair facility in the country. Besides being home to the largest dry dock in the world, Gosport was also a shipping depot that had tons of gunpowder and more than three thousand naval cannon in storage. Also at Gosport were eleven warships in various stages of repair, including the USS *Merrimack,* a forty-gun frigate. As the political crisis churned, the Union had been reluctant to remove those ships or even to appear concerned about their presence lest they insult supposedly loyal Virginians and push them into secession.

Gosport's value to North and South was obvious to both sides. It was a gold mine that had to be destroyed by the North or saved from destruction by the South.

The North's problem was an elderly, befuddled commodore commanding Gosport who was so focused on not offending the citizens of Norfolk that he made no plans to defend or destroy the complex should Secessionists attack it.

Paulding sailed for Norfolk with six hundred soldiers and eleven huge tanks of flammable turpentine. On arrival he was shocked when he found most of the ships had been scuttled at their moorings. This controlled sinking hardly made the ships useless to the Confederates. All the Secessionists had to do would be close the ships' sea cocks and pump out the water.

Paulding seized command, knowing Virginia had seceded three days earlier and militia forces would soon be moving against the base. He scattered soldiers all over the facility to spread turpentine, spike the three thousand cannon, and set charges to blow up the dry dock.

After midnight on April 21, Paulding and his wrecking crew set sail as the first of the fires and explosions attracted the attention of the gathering militia. A newspaper reporter described the fires as sounding like "the deep-toned roar of Niagara" and looking like "a universal sea of flames."

Despite the fires' ferocity, the Virginia militia was able to save much of Gosport, including the dry dock. It should have blown up first, but did not, leading to speculation that a Southern sympathizer among Paulding's crew may have broken the fuse leading to the tons of gunpowder that had been placed among its machinery. Of the three thousand cannon in storage, his men had been able to destroy only one thousand. The Secessionists saved tons of black powder. Though the *Merrimack* had burned to the waterline, the Confederates were able to raise it and use the hull to construct the ironclad CSS *Virginia*.

Months later, a congressional committee made up mostly of men whose only real sense of combat and danger was defeating someone at the polls, strongly criticized Paulding's ineffectiveness in destroying the facility.

Once word filtered back to the North that the *Virginia* was under construction, Congress authorized the construction of the Union's own ironclad. A board was formed to approve a workable design. Paulding, who had pleased Lincoln with his aggressiveness at Norfolk, was one of three members appointed.

The board could have been problematic. Two of its members, Paulding and Como. Joseph Smith, were old-line sailors who were also old in years, hardly the type of men to consider radical new ideas in shipbuilding. Neither was sold on steam-powered ships. Smith would later suggest to the inventor of the steam-powered, screw-driven ironclad that he add sails to his design in the event his steam engine broke down. None of the members of the design board had ever designed a ship or had any experience in evaluating ordnance damage.

In August 1861, after looking at eighteen proposals, the board approved two designs for ironclads which looked very much like standard ships with armor added. They were designs old blue-water sailors understood.

Within a few days the board was asked to review plans for a third ship that had not been initially considered. Its inventor, John Ericsson, had not entered the competition earlier because the U.S. Navy had blackballed him for years because of his involvement with an earlier ship on which a cannon had exploded, killing the secretary of the navy. President Lincoln had already seen and liked Ericsson's design and he asked the board to reconvene in his presence to consider the new model. Ericsson himself did not attend as he feared his presence would inflame the old navy men.

Lincoln set the tone for the meeting to consider Ericcson's model, which was initially called a "floating battery," when he cracked one of his jokes: "All I have to say is what the girl said when she stuck her foot into the stocking. It strikes me there's something in it!"

Paulding, knowing better than to vote against the president, voted for the approval of Ericsson's battery on the condition that the other two designs he had previously approved also be built. Smith also voted for Ericsson, but a third member who didn't mind bucking the president, Como. Charles Davis, voted against it out of the belief that the battery would never float. The panel had earlier agreed that all approvals had to be unanimous.

Ericsson came to Washington in a few days to demonstrate his model in person. Paulding voted for it again and persuaded Davis to change his mind. Paulding, a man who had never seen an iron ship and had spent fifty years on wooden ships, could have killed Ericsson's model, which would become the *Monitor,* but he had trust that the inventions of men much younger than himself would work.

"I advocated the *Monitor* because the amount of money appropriated would build several such vessels and the time of their construction would be much less than a ship of larger size. I relied upon the genius and pledges of Ericsson, while the admiral [Smith] claimed for *New Ironsides* greater power. The admiral and I compromised and agreed to build both," wrote Paulding. "Without knowledge of building ironclads, nothing was left to us to carry out the act of Congress but to exercise our judgment in the selection of the models and then depend upon the pledges and genius of the contracting parties to fulfill their promise."

Paulding did cover his bases with the *Monitor*. After verbally giving Ericsson work orders to start building the ship, he added a clause into the official written contract that said if the promised invulnerability of the *Monitor* was not proven, Ericsson would be forced to refund all of the money advanced to him for the project.

Later testing in wartime conditions would prove that Paulding's faith in the other two ironclad designs had some merit. One of the designs was built as the USS *New Ironsides,* which would actually see more service than the *Monitor*. The other design would become the USS *Galena,* which proved to have faulty armor penetrable by Confederate cannon. Both of these seagoing ships would be more serviceable than the low freeboard *Monitor* which was only stable in calm coastal waters.

Once he had approved of the *Monitor,* Paulding was forced into retirement at age sixty-two. Strings could have been pulled to keep him in service just as they were for other old sailors like David Farragut, just three years younger, but no effort was made to keep Paulding. Though Lincoln had brought him back into service, the president apparently bowed to political pressure to punish Paulding for not destroying Gosport.

Paulding spent the rest of the war in civilian service as the head of the Brooklyn Navy Yard. He watched the *Monitor* being built and often urged the workers to rush as he knew the *Virginia* was nearing completion.

Though out of the fighting in New York City, he still helped the war effort by making sure blockading vessels were repaired and put back to sea as quickly as possible. During the New York City draft riots in July 1863 he put several gunboats into the Hudson and East Rivers to show the rioters that he meant business if they did not stop the violence. He died at eighty-two, the first champion of a modern navy.

Gen. Fitz John Porter

(1822–1901)

A BLAMELESS MAN WHO TOOK THE FALL

★ MISFIRE ★

IF THE UNION'S TOP GENERALS AND POLITICIANS HAD spent as much energy fighting the Confederacy as they did going after fighting generals in their own ranks, the war would have ended sooner.

But destroying a man's reputation was fine sport among Washington's ditherers. They would not let a war disrupt that joyous hobby.

A destroyed reputation was all that Gen. Fitz John Porter had left to him in January 1863. The general who smashed Confederate Gen. Robert E. Lee's forces in June 1862 should have been a toasted hero in Washington. Instead, because he exercised measured judgment in a mismanaged battle two months after his victory, Porter was labeled a disloyal officer just six months after being labeled a hero. While his battlefield decisions proved to be correct, his superiors needed someone to blame for the battering of an army that came close to being destroyed. Porter was dismissed from the army and an entire career built on integrity and obedience to orders, even when questioned, was ended. Though he was right, Porter will always be remembered as a misfire.

An 1845 West Point graduate, Porter won two brevet promotions in the Mexican War before being wounded. Considered a fine officer, he was ordered to West Point to serve as an instructor.

Porter's early Civil War service must have made him cringe. First forced to bring the U.S. Regulars back from their January 1861 surrender in Texas, he was then assigned to the Shenandoah Valley under Gen. Robert Patterson. Patterson was a sixty-nine-year-old War of 1812 veteran who was easily duped and outmaneuvered into keeping his troops in the Valley while the Confederates once there rushed to fight at Manassas in July 1861. Patterson was replaced by Gen. Nathaniel Banks, a former governor of Massachusetts, whose skills were also lacking.

Finally, there was salvation. Porter's friend, Gen. George McClellan of the following West Point class of 1846, was appointed head of the Army of the Potomac. McClellan asked Porter to join him in capturing Richmond.

As McClellan's army crept up the Virginia Peninsula, they neared the Confederate defenses around Yorktown. Some of McClellan's generals sensed that those defenses were not very strong and asked Porter for the chance to probe the Confederate line.

Porter turned them down flat, reciting his mentor's view that the Confederates were much too strong at Yorktown and the best method to attack would be to wear the Confederates down by siege warfare. Later that same day an unauthorized probe of the Confederate line did find a weak spot, but the general who found it was given specific orders by Porter to return to Federal lines and not attack. The reason given was that several Confederate prisoners all agreed that the line held forty thousand men and nearly sixty thousand more were on their way.

In reality, fewer than ten thousand Confederates were in the line and that was all there ever would be. Those ten thousand Confederates would hold up McClellan's one hundred thousand for more than a month, giving the South time to gather more men and to build a defensive line around Richmond.

At the time McClellan did not understand that he had been duped. He thought a superior force of Confederates had run from their trenches as they watched Porter assemble his siege guns. Impressed with Porter's ability to make the Confederates retreat, McClellan gave his friend command of the Fifth Corps as they neared Richmond. He then sent Porter to the right flank, positioned northeast of Richmond and north of the Chickahominy River.

That right flank was critical to McClellan's plan to attack Richmond. McClellan anticipated that Irvin McDowell's corps would come down from Fredericksburg on the north and link with Porter's corps. That is why McClellan did not worry much about Porter's thirty thousand men being on the north side of the Chickahominy while the rest of his seventy-thousand-man army was on the south side. True, Porter's smaller force was exposed to attack at the moment, but McDowell would arrive soon.

Confederate Gen. J. E. B. Stuart noticed the river separation of Union forces on a ride around McClellan's army in June 1862. This report of Porter's exposure gave Lee, the newly appointed head of the Army of Northern Virginia, the opening he wanted. He planned to crush Porter with an army twice the Fifth Corps's size, then turn and roll up the rest of the Federal line.

Things did not work out for the Confederates. Porter sensed the impending attack and he dug in behind Beaver Dam Creek just east of Mechanicsville. When Stonewall Jackson did not appear on time, an impatient Gen. A. P. Hill threw thousands of men against Porter in an uncoordinated attack. Porter cut them up. The Confederates lost nearly 1,500 men while Porter lost barely 350.

Incredibly, though McClellan recognized that Porter had won a victory at Beaver Dam Creek, he ordered the Fifth Corps to retreat toward the James River. McClellan warned Porter that he would have to fight on his own, as darkness prevented the rest of the army from moving north to support Porter.

Porter argued that he should stay in place, but McClellan insisted on retreat. Porter dutifully retreated to Gaines's Mill, several miles to the southeast, after finding a creek with high ground behind it. Porter had chosen a second battlefield almost like the one he had at Beaver Dam Creek.

When Jackson was late attacking at Gaines's Mill, Porter again cut up the Confederates in front of him. Porter inflicted nearly eighty-eight hundred Confederate casualties while losing about sixty-eight hundred of his own. With Jackson really on his flank this time, Porter retreated again, but in good order.

Four days later the Confederates tried again to attack Porter at Malvern Hill. Again, Porter cut the Confederates to pieces; this time using one hundred massed cannon rather than massed muskets. The Confederates lost nearly fifty-four hundred men while Porter lost thirty-two hundred. In three different battles an unflappable Porter had won two of the battles and inflicted much heavier casualties on the Confederates in all three. As a reward for his fighting abilities, Porter was promoted to major general.

McClellan never understood he actually won most of the Seven Days' battles and could have won the entire campaign. Instead of pressing Lee's inferior forces, McClellan pulled back to the James River, abandoned his plan to attack Richmond, and evacuated his army. An exasperated President Lincoln finally removed McClellan from command in early August and transferred most of McClellan's troops into another army under Gen. John Pope.

This move spelled trouble for the loyal-to-McClellan Porter who had made frequent and public disparaging comments about Pope's ability to command. Word of those comments got to Pope before Porter did.

But before Pope could deal with Porter, he had to deal with Stonewall Jackson. At Groveton on August 28, 1862, near what would be Second Bull Run, Jackson surprised some of Pope's men by attacking, then retreating into an unfinished railroad cut. As Porter's Fifth Corps arrived on the field on August 29, Pope ordered him to immediately attack Jackson. Porter, unfamiliar with everything from the battlefield to the other generals who would be operating around him, took his time following those orders. His skirmishers discovered that Confederate Gen. James Longstreet had also arrived beside Jackson, a report Pope refused to believe.

Porter then specifically defied Pope by refusing to attack Jackson's right flank, citing that such an attack would leave his corps open to attack by Longstreet.

The next day, August 30, Pope believed that Jackson was in retreat and he still did not believe Longstreet was in the trenches. Pope again ordered Porter's corps to attack Jackson.

Against his better judgment, Porter ordered his Fifth Corps forward three times into galling fire from Jackson. Finally as the third attack was ebbing, Longstreet, who had kept his men quiet, launched his own attack. Pope's left wing crumbled, starting a general collapse of the rest of Pope's army.

After Second Bull Run and the following day's battle of Chantilly, an embarrassed Pope, who had come close to losing an entire army in just four days of fighting, looked for scapegoats for his mishandling of the battles. Porter, a friend of McClellan who had been slow to follow the orders of his new commander, seemed ready-made for the role. Within two weeks of Second Bull Run, court-martial charges were filed.

Luckily for Porter, Lincoln soon fired Pope and brought back McClellan to blunt Lee's move into Maryland. McClellan kept Porter in reserve during the battle of Antietam, although Porter begged to be released so he could smash through the Confederate line. Porter was trying to build up good will in case the court-martial charges ever came to trial. McClellan refused to release his reserves, a blunder that allowed Lee to escape back over the Potomac.

In early November McClellan was relieved of command of the Army of the Potomac and Porter was relieved of command of his corps.

In December 1862 and January 1863 Porter stood before a court made up of McClellan enemies. Every Republican from Lincoln on down had already decided that Porter would stand in for the sins of Democrat McClellan. The politicians did not want to attack McClellan directly because that risked alienating the common soldiers in the Union army who still idolized him. Porter, on the other hand, was only one field general among many. The politicians figured the common soldier wanted someone to take the blame for Second Bull Run. Had the politicians asked the soldiers, the men in the field would have court-martialed the pompous Pope, not the fighting Porter, but Pope had friends in Washington while Porter had none.

Porter, the man whose single corps had done more damage to Lee's army at Seven Days' battles than Pope's entire army had at Second Bull Run, was found guilty of disobeying orders and cashiered from the army.

For the next twenty-three years Porter demanded a fair hearing. In 1879 a congressional hearing dominated by Democrats found Porter blameless for the defeat at Second Bull Run. That did him little good because as long as a Republican was in the White House, he could get no action on the findings of the panel. In 1886 a Democrat president, Grover Cleveland, restored Porter to the rank of colonel of the army. He did not get any back pay, but he was able to retire at that rank. He died in 1901.

Gen. James Wolfe Ripley

(1794–1870)

THE GENERAL WHO HATED
WEAPONS OF MASS DESTRUCTION

⋆ MISFIRE ⋆

GEN. JAMES WOLFE RIPLEY NEVER THOUGHT OF HIMSELF as standing in the way of progress. But as ordnance chief for the United States Army from 1861 to 1863 he did exactly that. For the first three years of the war Ripley fulfilled his duty in his own mind by purchasing simple weapons that would work in the hands of quickly trained Union recruits. His job was to arm an army.

His job was not to evaluate every inventor's fancy, revolutionary weapon. Besides, some of the suggestions that crossed his desk chilled him, such as the artillery shell filled with chlorine gas. According to its inventor, the shell would explode over the Confederates, causing the heavier-than-air chlorine gas to settle down and kill everyone beneath the cloud. Ripley never asked for a demonstration.

But other more modern forms of standard weapons such as breechloading and repeating rifles, also caught the frown of Ripley. The Ordnance Chief rejected them out of hand because he believed rifles that fired too rapidly encouraged soldiers to waste ammunition. He believed in the muzzleloader, which had not changed in basic design for more than one hundred years and which forced the soldier to think as he loaded and fired.

Ripley was wrong. Had he endorsed several very good breechloaders and repeating rifles early in the war, their manufacturers would have geared up production and the Union army would have very rapidly out-gunned the Confederates. An old-style soldier caught up in the first modern war, Ripley never could adapt to newfangled and what he considered useless and wasteful technology. For refusing to endorse the rapidly advancing weapons technology, Ripley deserves the label of misfire.

Born in 1794, Ripley was one of the oldest generals to serve in the Union army. A graduate of the 1814 class of West Point, Ripley had little to do in the peacetime army until 1841 when he drew a plum assignment, supervising the Springfield Armory in Massachusetts. He was the right man in the right place at the right time working with the right arms.

Into the 1820s the primary method of firing a musket was for a piece of flint to strike a piece of metal under which a pool of black powder rested. The resulting flash fire was directed through a hole in the musket's breech, which would then set off the powder in the barrel, sending the musket ball toward its target.

Though flintlock muskets and pistols were still manufactured through the 1830s, the percussion cap had been invented in the 1820s and by the 1840s was finding its way into the mainstream. The cap was a self-contained, waterproof charge of mercury fulminate that when struck by the musket's hammer would send a controlled spark through that same breech hole. By the 1840s manufacturers such as Springfield were converting flintlocks into the much more reliable and waterproof percussion cap weapons. It was a period of modernization that Ripley endorsed.

Also coming along was the method of converting smoothbore muskets into rifled muskets. Smoothbores had a range of less than one hundred yards. Rifling increased the range to more than three hundred. Eventually better muskets would increase that range to six hundred yards. Again, Ripley approved of the advancements.

From 1848 until 1861 Ripley served in a variety of posts around the country, mostly inspecting arsenals. In the early winter of 1861 seceding Southern states began to seize those arsenals, though they rarely gained the latest weaponry. Most contained .69 caliber 1842 Springfields, a serviceable smoothbore percussion cap weapon that was nearly twenty years out of date compared to the best rifled muzzleloading muskets, the .58 caliber Springfield and the .577 caliber Enfield, imported from England.

Once the war started Ripley was named head of the Ordnance Department and quickly promoted to brigadier general. There seemed to be no unease about the appointment of the sixty-five-year-old to such an important post. He knew the most about the nation's arsenals so it made sense.

Ripley's job was big and he knew it. Since the country had been at peace since 1847 the army had been downsized and underfunded. A critical problem was that previous ordnance chiefs had not paid much attention to standardization of any type of weapon. Now, in a matter of months, the Ordnance Department would be expected to provide weapons to tens of thousands of volunteers flooding recruitment centers. Ripley would have to ramp up production of weapons at the Springfield Armory, contract out for weapons from other manufacturers such as Colt, and find instant sources of muskets from countries like England and Austria.

A methodical man, Ripley set out to do what he had been doing all his military life: manufacturing, inspecting, and purchasing muzzleloading, percussion cap, rifled muskets. That is what he best understood and what the Union's soldiers needed most.

What Ripley did not care about and what he did not want to know about were breechloading rifles, which loaded at the rear instead of by pouring powder down the muzzle. Though breechloaders had actually been around since the American Revolution, the design had never been proven on the battlefield. That, of course, was because men like Ripley had not been purchasing and evaluating them under combat conditions.

In Ripley's mind breechloaders encouraged soldiers to waste ammunition because they could be fired quicker than muzzleloaders. Shooting accurately required careful discipline that could not be achieved if soldiers fired much faster than three shots per minute, which was standard with muzzleloading weapons.

To a lesser degree, Ripley was also concerned about standardization of ammunition. Among the 1842 Springfield, the 1861 Springfield, and the 1858 Enfield, he already had three different calibers. Imported Lorenz muskets from Austria would be .54 caliber, yet another caliber. If he had to find ammunition manufacturers for breechloading muskets, each of which had a different cartridge design, Ripley would be complicating his mission even more.

Finally, Ripley may have been old, but he was no fool. He knew that every war brings out charlatans looking for government funding. He believed that some, if not most, inventors were con artists.

For those reasons Ripley made an early and firm decision not to support the purchase of breechloaders for any troops other than cavalry. He simply refused to meet with most breechloader and repeating rifle inventors.

While standardization of ammunition was a legitimate concern, Ripley was behind the times in his knowledge of the quality of many breechloaders. Even radical abolitionist John Brown recognized their value when he brought Sharps carbines along on his raid on 1859 Harpers Ferry a year and a half before the war started. During the war Hiram Brendan's sharpshooters would prove how deadly accurate Sharps rifles were. Union cavalry used a variety of breechloading carbines, including one designed by Ambrose Burnside, an infantry general.

Word got around about these new weapons. One battlefield report described how a Confederate company commander ordered his men to fire on one Union skirmisher in order to capture his seven-shot Spencer repeating rifle so it could be examined. President Lincoln himself took an interest in the Spencer, even personally ordering Ripley to buy some for evaluation. Ripley grumbled the whole time he was forced to evaluate the Spencer, but the president was the president.

Sometimes Ripley was right about breechloaders and inventors. The Colt revolving rifle looked like a pistol with a rifle barrel. When the rifle got hot, some or all of its rounds in the revolving cylinder could "cook off," or fire on their own accord. That would send minié balls down the length of the barrel—and take off the fingers of the shooter. After a few incidents like that, the Colt revolving rifle fell out of favor with men in the field, much to the delight of Ripley.

The .44 caliber Henry (forerunner of the Winchester so popular ten years later) was an example of a rifle Ripley judged too fragile and too expensive to be attractive to the Federal government. When Secretary of the Navy Gideon Welles was sent one as a gift, he ordered it tested. One test found the typical rifle could fire more than one thousand rounds without cleaning and still hit its targets. An accurate rifle, it cost the princely sum of forty-two dollars, more than three times the cost of a typical muzzleloader. That was too expensive for Ripley, but the governor of Illinois bought some for his state's regiments.

The men in the field were more impressed with the power of repeating fire than Ripley was.

A soldier writing in the *Army and Navy Journal* in 1864 wrote: "If those in authority have any doubts as to the propriety of thus adding to our efficiency, let them come to the front armed with one Springfield musket and oppose themselves to an equal number of Rebs, armed with repeaters or breechloaders. If they can stand that, let them go to the picket line, and while fumbling for a cap and trying to get it on the cone one of these cold days, offer themselves as a target to some fellow on the other side who has nothing to do but cock his piece and blaze away. Do our good friends ever reflect that the loss of time in loading is the great cause of haste, and consequent inaccuracy in firing?"

Ultimately it was articles like that getting back to home state politicians that forced Lincoln and Secretary of War Edwin Stanton to search the books for a law that would force Ripley out of the army. They eventually found an obscure statute that had something to do with continuous service. In September 1863 James Ripley retired from the U.S. Army after serving more than forty-five years in uniform. He would live another six years.

Once rid of Ripley, the purchase of breechloaders and repeaters accelerated. One accounting shows more than three hundred thousand breechloaders and repeaters were manufactured for the North, with the bulk of them coming after Ripley's departure in 1863. The two purchased most were one hundred thousand Sharps rifles and eighty-five thousand Spencer rifles and carbines.

There is something strange about the actions of the U.S. Army after the war. Though repeating rifles like the Spencer and Henry proved to be durable, the U.S. Army seemed haunted by the ghost of Ripley. After the war the army reverted to using single shot carbines as their standard weapon. When Lt. Col. George Armstrong Custer's soldiers faced the Sioux warriors at Little Big Horn in 1876, the soldiers were using single shot carbines and revolvers. Many of the Indians had the much more modern and faster firing Henry rifles. The U.S. government had once again underarmed its soldiers.

Gen. Truman B. Seymour

(1824–1891)

THE GENERAL
WITHOUT JUDGMENT

✯ MISFIRE ✯

GEN. TRUMAN SEYMOUR SO EXCELLED AT DRAWING AT West Point he became an instructor. Too bad he failed at battlefield tactics. Ask the dead black soldiers he commanded at Battery Wagner, South Carolina, in July 1863, or at Olustee, Florida, in February 1864.

Seymour's failure at Olustee has broader implications. Had he won, he would have been a key player in a virtual coup against President Abraham Lincoln.

A personally talented man, Seymour seems to have chosen the wrong career early in his life and he never corrected that mistake. Though sometimes a capable general, he more often proved to be one without good judgment, a character flaw that can get hundreds or thousands of men killed in one battle. For his errors in his political and military career, Seymour can be nothing but a misfire.

A native of Vermont, Seymour was in the fabled 1846 class, placing high enough that he was assigned to the artillery. A staff officer at Fort Sumter, Seymour's fifteen years of service marked him for promotion to brigadier general.

Seymour served for some time as a brigade commander in the Army of the Potomac, commanded by his friend George McClellan, before he was transferred to the Department of the South, which was charged with attacking and capturing Charleston, South Carolina. A proud man, Seymour, who kept track of his standing compared to other generals, must have been irritated at his posting. He now reported to Quincy Gillmore, a man four years his junior, but who had made general before him.

In July 1863 Lee had been defeated at Gettysburg and Vicksburg had fallen, putting pressure on Gillmore to match those Union victories with his own capture of Charleston. He started that campaign by focusing on Battery Wagner, a sand fort on Morris Island. Wagner's capture would bring Union guns into range of firing on Fort Sumter. After first failing to capture Wagner on July 11 with a surprise attack by three regiments, Gillmore then planned a massive assault by Seymour's division, fourteen regiments consisting of six thousand soldiers.

Seymour must have paused when he looked at the ground. The approach to the fort was just one hundred yards wide, bounded by ocean on one side and a creek on the other. There was no cover. Leading the attack would be the Fifty-fourth Massachusetts Regiment, a regiment of free blacks commanded by a colonel who told Seymour and Gillmore he wanted to prove to skeptical Union generals that black men were equal to white men.

Other commanders were skeptical. They could see little damage done to the fort by the heavy bombardment. One regimental commander who tried to warn Seymour that making the attack was a mistake later wrote that "Seymour is a devil for dash," meaning the general wanted to see the glory of the charge.

Two brigades of Union troops were shattered in front of Battery

Wagner. Seymour, who had not led the charge, was wounded by Confederate grapeshot. Only after his wounding did he call off the attack.

Before the attack, Gillmore and Seymour assumed they would be heroes for launching the attack that would lead to the eventual fall of Fort Sumter. After the attack, Northern newspapers called them racists for putting the mostly untested black troops at the head of the narrow line attacking the fort. Perhaps most damaging was that Seymour called off the attack after the Fifty-fourth Massachusetts had been shattered, but while there still were scattered pockets of black men fighting for their lives inside the fort.

Seymour defended charges of racism by writing: "It was believed that the 54th was in every respect as efficient as any body of men. It was one of the strongest and best officered; there seemed to be no good reason why it should not be selected for this advance."

Seymour's next chance at field command was a strange expedition to Florida that was designed not so much to defeat the Confederates, but to grab electoral votes.

Gillmore planned a raid in December 1863 aimed at capturing a railhead at Lake City, fifty miles west of Jacksonville, which would disrupt Confederate shipment of beef cattle north to Lee's army. The mission had a secondary purpose of freeing slaves and recruiting them into the Union army.

Not explicitly written into the mission's goals was setting up a puppet government that would bring Florida back into the Union before the 1864 presidential election. Both President Lincoln and his treasury secretary, Salmon Chase, had political operatives in the state charged with reorganizing the government so the voters would owe their allegiance to one or the other. Both Gillmore and Seymour knew of the political ramifications of the mission, with some evidence suggesting Gillmore backed Chase.

The raid commenced in February 1864 with mostly black troops, including the Fifty-fourth Massachusetts, the First North Carolina Volunteers, and the Second South Carolina Volunteers, the latter two made up of freed slaves from those states. The presence of these three regiments was historic in itself as it was the first time that the first regiments of freed slaves from two different states had joined with the first regiment of free black men to fight. If any of the black soldiers on the mission questioned the wisdom of following two white generals who had sent blacks into a slaughter just seven months earlier, they kept it to themselves.

Seymour led the brigade so slowly westward that Confederate reinforcements from Georgia had time to set up a defense in front of the unsuspecting Federals.

On February 11 Seymour wrote Gillmore a letter complaining that he was finding few Union sympathizers who would vote for either Lincoln or Chase. On February 14 Gillmore and Seymour met in Jacksonville to discuss the slow-going invasion. Gillmore returned to South Carolina after telling Seymour the operation would be pulled back to Jacksonville. Just three days later Seymour sent a letter to Gillmore, informing him that the force was moving westward again to capture the railhead at Lake City.

Gillmore was aghast. He rushed new orders demanding Seymour turn his force around and return to Jacksonville. While the letter was in transit, Seymour's own nervous commanders were telling him they felt exposed, fifty miles deep into Confederate territory. Seymour ignored them and pressed forward.

Theories abound about why Seymour went on without any direct orders and in violation of at least a verbal understanding with his superior. Seymour may have sincerely believed that he could wreck the railhead at Lake City and then return to Jacksonville with something to show for the invasion. He may have also wanted to burn a railroad bridge over the Suwannee River that would have further disrupted the flow of Confederate supplies northward. And he may have been completing some secret promise to agents of Chase or Lincoln to carry out the plan to set up a puppet government, even though Gillmore had cancelled the mission.

Another plausible theory is that Seymour may have been trying to restore the honor he lost at Battery Wagner. He may have hoped that if he could recapture Florida, he would regain his reputation in the eyes of his peers.

There could be another explanation of why Seymour pressed on with the invasion.

Perhaps he was mentally deranged.

"Seymour has seemed very unsteady and queer since the beginning of the campaign. He has been subject to violent alternations of timidity and rashness, now declaring Florida loyalty was all bosh, now lauding it as the purest article extant, now insisting that Beauregard was in front with the whole Confederacy, and now asserting that he could whip all the rebels in Florida with a good brigade," wrote John Hay, Lincoln's personal secretary. Hay had gone along on the expedition in order to set up Florida's new government so it would favor the president.

Seymour ran into the Confederate defenses on February 20 in open ground ten miles east of Lake City near a train stop called Olustee. The now-experienced Fifty-fourth Massachusetts went forward with a unique battle cry: "Three cheers for Massachusetts and seven dollars a month!" That was a reference to the Federal government's decision to pay black soldiers just half the wages of white soldiers.

"I think no battle was ever more wretchedly fought. I was going to say planned, but there was no plan," wrote one lieutenant of the Eighth United States Colored Troops.

Within a few hours the Federals were in full, unrestrained retreat. Olustee was the worst disaster suffered by the Union army during the war with more than 34 percent of the fifty-five hundred Federal troops killed, wounded, or captured. By contrast, the Union army lost about a quarter of its men to casualties at the war's largest battle in Gettysburg. Had the Fifty-fourth Massachusetts not stopped a poorly managed Confederate pursuit, it is conceivable that the entire Union force could have been surrounded and destroyed.

Seymour was soundly criticized by his regimental commanders for his incompetence on the field and once again wasting the lives of his black soldiers. Strangely, nothing happened to Seymour for his poor general-ship both at Battery Wagner and then at Olustee. In fact, he was taken out of the backwater of the Department of the South and brought back to the heavier fighting with the Army of the Potomac. He was given a brigade by U. S. Grant at the battle of the Wilderness. Eventually he was given a division and promoted to major general. He did fairly well over the next year. At least he had no more disasters.

Robert Smalls

(1839–1915)

No Small Man

⋆ BULL'S-EYE ⋆

IN THE 1860S THE WHITE POPULATION OF THE UNITED States, North and South, abolitionist and slave-holding, Republican and Democrat, did not believe black people, slave and free, were as civilized, intelligent, or capable as whites. Even John Brown, the radical abolitionist, thought of blacks as trainable children. When collecting weapons for the slave army he hoped to raise, he chose pikes over rifles as he was not confident all blacks understood how to use firearms.

Some Southern politicians claimed blacks were such inferior thinkers that slavery was the only thing they understood. Slave owners often believed it was their duty to take care of a race that could not make it on its own in civilized society.

While Northern politicians would eventually steer the war goal of the public to be freeing the Southern slaves, they did not think blacks were socially equal to whites. After raising the first black regiments, Northern military planners refused to pay the black soldiers the same monthly wages as white soldiers. Black people were not equal to whites as people so why should black soldiers be paid the same as white soldiers?

Then along came Robert Smalls. He would prove to both North and South that black people were not only as smart as whites but just as brave. Smalls was the first true black hero to emerge from the war, a man whose wartime success story was so fantastic that it was hard to believe in the North and generally disbelieved in the South. Smalls is a bull's-eye.

Born a slave to a slave owned by the McKee family in Beaufort, South Carolina, and possibly fathered by John McKee, Smalls never worked the muddy fields where Sea Island cotton was grown. When he was twelve he was sent to live with a McKee family member in Charleston. At eighteen he was employed as a ship's wheelman, the job closest to being a ship's pilot a slave could hold, a job reserved for supposedly much smarter white people.

Pilots knew the tides, where sandbars were forming and receding, where the shoals were closest to the surface, where floating trees lurked below the water. If a pilot forgot any of this information, his ship could sink.

In 1861 Smalls became a valued crew member of the 140-foot-long side-wheel steamer, the *Planter*. Built with a shallow draft so she could go up rivers, the *Planter* soon became a familiar and valuable ship in coastal South Carolina. When the war started she was used to run supplies to all of the coastal Confederate forts. Smalls was so good at his job of piloting that the *Planter* became the dispatch boat for the Confederate commander of Charleston's defenses. Smalls became very familiar with the water approaches to Confederate installations around Charleston. That information would come in handy.

As 1862 rolled around, a blockading Union fleet anchored off Charleston Harbor. An idea must have formed in Smalls's head associating that Union fleet with freedom.

That idea crystallized one night when the slave crew was below deck on the *Planter*. Smalls playfully took the captain's white wide-brimmed hat, clamped it on his head, and then crossed his arms, striking a pose like the white man invariably did standing in the bow of the *Planter* as it left port. The slaves all laughed, claiming Smalls looked just like the captain. Then the laughing stopped.

On the night of May 12, 1862, Smalls and the crew fired up the boilers of the *Planter* just as they would on any normal day—just several hours sooner. They headed up the Cooper River. No one on shore, least of all the supposedly watchful Confederate sentries, paid the ship any mind. The *Planter* pulled next to another small steamer, allowing the families of the slaves to leap aboard the *Planter.*

The *Planter* then headed down-river toward the sea and the U.S. Navy. Smalls donned the white hat and stood in the bow to pose as the captain. Whenever anyone would hail the ship from the shore, Smalls would wave his hand then turn away "so they would not see the color of my skin" as he explained in a written account.

As the ship approached Fort Sumter, Smalls blew a recognition signal on the *Planter's* whistle. The watchful sentries, now knowing the *Planter* was a Confederate ship, waved as it passed.

Normally the *Planter* would turn south, hugging the shoreline and staying out of reach of the Union vessels. But as soon as Smalls was out of range of the fort's cannon, he swung the ship out to sea.

As the *Planter* neared the Union blockade, the danger shifted from being sunk by Confederate Fort Sumter to being sunk by Federal blockading ships. Seeing a vessel approaching in the predawn darkness from the direction of the Confederates, the Federals assumed they were being attacked. Before they could fire, Smalls unfurled a white bed sheet and called to the nervous men on the decks that he was surrendering the *Planter* to them.

The stunned Federals were presented with a shallow-draft ship armed with three cannon, plus four unmounted cannon scheduled for delivery to a Confederate fort. What was more valuable was that the ship, personally used by a Confederate general, was crewed by black slaves who had stolen it right from under the noses of thousands of Confederates. It was a public relations disaster for the Confederates and a boon for the Federals.

Harper's Weekly published a photograph of Smalls and wrote of the "daring and intelligent Negro" who stole the *Planter*. Not every newspaper got it right. One account said "a very ancient old darky" stole the ship. Smalls was twenty-three years old.

The *New York Commercial Advertiser*, unconscious or uncaring about racist beliefs, wrote: "We suppose few events that have taken place during the war have produced a heartier chuckle of satisfaction than the capture of the rebel armed steamer *Planter*. It is a remarkable instance, even in these times, of riches taking themselves to wing and flying away. Here were eight contrabands made out of the commonest clay imaginable, with souls so vulgar that their very existence has been questioned, yet they actually emancipated not only themselves, but as many others, bringing a highly valuable present to Uncle Sam. The fellow who managed this affair proves that, in spite of his name, he is no Small man."

Recognizing the promotional value of the incident, the U.S. Congress passed a bill, virtually without any debate, that appraised the value of the *Planter* and awarded the sum to the crew. Of the nine thousand dollar appraised value, Smalls was given one thousand five hundred dollars. He was sent North on a speaking tour of black and white churches to display this first black hero of the war.

Smalls returned to become a pilot first for the Union navy and then for the Union army, which used ships to run up rivers. Smalls's U. S. Navy experience must have left him thinking about the intelligence of white people. He was the pilot of a Union ironclad called the *Keokuk*, which was part of a fleet of ironclads that had attacked Fort Sumter in the spring of 1863. The *Keokuk* was hit ninety times by fire from the fort but was able to fire only three shots itself. It sank in shallow water. Smalls survived with some minor wounds to his face.

Not impressed with the white man's ability to build ironclads, Smalls returned to the *Planter*, which he piloted on plantation raids to free slaves. During one unexpected engagement with Confederates, the white captain became so rattled that he ran below deck and hid. Smalls took over command of the ship.

Satisfied with that performance, the government made Smalls the official captain of the *Planter*. He performed well, participating in at least seventeen raids. In 1864 he took the *Planter* to the Philadelphia Shipyard for a three-month refitting. While there he learned to read and write. During his stay in the North he was thrown off of a streetcar because the line did not allow blacks to ride public conveyances.

Though Smalls was nationally known during the war, bureaucrats quickly forgot. After the war he applied for a United States government pension based on his service aboard the *Planter.* Because he had lost the original order naming him captain and because other paperwork on his service was not in the navy's files, Smalls was denied the pension. The widely publicized accounts of his service were not good enough for the U.S. government to grant pensions to a black man.

After the war Smalls entered politics. In 1874, running as a Republican, he became the first black U.S. congressman from South Carolina. Smalls served off and on in Congress for a decade. In 1882 he introduced a bill calling for the expansion of a small U.S. Navy coaling installation at Port Royal, South Carolina. After much lobbying of his fellow congressmen, he managed to get the bill passed. That little coaling station kept growing. Today it is the Parris Island Marine Corps Training Depot, where more than nineteen thousand marines get their basic training each year. The slave who stole a Confederate ship and used it to become one of the first black ship captains and first black heroes of the Civil War helped to create one of the most famous military bases in the world.

Smalls kept his sense of humor even when faced with racism. He was once approached on the street by a white woman who called him "Uncle," a vernacular address applied to many older black men of the day. Smalls, who always dressed in the latest fashions, looked at the woman and loudly proclaimed, "Madam, I am no relative of yours. Good day!"

Smalls died in 1915.

Smalls's military adventures are insignificant when judged only by destroyed Confederate facilities. Nothing he did on the *Planter* changed the outcome of any battle. His real contribution to the war effort was to prove to North and South that black people were not intellectually inferior to white people. It would be nearly a year after he became nationally known before the Lincoln administration would recognize that by allowing the raising of black Union regiments.

The process of treating black and white soldiers equally started with one twenty-three-year-old slave who was good at imitating his white captain. By the time the war ended more than 180,000 black men would be serving in the Union army and navy. Putting them in the service allowed the Union to attack on many more fronts than was possible when only white soldiers were recruited. Blacks would provide the man-power to finally push the war to conclusion.

Gen. William F. Smith
(1824–1903)

THE TIMID GENERAL WHO
TWICE FAILED TO END THE WAR

✴ MISFIRE ✴

WITH FRIENDS WHO NICKNAME YOU "BALDY" WHILE YOU are still a young West Point cadet, who needs enemies?

Actually Gen. William F. "Baldy" Smith, the man who may have invented the comb-over, was his own worst enemy. Confident of his own command abilities, he enjoyed criticizing the abilities of others, particularly his superior generals. Eventually those superiors got around to pulling this thorn from their side.

It did not help Smith's image that he missed one opportunity in spring 1862 to crush the Confederate army before him at Yorktown and then again in summer 1864 when he could have captured Petersburg without a fight. Few generals are given a single chance to affect the outcome of a battle and perhaps an entire war, if they make the right decision. Smith was cursed by the fact that he was given not one, but two, clear-cut, easily seen chances to crush the Confederates in front of him. He failed to take both of those chances. For that he is a misfire.

A Vermont native, Smith graduated in 1845 fourth in his class and was ordered to remain at the academy to teach mathematics while his classmates fought the Mexican War.

Finally getting his chance to fight in 1861, he performed well at Bull Run. Promoted to brigadier general, he was given a division command in the Army of the Potomac during the 1862 Peninsula campaign.

Smith's engineering training made him suspicious about the Confederate defenses at Yorktown as the army crept up the peninsula toward Richmond. He did not believe there were enough Confederates on hand to cover a trench line stretching across the entire peninsula. Without asking permission from McClellan, Smith sent two regiments forward to probe the Warwick River line. He told Gen. Winfield Scott Hancock to attack if he thought he had found an exploitable hole. The sound of the fighting would be a signal for Smith to send in reinforcements.

Working under the principle that it is better to do something and apologize for it later than to ask in advance for permission and to be refused, Smith rode to his corps commander's headquarters and casually told him about the scouting mission he had ordered. The corps commander handed Smith a blanket order from army commander George McClellan refusing permission for any general to probe the Confederate defenses until his engineers investigated the strength of the line.

Seeing his career flash in front of his eyes, Smith ordered Hancock to return without attacking. Hancock protested that he had indeed found a weak spot in the Confederate line. One simple rush would take it.

Smith was in a quandary. If Hancock attacked, Smith's corps commander would know that it was in violation of McClellan's direct order. If Hancock ran into trouble, it would mean the end of Smith's career. Even if Hancock succeeded in breeching the Confederate line, it would still be against express orders. Smith recalled Hancock, who protested again that they were losing a chance to crack the Confederate line.

Smith later privately wrote that had he not received McClellan's order, he could have broken the Confederates and there never would have been a month-long siege of Yorktown.

In a few weeks Smith faced Stonewall Jackson at White Oak Swamp in the Seven Days' battles and did well enough to be rewarded with a major general's promotion.

Smith continued climbing the command ladder after Antietam when his boss, Gen. William B. Franklin, was promoted to command the "Left Grand Division" in the reorganized Army of the Potomac under Gen. Ambrose Burnside. At Fredericksburg, Franklin, unsure of his orders from Burnside, did not fully commit all of his troops, including Smith's division. Franklin's weak attack faltered though he outnumbered the Confederates.

After the battle Franklin and Smith wrote a letter to Lincoln blaming Burnside for the Fredericksburg debacle. That was a colossal mistake on their part. Lincoln did not like underling generals criticizing the man he had just put in charge of the army. Lincoln noted that both Franklin and Smith were close friends of McClellan, whom he had just fired in favor of Burnside.

If Smith expected the thanks of his president for exposing Burnside's flawed battle, he did not get it. Instead, his promotion to major general was revoked, and he was transferred away from the Army of the Potomac and given a minor job as commander of a division of Pennsylvania militia.

Having performed valuable service by protecting the roads and railroads threatened by Lee's invasion of the North, Smith was rewarded by being reactivated as chief engineer for the Army of the Cumberland. He was sent west to Chattanooga, Tennessee, to help break the siege of that town by surrounding Confederates.

Still unable to break his habit of criticizing his commanders, when he got to Tennessee, he quarreled with Gen. George Thomas over meaningless credit for placing a pontoon bridge over a river. U. S. Grant soon was put in command of the army, replacing Thomas.

At first Grant loved Smith, finding his engineering skills of the highest order. He suggested him again for promotion to major general and forced through the nomination. The love affair with Smith would soon end, however, once Grant came east, bringing Smith with him. In his memoirs Grant would write, "I was not long in finding out that the objections to Smith's promotion were well founded."

Back east Smith first went into the Army of Virginia, commanded by Gen. Ben Butler, a political general from Massachusetts who caused Smith to grumble still more. At first Smith's whining was not hard to take as it was directed at Butler whom Grant did not like.

Then Smith was transferred back to the Army of the Potomac under George Meade, who was Grant's immediate subordinate. After several devastating charges across open ground at the battle of Cold Harbor in early June 1864, Smith started complaining about Meade. While Meade was the recognized head of the Army of the Potomac, Grant actually made most of the major decisions about what that army would do. So when Smith was criticizing Meade, he was also criticizing Grant. General Grant knew he had made a major mistake at Cold Harbor and he didn't need someone reminding him of it.

In mid-June 1864 Smith sealed his fate when he failed to show the initiative Grant liked to see in his generals. He did not capture Petersburg when there were virtually no Confederate troops defending it.

After flinging his troops fruitlessly into Lee's dug-in forces at Cold Harbor northeast of Richmond, Grant realized that continued fighting like that would only wear down his own army. Therefore he conceived a mammoth alternate plan. He would move his ninety-thousand-man army across the half-mile-wide James River and attack Richmond's main source of supplies, the railroad town of Petersburg, thirty miles south of Richmond.

Smith commanded the 12,500 men of the Eighteenth Corps. They led the movement toward Petersburg, which was defended at the time by just twenty-two hundred soldiers. As Smith approached the trenches east of Petersburg on June 15, 1864, his old engineer's caution began to play tricks on his mind. Why was his approach so easy? Was he about to make the same mistake that Grant had made at Cold Harbor just two weeks earlier when more than one thousand of Smith's corps had fallen in less than half an hour?

Smith was so conscious of putting men in danger that he even insisted on doing his own scouting of the Confederate defenses, hardly the sort of thing a corps commander should be doing.

What he saw disturbed him. The trenches were well dug and the artillery redoubts were high around each of the cannon he could see. In front of the trenches were steep ditches. What was strange was that he could see few infantrymen in the trenches. That frightened him too. Were there extra men hiding in the bottom of the trenches, waiting to spring to the firing wall and cut down more of his corps?

Finally, Smith sent a heavy skirmish line forward toward the Confederate works. To his surprise the line went up and over the works. Within minutes Smith's corps, without trying, had captured four cannon and two hundred prisoners. When the main attacking force reached the trenches, they fanned out and captured another twelve cannon. By nine o'clock Smith's night attack had captured more than a mile and a half of the defenses of Petersburg.

Soon a trickle of Confederate brigades arrived from the outer defenses of Richmond, alerted by the first troops to detect Smith's presence. But those brigades faced an entire corps. If Smith were to push, those Confederates would be swiftly dispatched.

Smith did not push. Surprised and suspicious that he had been allowed to capture these defenses so easily, he stopped to evaluate a rumor that Lee's entire army had already crossed the James River and was on its way to wipe him out.

When Hancock arrived, he told Smith he had two fresh divisions ready to move out in any direction Smith chose. Smith told a surprised Hancock that no one was moving anywhere. They were digging in and defending what they had captured.

Incredibly, more than five hours after the Petersburg trenches had fallen to Smith, Lee still did not believe that Grant had moved his entire army. Petersburg's main defender, Gen. P. G. T. Beauregard, kept sending frantic notes to Lee while shifting men from Bermuda Hundred, which was under his command. At one point Beauregard had just fourteen thousand men facing nearly eighty thousand Federals.

Luckily for the Confederates, the Federals coming along behind

Smith had exhausted themselves on a fast march to Petersburg and they too did nothing to capture Petersburg.

Lee finally realized that Grant had fooled him and he rushed reinforcements south. Four days later the Federal assault had fizzled after suffering more than ten thousand casualties compared to just four thousand Confederate casualties. Five days after Smith had taken the trenches, Grant put Petersburg under siege.

Grant demanded answers. He had duped Lee into staying in his Richmond trenches while most of the Union army got across the pontoon bridge close to Petersburg. He had overwhelming numbers, but the city had not fallen.

His eyes fell on Baldy Smith. Smith had captured more Confederate territory in a few minutes of unspirited fighting than the entire Union army had captured in the previous several months. Yet Smith had let the opportunity to capture the entire city slip through his fingers. Had Smith rushed in either direction and ordered Hancock to do the same, Petersburg would have fallen on the first night. Instead, Smith sat in the captured Confederate trenches as if he were paralyzed.

That did it. Barely a month later, Smith was relieved of command of the Eighteenth Corps and ordered to New York "to await orders." Those orders never came. All that did come were minor appointments to review boards that never brought Smith close to combat again. He spent the rest of his life doing civil engineering projects and writing articles explaining why a Union corps could not capture Petersburg from two thousand Confederates.

Smith never did come up with a plausible explanation. He died in 1903, never admitting but probably wondering if he could have ended the war in June 1864.

Elizabeth Van Lew
(1818–1900)

GRANT'S BEST SPY

⭐ BULL'S-EYE ⭐

ELIZABETH VAN LEW OF RICHMOND, VIRGINIA, WAS crazy. She must have been. She wore tattered old clothes though she lived in a fine mansion. She talked to herself in public. She kept a bedroom made up in the event Union Gen. George McClellan should visit as a conquering general.

"Crazy Bet," as taunting children called her, was not crazy. She wore those shabby clothes and talked to herself to make her neighbors—and more importantly, Confederate government officials—think she was crazy.

A Union spy is what Crazy Bet was.

"For a long, long time, she represented all that was left of the power of the United States government in Richmond," was the way Gen. U. S. Grant's chief of military intelligence described Van Lew.

114

That kind of powerful assessment by a man who knew Van Lew's contributions to the war effort makes her a bull's-eye. As might be expected of a spy, no one today can tell exactly what role she had in shortening the war but Grant paid her more respect than he did many of his own generals who were doing the fighting.

Van Lew may have run the best spy network the United States government ever had. Her network was so efficient she may have successfully placed an operative inside the Confederate White House who was able to see, read, and memorize important documents and overhear meetings between Confederate President Jefferson Davis and his generals. One story told about the strength of Van Lew's network was that she could cut flowers in her garden in the morning and have them on the camp desk of General Grant by that afternoon.

"May have run the best spy network" is an important distinction. Many of Van Lew's actual accomplishments were never documented and those that were recorded were later expunged from the records. Though she kept a diary of the war years, at least half of the pages are missing and presumably destroyed by her, or unaccountably lost. Numbered pages appear to have been ripped out of the diary as if upon reflection she decided she did not want anyone to read them. In one portion of her diary Van Lew mentions that she was afraid to write down everything out of fear that her house would be searched and her complicity discovered. She never got around to reconstructing that diary or writing a comprehensive autobiography that would have detailed all of her wartime contributions.

One way that history can prove Van Lew was important to the Union cause is that President U. S. Grant named her postmistress for the city of Richmond in 1869. That was a valuable patronage job, indicating that even four years after the war Grant still wanted to find a way to thank Van Lew.

Born a southerner in Richmond, Van Lew was the daughter of a New Yorker who made his fortune selling hardware in Richmond. Educated in Philadelphia, she grew up believing slavery was wrong. After her father died, she convinced her mother to free the family slaves in the 1850s. Most of those slaves stayed on as free employees.

Early in the war Van Lew and her mother visited Union prisoners, quizzing them about information they overheard from their guards. She then sent that information through the lines, first to Union Gen. Ben Butler and later to U. S. Grant.

Her first level of spies was her servants who maintained a small farm outside of town. Their going back and forth carrying produce in one direction and tools in another did not attract attention. One story says that messages to other Union spies were often written in code, put in a hollow egg that was placed at the bottom of a basket of eggs that slaves would peddle between the farm and the Van Lew house. Another favorite hiding place was in the double-soled shoes of her servants. Messages would be folded into the hollow shoe soles and the servant would then walk through the nearest, freshest mud puddle. The muddy shoes would dissuade any suspicious Confederate picket from examining the black man or woman too closely.

A story that has persisted through the years is that Van Lew placed a spy in the Confederate White House, Mary Elizabeth Bowser, a young black woman whom Van Lew had sent to Philadelphia to be educated, just as she would have sent a white daughter. While in Philadelphia, Bowser learned to read. Van Lew supposedly called her back to Richmond where she was employed by Varina Davis, the Confederate first lady. Bowser would clean up around President Jefferson Davis's office, reading his papers when she got the chance and otherwise keeping her ears open when Davis was meeting with high ranking officers.

Bowser's activities are shrouded in even more mystery than Van Lew's, making her contributions difficult to ascertain. According to modern historical legend, Bowser's own diary mentioning Davis, Lee, Longstreet, and other generals was supposedly thrown out in the 1950s by her descendants who seemed unaware of or uninterested in their ancestor's account of her life in the 1860s. References to the contributions of Bowser do not appear in the surviving portions of Miss Van Lew's diary. The only indication of how valuable Bowser might have been comes from the account of a male spy who was part of Van Lew's spy network. After the war he told his grandson that Bowser had a photographic memory and could recite what she saw on Davis's desk word for word. The man claimed Bowser would deliver hollow eggs to him and he would smuggle them out of the city and into Union hands.

One problem with the story about a black spy in the Confederate White House is that First Lady Varina Davis said after the war that she never employed anyone named Mary Bowser. While Bowser could have used an alias, another problem is that Van Lew was very well known and very disliked in Richmond. It seems unlikely that Mrs. Davis would have hired anyone suggested to her by Van Lew. It is possible that Van Lew hid her relationship with Bowser by going through a friend, but Van Lew supposedly was without friends in the city because of her outspoken Unionist stands. Any friend of Van Lew's would have been suspect as well. Perhaps the friend was another undercover female Union spy who only pretended to be friends with the Davis family.

One bizarre episode that proves that Van Lew had resources, connections, and the nerve to use them occurred in February 1864. Four thousand Federal cavalrymen moved on Richmond in two columns, one of which was commanded by a twenty-two-year-old colonel named Ulric Dahlgren, son of Union Adm. John Dahlgren. The mission's true purpose is still murky today, nearly 140 years later, but papers supposedly found on Dahlgren when he was killed in a skirmish showed that he planned to kill or kidnap the Confederate cabinet. While a controversy over the authenticity of the papers was raging in Richmond, the body of Dahlgren was buried in a Confederate cemetery not far from Van Lew's house.

Apparently without being asked or ordered but out of concern for Dahlgren's famous father's feelings, Van Lew had the body dug up and spirited out of Richmond six weeks after he had died.

As Grant's army approached Richmond, Van Lew's spying began to take on a different importance. She began to smuggle out information about the strength of troops in and around Richmond. According to a story in the *Richmond Times Dispatch* in 1883, one of her sources was a clerk in the Confederate adjutant general's office who was able to show her the strength of all of the units in the whole army. Another spy was able to make maps of the defenses around Richmond for her. She was able to funnel all this information to Grant, who made his headquarters about forty miles southeast of Richmond at City Point.

As Lee's army left Petersburg and Richmond, Van Lew unfurled a large American flag from her house, the first house in Richmond to display the flag in four years. Soon an angry crowd began to gather outside the house. Van Lew moved among the men saying: "I know you and I know where you live. If you burn my house, I will tell General Grant you did it and he will burn your house down as well." The threats worked.

Grant made Van Lew's house one of his first stops in Richmond after he returned from Lee's surrender at Appomattox. He shocked his wife when he told her he had to go visit a woman in Richmond. Van Lew's activities had been so secret that even the general's wife, who often sat in on military briefings, had never heard of her.

Van Lew kept her job as postmistress only as long as Grant was in office, from 1869 through 1875. Succeeding presidents demoted her to clerk and ignored her contributions to the war effort. She was even savaged in a northern newspaper editorial as being a "relic" of a long-gone era, someone who did not need to be on a public payroll any longer.

Richmonders never forgave their native daughter for siding with the enemy in the war. When Van Lew finally died in Richmond in 1900 not a single person attended her funeral. A boulder from Massachusetts shipped south to act as her tombstone was fitted with a plaque reading: "She risked everything that is dear to man—friends, fortune, comfort, health, life itself—all for the one absorbing desire of her heart, that slavery be abolished and the Union preserved."

Exactly what Van Lew did for the Union army will probably never be known. At her request in 1866 all of the surviving messages she sent to Generals Butler and Grant were returned to her and she promptly destroyed them out of fear that she would anger her Richmond neighbors even more than she already had. Only one message she sent to General Butler survives in the Official Records.

Gen. Lew Wallace

(1827–1905)

THE MAN WHO
SAVED WASHINGTON

⭐ BULL'S-EYE ⭐

HAD GEN. LEW WALLACE FAILED IN HIS DEFENSE AT
Monocacy Station, Maryland, in July 1864, the Confederates might have
captured Washington, D.C., and President Lincoln. Had Lincoln been
captured, the South would have had a prisoner who could have been
exchanged in return for a negotiated peace. Had Washington been captured or burned, an embarrassed President Lincoln might not have been
reelected and his replacement might have settled with the South.

Neither of those scenarios played out because Wallace, a man who
had been fired from his command position two years earlier, had put
aside his personal pride in favor of saving his nation's capital. His military instincts, generally accurate compared to his superiors, proved to be

correct, and he can be credited with saving Washington from an uncertain fate. For that he is a bull's-eye.

Self-educated in warfare, lawyer Wallace was always fascinated with the military, raising his own regiment for the Mexican War and his own militia unit in the 1850s.

His professional military compatriots did not immediately embrace this amateur. He attracted irritated envy from other generals when he drove the Confederates out of Romney, Virginia, in June 1861, an early Union victory after the defeat at Fort Sumter.

Sent west, Wallace helped Gen. U. S. Grant capture Forts Henry and Donelson. In March 1862 he was promoted to major general, a somewhat rare honor for a man who had never attended West Point and who did not have political clout in Washington. Again, the professional generals were irritated at this pretender.

They would get their revenge.

On April 6, 1862, Wallace was camped several miles north of the main body of Grant's army when Confederate Gen. Albert Sidney Johnston launched a surprise attack at Shiloh. Grant ordered Wallace: "Hold yourself in readiness to march upon orders received. Hold your division in readiness to march in any direction."

It was nearly noon before Wallace received a simple unsigned order to "march and form junction with the right of the army. Form line of battle at right angle with the river and be governed by circumstances." Grant's courier who delivered the order told Wallace, "We are repulsing the enemy."

That was untrue. The Confederates were pushing Grant's surprised army back toward the river. Based on the courier's information, Wallace started marching to where the army's right under the command of Gen. William T. Sherman would be if it was repulsing the Confederates.

After several hours of marching, two different officers sent by Grant intercepted the column to tell Wallace to "hurry up!" An irritated Wallace insisted he was hurrying toward Sherman. The second officer then told Wallace for the first time that Sherman had been pushed back toward the Tennessee River. Wallace's division was marching away from the fighting rather than toward it.

Wallace pondered his position. If he continued marching in his present direction he would have four thousand men coming in on the rear of Confederates who probably had no idea his division existed. He asked the officer if Grant had orders for him.

"He wants you at Pittsburg Landing and he wants you like hell!" came the reply.

Abandoning his better judgment in favor of specific orders from Grant, Wallace headed for Pittsburg Landing.

Grant's aides, desperate for fresh men, demanded Wallace rush his leading regiments toward the fighting. Wallace, reluctant to abandon his artillery in the middle of the woods, refused. When Wallace finally arrived at Pittsburg Landing near nightfall, most of the fighting was over. His men had done nothing in the epic battle that almost saw Grant himself pushed into the Tennessee River. The next morning Wallace's division participated in the attack that finally won the two-day battle.

Blamed by many of Grant's generals for the near-defeat because he arrived after the fighting was over, Wallace defended himself by saying he had followed Grant's vague orders to the letter. Made the scapegoat for Grant's own poor deployment of his troops, Wallace was removed from command.

Though Wallace could have resigned from the army, he swallowed his pride and went back to recruiting soldiers. In March 1864 he was offered command of the Middle Department, which included the defense of Washington, more than one hundred miles from the front.

No one, including Wallace himself, thought he would ever do anything important again. It would take a second lapse in judgment by Grant to bring Wallace back into prominence.

By early June 1864 Grant had trapped Lee's army around Richmond and Petersburg. In mid-June Gen. Jubal Early and fourteen thousand men slipped out of Grant's encirclement and swept north through the Shenandoah Valley. Lee had given Early two goals: sweep the Federals from the Valley to protect the farmers and then "demonstrate" on Washington in hopes that Grant would peel troops away from Petersburg and Richmond to defend the capital.

Lee had not counted on Grant sometimes being a dense commander.

Grant refused to believe that Early had left Petersburg. As Early neared the north end of the Shenandoah Valley in early July, Grant still had not moved any troops to protect Washington.

The opportunistic Lee now changed plans. He had intended only to make Grant believe he would attack Washington. If Grant was not sending reinforcements to the forts around Washington, a raid on the capital city had real potential. Early crossed the Potomac and made a beeline for Washington.

The only troops who stood in Early's way were the five thousand untested garrison troops commanded by Wallace. Responding to reports about mounted men in the mountain passes of Maryland, Wallace headed for Monocacy Junction, a rail stop just south of Frederick, Maryland. Wallace guessed the mounted men were advance Confederate scouts. He sent a telegram to his Washington boss, Gen. Henry Halleck, the same man who had fired him after Shiloh, warning him that Washington would soon come under Confederate attack. Halleck refused to believe that any Confederates were even in the area. Ignored himself, Wallace cut off any more input from his superior as he prepared for what he thought to be a suicide mission.

"Twenty-three hundred men was the utmost I could make of my force. Of that number the major part were raw and untested. On the other side, out of the great uncertainty respecting the strength of the enemy, everything known and everything surmisable fixed it that he outnumbered me and largely. With a conviction then of my own comparative weakness, did I have a right, morally speaking, to subject those under me to the perils of a battle so doubtful, if not so hopeless?" Wallace wrote.

Wallace went into the battle of Monocacy on July 9, 1864, knowing that he would lose, but hoping he could slow the Confederates until Grant realized the raid was real and could rush reinforcements to Washington.

There is an interesting contrast to the way Wallace fought at Monocacy and the way Grant fought at Shiloh. Wallace positioned all of his men on the east side of the Monocacy River, using it as an effective defensive position against the Confederates who were attacking from the west. At Shiloh Grant allowed himself to be pushed all the way back to the west bank of the Tennessee River as he faced Confederates also attacking from the west. Amateur soldier Wallace's defensive use of a river was by the book while professional soldier Grant's placement of his troops with their backs to a river showed military incompetence.

All day long Wallace's reserve troops and a division finally rushed by Grant to help performed well because Wallace knew which river fords had to be defended while the Confederates had to look for those fords. As the sun was going down, Wallace finally retreated in the face of overwhelming numbers. His green garrison troops had held up the battle-hardened Confederates for more than twelve hours. The delaying battle had been costly to the Federals, with casualties of nearly thirteen hundred of the fifty-eight hundred men on the field. But what Wallace had lost tactically, he had won strategically. It took Early a full day to regroup his men. Grant used that full day to rush reinforcements from Petersburg to Washington.

On July 11 Early was within six miles of the White House, eyeing the single fort standing between him and the seat of Federal government. Just two days earlier the fort had been manned by nervous home guard troops. Now two veteran corps were occupying the fort. Early would leave Washington with the remark, "We didn't take Washington, but we've scared Abe Lincoln like hell!"

Though he had saved Washington from capture, Wallace was never thanked by being given another field command. Instead, after the war he was assigned the distasteful duty of serving on both the Lincoln assassination trial board and the commission that hanged the Confederate commander of the prisoner of war camp at Andersonville, Georgia.

After the war Wallace was appointed territorial governor of New Mexico. In his spare time he wrote *Ben Hur*, still one of the world's best-selling novels.

What would have happened had Wallace, the goat of Shiloh for his misdirected march, not sacrificed his troops at Monocacy Junction? What if Early's fourteen thousand troops had reached Washington on July 9 or 10, 1864?

Even if President Lincoln had escaped the capital, Washington itself would have been left open to the Confederates. Millions of dollars in bonds sitting in the Treasury Department could have been captured. Government buildings could have been burned. Losing the United States capital and the Capitol building itself would have been embarrassing to a Lincoln administration up for reelection in just four months. Even if Early had been forced to vacate the city within hours or days after capturing it, he would have made his exit very dramatic.

None of that happened because Gen. Lew Wallace, the self-taught soldier, recognized the danger his nation's capital was in and threw himself into the job of saving it. The politicians and professional generals may have ruined his military career, but he would not allow the Confederates to ruin his capital.

Gen. Thomas J. Wood

(1823–1906)

THE GENERAL WHO
FOLLOWED ORDERS

✭ MISFIRE ✭

WHAT IS A DIVISION GENERAL TO DO WHEN HE IS GIVEN a direct, if stupid, order by the general in charge of the entire army? Does he carry it out without question? Or does he stand his ground, ignore the direct order, and hope that he will be able to withstand the wrath that will surely fall upon his head for defying a commanding general?

Gen. Thomas J. Wood had to answer that question at the battle of Chickamauga, Georgia, on September 20, 1863, when he was specifically ordered to move his division out of line by his superior, Gen. William Rosecrans. When he followed those orders, the Confederates poured through the hole Wood knew he was creating in the line, and the Federals lost the battle. Always a soldier who had proven his bravery and

125

skill, Wood let his emotions get the best of him in this battle and he obeyed orders he knew instinctively could not be proper. For that he is a misfire.

Wood was a well-rounded soldier in 1861, having moved from the engineering corps to the dragoons in the Mexican War and then on to fighting Indians as a cavalryman in the 1850s.

Appointed a brigadier general in the fall of 1861, Wood performed well in the Army of the Ohio under Gen. Don Carlos Buell, helping win Shiloh and later Perryville, Kentucky. Late in 1862 the Army of the Ohio got a new commander, Gen. William S. Rosecrans.

There must have been early tension between Rosecrans and Wood, since Wood was a professional soldier while Rosecrans had resigned his army commission in 1854 to become a civil engineer. Rosecrans had not fought in the Mexican War so he had very little combat experience compared to Wood's proven bravery.

By September 1863 the presidents of both the United States and the Confederacy were irritated with their respective western theater commanders. Confederate Gen. Braxton Bragg had abandoned Tennessee without a fight, which angered Jefferson Davis. Rosecrans was slow in bagging Bragg, which angered Lincoln. Both presidents were demanding that their generals come to blows with the enemy.

Bragg stopped his retreat in north Georgia along the Chickamauga Creek. His battle plan was to flank march around Rosecrans and attack him from the north rather than from the south, which Rosecrans would expect. If the plan worked, the Federals would be cut off from their supply lines to Chattanooga, the city they had just occupied.

On the night of September 18, Rosecrans figured out what Bragg intended to do and shifted Gen. George Thomas's corps north to counter the Confederates.

Bragg now canceled his plans for a flank march. All day on September 19 the two armies sparred with each other but no major battle erupted. That night Confederate Gen. James Longstreet arrived on the battlefield with five brigades borrowed from the Army of Northern Virginia.

On the morning of the twentieth, Thomas, concerned that his left wing might be cut off from the rest of the army, sent word to Rosecrans that he needed reinforcements on his left. Rosecrans began shifting divisions northward. Under the plan, nearly three-fifths of the Union army would be on the left, leaving the right and the center much weaker. That defensive plan would work if the Confederates attacked on the left, as Thomas had been telling Rosecrans they would do, but it would be dangerous if the Confederates attacked the Union center or right.

The Federals had no idea that Longstreet was on the field near the center of their line.

About midmorning on September 20 Rosecrans had ordered a division under Gen. James Negley to pull out of the center and move closer to Thomas. Negley's division was to be replaced by Wood's division. When Rosecrans was checking the distribution of his troops, he found that Negley had not yet joined Thomas and that Wood's men were not yet where Negley had been. Rosecrans found Wood and began shouting at him.

According to one cleaned-up, expletive-deleted version of Rosecrans's confrontation with Wood, which was conducted in the presence of Wood's staff, Rosecrans screamed: "What is the meaning of this, sir? You have disobeyed my specific orders! By your damnable negligence you are endangering the safety of the entire army, and, by God, I will not tolerate it! Move your division at once, as I have instructed, or the consequences will not be pleasant for yourself!"

According to accounts, Wood simply saluted and moved off to get his brigades into the space that Rosecrans wanted filled. Wood did not protest at the time that he had been publicly embarrassed in front of his staff, something that West Pointers did not do to each other. He must have been simmering.

Later that morning, perhaps an hour after that exchange, an aide to Thomas rode to Rosecrans to request still more troops for the left side. As he rode along the Federal positions, Thomas's aide looked at the center of Rosecrans's army and saw nothing but woods. The startled aide thought he had discovered a hole in the Union defenses, a hole that the Confederates might also discover. When the aide reached Rosecrans he informed the commanding general that a gap existed in the center of the Federal line.

Rosecrans exploded again. After all of the work he had personally done this morning in arranging troops, his subordinate generals still had failed to follow his orders. Now there was a gap in his center.

There was no gap. Thomas's aide, who was not a professional soldier, had simply missed seeing the entire division of Gen. James Brannan. Brannan's men were staying under cover in the heavy woods between the divisions of Wood on the right and Gen. Joseph J. Reynolds on the left.

Apparently Rosecrans did not even ask around headquarters if the report could be true. Instead Rosecrans got some aide to write out an order to Wood to "close up on Gen. Reynolds as fast as possible and support him."

Wood was puzzled by Rosecrans's order. The first part literally made no sense. By military definition "closing up" meant to shift left until his left flank touched Reynolds's right flank. Brannan's division, taking up several hundred yards, was in the way of that particular maneuver.

Neither did the second part of the order, "support" Reynolds, make any sense. Support meant to line up behind Reynolds. In one order, Wood had first been ordered to march left through an existing division, and then to line up behind a second division that was already in line, thereby creating a hole where none existed.

Had Rosecrans not dressed down Wood earlier that morning, Wood likely would have ridden to headquarters himself to confirm the order. He did not. He had been told by his commander to obey direct commands and he would do just that.

Wood pulled his division out of line and marched it to the rear of Reynolds's division in order to "support him." He chose to obey the part of the order he understood since he could not "close up" on Reynolds because Brannan's men occupied that position.

Wood later said: "The order was not only mandatory, but peremptorily mandatory. It directed me to close up on Gen. Reynolds, a movement of one body from the rear to another body in front of it."

Within minutes after Wood left his place in line, Longstreet's Confederates plunged through the quarter-mile-wide gap with an arrow-shaped column of more than sixteen hundred men.

The Federal weak right and center collapsed. As the Confederates wheeled north toward Thomas, the rest of the Union army, including its commander, Rosecrans, beat a hasty retreat toward Chattanooga. Only Thomas and a hastily thrown together force, which included Wood's and Brannan's divisions, formed a rear guard on top of Snodgrass Hill that successfully stopped the Confederates from annihilating the routed Federals. Just as he had in every other battle, Wood performed well.

Rosecrans tried to pin his devastating defeat on Wood, saying that it was obvious that the order pulling the division out of line was a mistake and Wood should have questioned it.

Wood's defense was simple. Earlier that morning, Rosecrans had screamed that any future order be immediately obeyed.

Rosecrans was fired, but Wood stayed. He won unexpected accolades when his troops were among those to carry the crest of Missionary Ridge outside Chattanooga in November. His troops had only been ordered to capture the rifle pits at the base of the ridge. He lived until 1906.

What would have happened had Wood ignored the order and stayed in place at Chickamauga or had ridden to headquarters to find out why he was getting such a strange order? There is no doubt that Wood's division would have borne the brunt of Longstreet's attack. Wood's division likely would have suffered heavy casualties within minutes of coming under fire.

Longstreet, however may have been slowed up enough so Rosecrans might have had time to shift all those divisions he had been sending north back south where the main attack was coming. Had Longstreet's attack failed, Chickamauga might have been a Union victory. Had it been a Union victory, the Union army would have been moving into Georgia six months before it did.

Gen. John Ellis Wool

(1784–1869)

ONE OLD GENERAL STOPS FORTY THOUSAND CONFEDERATES

⭐ BULL'S-EYE ⭐

GEN. JOHN ELLIS WOOL, THE OLDEST GENERAL TO SERVE in the war, may have saved Pennsylvania and perhaps even the entire war for the Union by issuing one order.

That order must have been hard to issue because it meant admitting defeat and surrendering more than 12,500 men to an enemy force. Giving in to an enemy is always difficult for a commander; but in this case, wily old Gen. Wool knew that the sacrifice of a Union garrison might mean that an entire Confederate army could be bagged. For that, Wool is a bull's-eye.

Orphaned at age four, Wool grew up determined to succeed. He set aside his goal of becoming a lawyer to volunteer during the War of 1812.

Wounded in both legs at one battle, he still managed to lead his men in capturing a vital position. That action made him a national hero and started him on a fifty-year career in the U.S. Army.

After the War of 1812, the nation was safe from outside invasion, which allowed its politicians to concentrate on other interests, such as westward expansion into Indian lands. In the mid-1830s President Andrew Jackson was angered when Wool, who sympathized with the Indians, slowed the Indian removal process as long as he could. Wool's reluctance prompted Jackson to replace him.

This apparently did not block Wool's career advancement, as he was promoted to brigadier general in 1841, the highest rank a regular army officer could attain other than commander of the army.

When the Mexican War came along, Wool saw action for the first time in thirty years. Gathering an army in San Antonio, Texas, in August 1846 in anticipation of invading Mexico, Wool issued the first wartime order to Lt. Robert E. Lee, whom he had met a decade earlier when Lee was doing engineering work at Fort Monroe, Virginia. Wool's order to Lee was simple: Go find some picks and shovels for building roads.

When the army finally moved out of San Antonio and crossed the rushing Rio Grande, Wool ordered Lee to dig earthworks to protect the rest of the waiting forces. It was the first time Lee had ever dug field entrenchments, something he would be a master of in just sixteen years.

Lee was soon transferred from Wool's army to Winfield Scott's. It was a good career move as Scott took a liking to Lee, which would last for the rest of their mutual U.S. Army careers.

Sixteen years after the transfer, Lee and Wool did not exactly cross paths, but Wool still played a major role in Lee's career.

After returning from Mexico Wool made the rounds of the departments, including acting as head of the U.S. Army, first on the Pacific and then on the Atlantic coast. When the Civil War started, Wool rushed reinforcements to Fort Monroe on the tip of the Virginia Peninsula. The arriving U.S. soldiers so cowed the inexperienced new Confederates they did not attack. Fort Monroe would remain in U.S. hands for the rest of the war.

Though Wool had shown military skill and sharp presence of mind in saving Fort Monroe, his seventy-seven years greatly bothered the new president, Abraham Lincoln. Lincoln already had one old general to deal with, General of the Army Winfield Scott. He did not want one even older. Lincoln passed over Wool when it came time to name three new major generals, all of whom were decades younger than Wool.

Thus Wool's Civil War career started sliding. Though he commanded Fort Monroe's garrison, Lincoln ignored military protocol and gave those troops to Gen. George McClellan. Lincoln knew he couldn't fire Wool, New York State's most famous and prominent hero, but he allowed his newly found, thirty-four-year-old golden boy McClellan to push Wool around in hopes that the old general would resign. To the disappointment of Lincoln and McClellan, Wool hung on.

In June 1862 Wool was transferred to command the Middle Department, which included New Jersey, Delaware, Pennsylvania, and some eastern parts of Virginia and Maryland. That was far from any fighting so Lincoln would not have to worry about Old Man Wool slowing down Golden Boy McClellan who would be marching up the Virginia Peninsula to capture Richmond.

Within a few weeks Lincoln's Golden Boy McClellan was running back to Washington with his tail between his legs, licked by Lee in the Seven Days' battles. Wool must have at least smiled at his tormentors' misfortunes.

In early September 1862 Lee launched a campaign that would take him right through the supposed backwater controlled by Lee's old commander and the man the North considered too old to fight.

Lee's strategy was relatively simple. Cut through Maryland like a knife, plunging into Pennsylvania to capture the capital of Harrisburg or another major city like Philadelphia before the disorganized remnants of the Union army could catch up with him. With a victory on Northern soil, the Confederacy hoped that England and France would recognize it as a legitimate nation.

Only one thing stood in Lee's way. Actually it would stand in his rear once he crossed the Potomac. That was the 12,500-man Union garrison at Harpers Ferry, Virginia, now West Virginia. That garrison could disrupt

Lee's supply and communication lines going into Virginia unless it were eliminated.

Actually Lee was not too worried about Harpers Ferry. He figured once the Federals in Washington realized the 50,000-man Army of Northern Virginia, which had beaten two separate Union armies over two months, was on the move north, Harpers Ferry would be evacuated. That would solve Lee's concerns without any time or blood lost.

To Lee's surprise, his spies told him that not only was the garrison still in place, it was reinforcing its position. That was puzzling. In violation of all military thinking, the Federal army was keeping an inferior garrison in place as a vastly superior army bore down on it. That garrison would be trapped unless it was evacuated.

What Lee may not have known was that his old commander Wool had sent a telegram on September 12 to the Harpers Ferry commander. The telegram must have chilled the telegraph operator who received and transcribed it: "You will not abandon Harpers Ferry without defending it to the last extremity." Later that day, a second Wool telegram arrived: "There must be no abandoning of a post. Shoot the first man that thinks of it."

That was pretty clear.

It took nearly four days from the time Lee issued the orders, until the evening of September 13 for the Confederates under Stonewall Jackson to surround Harpers Ferry. After enduring nearly two days of shelling, on September 15 the garrison finally surrendered.

From Harpers Ferry Jackson rushed to join Lee where the reconstituted Army of Northern Virginia fought McClellan to a standstill at Antietam on September 17. The capture of the Harpers Ferry garrison had taken up more than a week of precious time that Lee had anticipated using to invade Pennsylvania.

After McClellan lost his chance to destroy Lee's army at Antietam, he looked for a scapegoat to blame. He found him in old soldier John Wool. To divert attention from his failure to crush Lee's forty-thousand-man army (nearly ten thousand of Lee's men had refused to invade the North by crossing the Potomac) with his eighty-thousand-man army, McClellan charged Wool with allowing Harpers Ferry to be encircled and surrendered. A censure board, then still enthralled with McClellan as a leader, rubber-stamped the charge. They conveniently ignored evidence that McClellan could have rushed divisions to relieve Harpers Ferry. McClellan could have saved the garrison and caught Jackson's portion of the army separated from Lee, but he did not.

The board ignored or never understood what Wool had done by ordering the Harpers Ferry garrison to stay rather than retreat. Wool's refusal to abandon Harpers Ferry had stopped Lee in his tracks, forcing him to split his army into four pieces until the garrison threat was eliminated. Wool had handed Lee, his old subordinate, to McClellan, his new antagonist, on a silver platter. McClellan never admitted that he had badly bungled the opportunity Wool had presented him.

A disheartened Wool was reassigned yet again. This time he was sent to head the Department of the East, consisting of New York, New Jersey, and the other New England states. Surely, Confederates would never invade that region.

Tired of fighting enemies both outside and within his own army, the old general faced another unexpected threat to his career when the New York City Draft Riots erupted in July 1863. Though stunned by the violence raging in the streets, Wool was reluctant to fire into crowds of civilians. It took several regiments of troops rushed from the Gettysburg battlefield to quell the disturbance.

Wool finally realized that he could no longer cope with the stresses of command. He resigned on August 1, 1863, after more than fifty-one years of service to his country dating back to the battles that forever freed it from the British.

No one in power ever thanked Wool for holding up the Army of Northern Virginia with a simple telegram. None of them ever recognized what old soldier Wool instantly realized: a Federally occupied Harpers Ferry would be a giant deterrent to a Confederate invasion of the North.

CONFEDERATES

Gen. Edward Porter Alexander

(1835–1910)

THE MAN LEE
THANKFULLY IGNORED

⭐ BULL'S-EYE ⭐

HAD GEN. ROBERT E. LEE TAKEN THE ADVICE OF YOUNG, cocky, and impulsive Gen. Edward Porter Alexander, the war would have lasted decades and may have never ended.

Though he made a bone-headed, misfired suggestion on the last day of the war, which could have kept the South fighting well beyond Appomattox, Alexander's overall military career must be judged as one bull's-eye after another—with one other misfire on July 3, 1863.

Alexander always seems to have been in the right place at the right time to greatly contribute to the Confederate war effort. Though known primarily for what he did at Gettysburg while directing a battle the old-fashioned way, Alexander helped usher in new methods of fighting that would revolutionize combat decades into the future.

A brilliant student from Georgia, Alexander was asked by Lee, the West Point superintendent, to stay on after graduating in 1857 to teach engineering. Restless, Alexander finally wrangled an assignment to build forts in California where he was when the war began. He made his way South, ignoring pleas from friends and superiors that he sit out the war so as not to damage his budding engineering career.

Alexander's first duty at the front at Manassas, Virginia, was finishing the development of a Confederate signal service based on waving large flags in coded signals, the "wig-wag" system he had helped create for the United States. Alexander also built several tall towers so he could keep watch on the approaches to Manassas from Washington. It was while looking through his telescope on July 21, 1861, that a glint of sunlight caught his eye. The flash came from the sun hitting a brass cannon barrel being pulled to the north. Adjusting his telescope, Alexander spied a stealthy Federal column unaware that their shiny bayonets also were catching the sun.

Alexander used his flags to signal a detachment guarding the Stone Bridge over Bull Run.

"Look out for your left. You are flanked," Alexander waved. A Confederate force rushed northward. The battle of Manassas was under way.

Thanks to Alexander's sharp eyes and trained signalmen, the crafty Federal plan to cross at unguarded Sudley Ford was foiled. The detachment held up the initial Federal advance until reinforcements arrived. Those men fought back to Henry House Hill held by Gen. Thomas J. Jackson, whose resistance and counterattack assured a Confederate victory. The battle, however, really hinged on Alexander's early notice of that sneaking Federal column.

During the Seven Days' campaign in June 1862, Alexander reluctantly pioneered another method of observing the enemy—from the air. He ascended in a hot air balloon to determine if Federals were moving north over the Chickahominy River to join in the upcoming fight at Gaines's Mill.

"I was not at all enamored of my prospective employment," Alexander later wrote, because he harbored an "almost irresistible impulse to jump" from heights. To his surprise, Alexander felt so comfortable aloft in the balloon that he speculated he could develop a "balloon habit" just so he could look at the little people on the ground.

As the war progressed, Alexander began to feel important. Displaying pomposity that bordered on insubordination, Alexander had a run-in with Lee about the placement of cannon on Marye's Heights at Fredericksburg in December 1862. Alexander had placed the guns down the hill, but Lee asked that they be moved farther up so they could fire a longer distance. Alexander reluctantly moved the guns.

After the battle, during which the guns were used at much closer range, Alexander purposely shouted at a friend standing near Lee that it was a good thing the guns could fire at close range. Lee did not say anything, but Alexander wrote, "I could not resist the temptation to have one little dig at him, but he took it in silence and never let it on that he was listening to us."

Seven months later Alexander was told he was in charge of the artillery barrage that would precede the third-day assault against the Union center at Gettysburg. The plan was of concern to Alexander from the beginning. He knew that his cannon ammunition was already low from two days of fighting and he would be unable to sustain a barrage that would "drive off the enemy or greatly demoralize him," as Gen. James Longstreet had put into his order.

Sometime during that morning Gen. William Pendleton, Lee's "so-called chief of artillery" (Alexander's description) came to Alexander with the news that he could have nine twelve-pounder howitzers, short-range guns that could not reach the Federal lines at that distance. Alexander immediately accepted them with the idea that they would follow "Pickett's infantry in the charge," as he later wrote.

Alexander personally led the gun crews to a protected hollow and told them to wait for orders from him.

Just before the cannonade was to start, Alexander received a note from Longstreet: "Colonel, If the artillery fire does not have the effect to drive off the enemy, or greatly demoralize him, so as to make our efforts pretty certain, I would prefer you should not advise Gen. Pickett to make the charge. I shall rely a great deal on your good judgment to determine the matter and shall expect you to let Gen. Pickett know when the moment offers."

Longstreet, a lieutenant general and corps commander, had just handed responsibility for the success of the charge to a colonel of artillery.

After a half hour of firing, Alexander frantically sent two notes to Pickett to move out. More than twelve thousand men marched out from the woods toward the Federal line a mile away, but without those supporting howitzers. Without telling Alexander, Pendleton had reclaimed some of the guns and their commander had moved the rest. Alexander never saw those guns again.

Alexander has been criticized for not placing all his guns in an arc that would have caught the Federals on Cemetery Ridge in a crossfire, but Alexander answered his critics by saying his guns were placed according to orders. He also believed Lee should have attacked Cemetery Hill, several hundred yards north of Cemetery Ridge, the actual object of the attack. Alexander said his First Corps guns, combined with those of the Second Corps on the north, could have pulverized Cemetery Hill just as his critics wanted to do to Cemetery Ridge.

Could an effective cannonade against Cemetery Ridge have won the battle of Gettysburg on the third day? Maybe if there had been enough room to put the cannon in an arc for enfilading fire. However, even if Alexander's guns had had enough ammunition, he simply did not have enough long-range guns or properly placed guns to do damage to the Federals.

Could those nine howitzers have made a difference to the infantry? If those howitzers had accompanied the infantry and fired canister to knock down the wooden fences in front of the charging Confederates, that would have saved precious minutes and lives, because each marching man had to stop to climb through the fence rails. Alexander first thought an unimpeded charge might have been successful, though he doubted it years later while writing about the battle.

In August 1864 at Petersburg Alexander again had a single-handed impact on a battle.

Alexander noticed that if he walked to the left or the right of the Elliott salient, a bulge in the Confederate trench line aimed at the Union line, Federal sharpshooters would not fire on him. If he looked over the salient breastworks, he became an instant target.

"This satisfied me very soon that something was going on there and the next attempt of the Federals would be made at this point," Alexander wrote.

Alexander put reinforcements behind the salient, even stationing cannon to sweep his own trenches and designing makeshift hand grenades that could be launched by swinging them from leather thongs, much like David's biblical slingshot.

Alexander was wounded in July and was not on duty when his suspicions about the Federal intentions were realized. A mineshaft dug under the salient by Federal coal miners and then filled with gunpowder blew up, killing two hundred South Carolinians. Alexander agonized that he should have guessed what the Federals were doing.

Alexander's last contribution to history came on April 9, 1865, the day Lee met with Grant to discuss surrender terms. Alexander, now a general himself, found himself in a private talk with Lee early that day.

"Well, here we are at Appomattox and there seems to be a considerable force in front of us. Now, what shall we have to do here today?" Lee asked.

Alexander replied: "Well sir, then we have only two alternatives to choose from. We must either surrender, or the army may be ordered to scatter into the woods and bushes and either to rally upon Gen. Johnston in North Carolina, or to make their way, each man to his own state, with his arms, and to report to his governor. This last course is the one which seems to me to offer us much the best chances. If there is any hope for the Confederacy it is for delay."

Alexander was advocating guerrilla warfare.

Lee then asked: "If I took your suggestion and ordered the army to disperse, how many would get away?"

"Two-thirds of us," Alexander replied. "We would scatter like rabbits and partridges in the woods and they could not scatter to catch us."

Lee thought for a moment and then replied that though ten thousand escaped, that would be too few to carry on a war. They would not be the same proud army that had resisted overwhelming numbers of Federals.

"The men would have no rations and be under no discipline. They are already demoralized by four years of war. The country would be full of lawless bands. And as for myself, while you young men might afford to go bushwhacking, the only proper and dignified course for me would be to surrender myself and take the consequences of my actions," Lee said.

Alexander later wrote: "I had never half known before what a big heart and brain our general had. I was so ashamed of having proposed to him such a foolish and wild cat scheme as my suggestion had been that I felt like begging him to forget that he had ever heard it."

Had Lee followed Alexander's suggestion and disbanded the army, the Federal army would have spent years trying to root out Confederate resistance in every state of the South.

Alexander's postwar career was spent in building a railroad. He also wrote his extensive memoirs, published nearly one hundred years later as *Fighting For The Confederacy.*

Alexander died in bed, an old man, probably of a cerebral hemorrhage. The man who had witnessed and maybe changed so much Civil War history had finally become part of it.

Gen. Joseph Reid Anderson

(1813–1892)

THE CONFEDERACY'S IRONMAKER

✵ BULL'S-EYE ✵

THE SOUTH HAD MANY MILITARY GENERALS LEADING soldiers on the battlefield. It had only one businessman general leading factory workers.

That was Gen. Joseph Reid Anderson.

Without the business acumen mixed with the engineering knowledge that Anderson possessed, the South never would have armored the CSS *Virginia*. It never would have armed that ironclad with the best cannon manufactured during the war. It never would have supplied Confederate forts and field artillery units with thousands of cannon. Without Anderson managing two thousand employees in the South's largest manufacturing operation, the industrial North would have quickly smashed the South.

While "business sense" might not normally seem to be a fighting quality, it was just what the South lacked, what it most needed, and what Anderson had. Although he allowed his ego to cause him to make one almost fatal misfire on the battlefield, and he was too bull-headed to modernize his factory when he had the chance in antebellum America, it was Anderson's skills behind the desk that make his overall war career a bull's-eye. Thanks to Anderson, the Southern army had cannon and the Southern navy had iron plating for its formidable ironclads.

Anderson's ambition after graduating from West Point in 1836 was to quickly move into the private sector where he could make much more money. After barely a year in the U.S. Army, Anderson resigned to take a civilian job as engineer on the Valley Turnpike. Designing such a highway would be a feather in the cap of any young civil engineer, but Anderson wanted still more money. Within a few months he was eyeing employment with Tredegar Iron Works in Richmond.

In the late 1830s Tredegar was a small iron works manufacturing railroad rails. As that market was drying up, Tredegar's owners were looking for someone to open up new markets when they discovered Anderson. What they saw in Anderson was what he saw in himself—a bright young man who understood engineering and who had a driving ambition to make money. Anderson had the careful, analytical nature of an engineer combined with the marketing sense of a businessman. That was a rare combination of skills in a southern economy dominated by agriculture.

Anderson eagerly job-hopped again to become Tredegar's chief commercial agent or salesman in March 1841. There he found his calling, staying at Tredegar for the next thirty-five years, first as employee, then as manager, then as owner.

Hitting the ground running, Anderson won contracts from the army to manufacture ammunition for existing cannon and contracts from the navy to manufacture cannon. Tredegar's catalogs had never before contained cannon, but Anderson the salesman convinced his U.S. government buyers he could deliver.

The company's reputation grew in the 1850s as Anderson pursued government and private contracts in the North as well as in the South. At a time when most northern factories were segregated by race and even European origin, Anderson integrated his work force by hiring slaves from local owners.

In 1859, as war seemed inevitable between North and South, Anderson and U.S. Secretary of War John Floyd, also a native Virginian and future Confederate general, engaged in a strange battle of wills and opinion of technological advances. Floyd asked Anderson to start casting his cannon using a process developed by U.S. artillerist Thomas J. Rodman. The Rodman method involved pouring molten iron around a hollow core, then circulating water around the core until it cooled. Until Rodman's technique, most cannon, including those from Tredegar, had been manufactured by boring out a solid tube of iron. Rodman's method allowed the iron to cool from the inside out, a process that made it stronger and less likely to burst after multiple firings.

Anderson refused to invest in new equipment to manufacture Rodman cannon, saying he had provided reliable guns for years to the U.S. government using his bore-out method. Floyd, just as stubbornly sticking to his desire to modernize the U.S. Army, responded by reducing orders for Tredegar cannon.

Though on balance, Anderson's instincts were a great asset to the Confederacy, his refusal to invest in the Rodman method was the greatest mistake of his professional career. As the war began, all of the Northern cannon manufacturers were using the Rodman method. While the North manufactured fifteen-inch Rodmans, cannon that could lob a 320-pound shell more than three miles, Tredegar Iron Works could not manufacture anything with a bore larger than ten inches.

Ironically, Floyd would be accused of trying to arm the South just before the war while in reality he canceled contracts for cannon that could have been placed in Confederate forts.

In the summer of 1861 Tredegar processed its most famous order, rolling the two-inch armor plate for the ironclad CSS *Virginia*. The same thickness of plating would go on other Confederate ironclads like the *Albemarle* and the *Arkansas*. Tredegar would also manufacture the rifled Brooke cannon that would give the *Virginia* its formidable punching power.

In mid-1861 Anderson's ego got the best of him as he demanded a generalship and a field command. Amazingly, Anderson complained to President Davis that three of his classmates had been appointed Union generals but he had not been appointed as a Confederate general.

"I would not consider it boastful in me to compare my qualifications as a soldier with theirs," Anderson wrote.

What makes Anderson's complaints remarkable is that he had spent barely a year on active duty while the three Union men he complained about were all twenty-five-year Army veterans when appointed generals.

Many high-ranking Confederate officials counseled Davis not to appoint Anderson, believing him to be more valuable in the factory than in the field. Davis, however, gave in to Anderson's demands. Several months later a spent rifle ball hit Anderson in the head during the Seven Days' campaign. That lucky blow was enough to knock some sense into Anderson. Nearly three weeks after his close call, Anderson resigned from the army and returned to Tredegar where he would remain for the rest of the war.

Anderson's business skills were constantly taxed as he struggled to keep the flow of coal and pig iron coming to Richmond and to find enough workers to man his furnaces. Though it could employ more than two thousand men, Tredegar never operated at more than a third of its ideal capacity during the war because of shortages of raw materials and skilled workers.

Tredegar's production problems would not only affect the overall war effort, they would almost kill the commanding general of the Army of Northern Virginia.

After the battle of Sharpsburg in September 1862, Lee asked Anderson to use the lull in the fighting to melt down his obsolete six-pounder smoothbore cannon and recast the metal into heavier rifled cannon. Anderson rushed production of twenty-pounder and thirty-pounder Parrott rifles through his factory. The guns were delivered to Lee at the front in Fredericksburg in October and November 1862.

Barely three weeks old, two thirty-pounders were throwing a devastating fire into the Federals on December 13 when they exploded while firing. Shrapnel flew everywhere but into Lee and Longstreet, the top two commanders who had been standing near the cannon. While it appears that the Confederate artillerists overheated the guns, Anderson and Tredegar were blamed for the near disaster.

As Federals captured Confederate iron ore and coal mines in 1864, Tredegar's production continued to drop. Anderson's administrative talents could not produce weapons without raw materials and skilled production workers. During the first four years of the war, including the four months building up to the firing on Fort Sumter, Tredegar manufactured 1,064 cannon. In the first three months of 1865 it produced only thirty-five. Still, Tredegar kept producing right up to the end, manufacturing four cannon in March 1865, when Richmond and Petersburg were virtually surrounded.

Anderson's postwar Tredegar Iron Works was a model of fairness for workers now again producing railroad rails. Anderson hired many of the same blacks that he had employed as slaves, paying them the same wages he did whites. That policy angered some white Philadelphia iron workers he was trying to recruit. The northerners demanded that he fire the blacks if he wanted them to move south to work at Tredegar.

Anderson replied, "We southern men regard Negroes as an inferior race, but we make no distinction of color in employing men and pay all the same wages as we all have to live." When Anderson died in 1892, the black newspaper in Richmond praised him as a man "too great to know any prejudice, either on account of race or color." The company was successful until 1876 when some railroads that it depended on as customers went bankrupt, forcing Tredegan into bankrupcy.

None of Anderson's subordinates had the managerial ability of Anderson. During the seven months that Anderson indulged his ego to play battlefield general, Tredegar suffered its worst bouts of poor quality production. Once Anderson returned to daily supervision, Tredegar's quality problems lessened.

Anderson the iron manufacturer contributed much more to the Southern war effort than Anderson the general ever could have.

Gen. Turner Ashby

(1828–1862)

HIS DARING WAS PROVERBIAL

✴ MISFIRE ✴

ONE HEAVILY BEARDED, RECKLESS, SPOILED, UNDISCIPLINED Confederate general inadvertently fueled the Union image of an invincible Stonewall Jackson when he foolishly led Jackson into a trap. Though that resulted in Jackson's only battlefield loss in the war, it was a good thing. Jackson's defeat may have saved Richmond from capture during the Peninsula campaign.

Both South and North had Turner Ashby to thank and to blame for that turn of events.

While Ashby made only one major misfire, it was one that could have wiped out not only his cavalry command, but that of his infantry boss, Stonewall Jackson. He made the mistake of believing a rumor. By trusting the people of Winchester, Virginia, to tell him what they had seen instead of checking out the rumor himself, he endangered Jackson's command. Amazingly enough, while that normally would have been a disaster, it turned out to be the best thing that ever happened to Jackson.

Because his father had died early, Ashby learned riding and shooting from his mother. She was a great teacher. By 1859 he headed his own private mounted militia made up of area youths. It was easy to hear the militia coming, as Ashby's boys adapted a roaring cheer that in two years would become the famous and feared Rebel yell.

Named captain when his militia was converted into a cavalry regiment, Ashby was fearless. He once donned homespun clothes and posed as a horse doctor to collect intelligence from Federal camps. After his brother was killed, perhaps murdered by a Federal patrol, Ashby became even more personally reckless and less responsible for his men. He refused to treat his childhood friends as subordinate soldiers.

Lack of discipline in the ranks irritated Jackson in whose command Ashby served. Still, Jackson was surprisingly patient with Ashby as he valued his cavalry's knowledge of the Shenandoah Valley.

In mid-March 1862 Ashby failed Jackson, but that turned out to be an advantage the South would enjoy. If most Union generals feared Jackson before the battle of Kernstown, Virginia, they all did afterwards.

In March 1862 Union Gen. George McClellan made the capture of Richmond the focal point of the war, believing if the Confederate capital fell the Confederacy would fold. McClellan began slowly marching up the Virginia Peninsula, asking for reinforcements from Washington with every step he took. Faulty intelligence had told McClellan he was outnumbered two to one, though his army was really five times the size of the Confederates.

McClellan demanded that thirty thousand Federals in the Shenandoah Valley, just north of Winchester, join him on the peninsula. Lincoln was reluctant to send the men because Jackson was still in the Valley less than one hundred miles from Washington. Lincoln imagined Jackson could march on Washington without a force to stop him.

What Lincoln did not know was that Jackson had only forty-five hundred men facing the Union's thirty thousand. Lincoln and his generals imagined tens of thousands of soldiers who did not exist standing behind Jackson who was only too real.

Jackson had no intention of marching on Washington. His strategy was to hit and run, forcing the Federals to keep after him and away from Richmond. Jackson was retreating south from Winchester with the Federals in slow pursuit when he heard from Ashby that the Federals had reversed their march.

Jackson surmised that the Federals chasing him had now been ordered to the peninsula. Now he had to attack to keep them in the Valley. It was a strange, necessary strategy: Keep the threatening Federals in the breadbasket of the Confederacy in order to keep them from advancing on the capital of the Confederacy.

Jackson reversed his march and started trailing the Federals. The stalked Confederates were now the stalkers. Jackson sent Ashby's cavalry forward to Winchester on a scout to determine the strength and location of the Union divisions.

Ashby now made the mistake that would make Jackson a legend.

Instead of sending his riders out to actually find the Federal infantry, Ashby asked the residents of Winchester what they knew about the Federals' location. Some residents Ashby questioned told him the Federals were already heading east along the road toward Washington. That information was critical. It must mean the Federals were heading to the peninsula. Ashby himself saw just four regimental battle flags around Winchester, a nominal force Jackson could easily handle.

What Ashby didn't learn from his scout but what Jackson would soon discover was that the Federals were hiding a nine-thousand-man division. That was more than twice the number Jackson had at full strength. Ominously, Jackson was not at full strength. He had marched so hard to reach Winchester that no more than three thousand very footsore men were available to face three times their number.

Jackson arrived at Kernstown, four miles south of Winchester, just in time to see a sizeable force of Federals rushing for the same stone wall Jackson's men wanted. Jackson's men won the footrace to the wall, but were astonished to see wave after wave of Federals arriving from Winchester.

Jackson quietly summed up the coming battle when he turned to an aide and said, "We are in for it."

Kernstown was an obvious, painful defeat for Jackson. His losses were more than seven hundred compared to just six hundred for the Federals who drove his fabled Stonewall Brigade off the field in a near rout. Jackson blamed Ashby for performing slipshod intelligence.

Incredibly Ashby's blunder turned out to be golden. As Jackson retreated south, the Federal generals puzzled over why Jackson would attack a force three times his size. The conclusion they reached was chilling. Jackson must have hidden reinforcements nearby! He must be ready to march on Washington!

When Lincoln read those reports, he immediately ordered one eight-thousand-man division that was on its way to McClellan to be turned around and sent back to the Valley. He ordered another thirty thousand men at Fredericksburg who were supposed to have moved toward Richmond to come back to defend Washington. Finally, Lincoln ordered another ten-thousand-man division already with McClellan to another Union army operating west of the Alleghenies.

The humiliating defeat of Jackson's three thousand men at Kernstown took fifty thousand Federals out of the Peninsula campaign to capture Richmond.

Jackson soon realized that his tactical defeat had turned into a strategic victory.

"Time has shown that while the field is in possession of the enemy, the most essential fruits of the battle are ours," Jackson wrote.

Jackson disciplined Ashby for his lack of discretion by dispersing his cavalry. Ashby responded by resigning from the army. Jackson backed down and returned Ashby's men to his command. Only Ashby could control his men and Jackson needed every man for the coming campaign to finally rid the Valley of Federals.

Jackson reluctantly nominated Ashby for brigadier general, figuring that was one way to keep his volatile cavalryman happy but really believing Ashby didn't think critically about situations or control his men, necessary skills in a general.

Just two weeks after his promotion, Ashby was fighting in a rear-guard action near Harrisonburg, Virginia, when his horse was shot out from under him. The leader of Jackson's cavalry, a man who had been riding since before he could walk, charged forward on foot. He was dead before he hit the ground when a bullet pierced his heart.

Jackson prayed over Ashby's body as it lay in a house before a photographer took Ashby's image, the only known photograph of a dead Confederate general.

Jackson said of Ashby, "His daring was proverbial; his powers of endurance almost incredible; his tone of character heroic; and his sagacity almost intuitive in dividing the purpose and movements of the enemy."

Ashby whose scouting mistake almost wiped Jackson's command from the Shenandoah Valley, was the same man who had convinced the North that Jackson was invincible.

Maj. John Decatur Barry
(1839–1867)

I Met Him A Pygmy
And Left Him A Giant

✷ MISFIRE ✷

MAJ. JOHN DECATUR BARRY OF THE EIGHTEENTH
Regiment of North Carolina Troops was a rising star in the army, having rapidly worked his way up from the bottom rank of private. On May 2, 1863, he would make one split-second decision that would change the course of the war.

He would order Stonewall Jackson shot.

This is not implying that Barry executed Jackson. Rather, Barry was doing exactly what he was supposed to be doing and what Jackson would demand he do: defeat suspected enemies before they could attack. While Barry did everything by the book, killing a lieutenant general in your own army, even by accident, has to be considered a misfire.

A baby-faced bank clerk before the war who could barely grow facial hair, Barry did not look the part of a regimental officer, but he must have been an inspiring leader. Though he joined his company as a private, he was soon elected captain, somewhat unusual for a twenty-three-year-old with no military training.

Barry and the Eighteenth North Carolina found themselves in heavy fighting almost from the beginning of the war as they were assigned to Jackson's Second Corps. Barry and his regiment would prove themselves at the Seven Days', Cedar Mountain, Second Manassas, Chantilly, and Sharpsburg battles. His name is mentioned repeatedly in battle reports, with his superiors praising him for coolness under fire. Barry was promoted to major in November 1862, nine months away from his twenty-fourth birthday.

His meeting with destiny came at Chancellorsville.

The Eighteenth North Carolina was part of Gen. James Lane's brigade, which spearheaded Jackson's flank march. The late afternoon attack smashed the Union flank, but as darkness grew, Jackson's line lost shape as regiments encountered resistance. The attack lulled as the Confederates gathered themselves. The Eighteenth North Carolina positioned itself on the north side of the Plank Road at the very front of the battle lines. Lane, in the process of reorganizing his brigade, ran into Jackson, who ordered Lane to "push ahead." Lane cautiously did so, discovering Union troops just yards in front of his position. One mounted Union scout fooled the Confederates into not firing on him by shouting that he was a "friend."

Out of direct sight of Lane's brigade, including the Eighteenth North Carolina, which was closest to him, Jackson and eighteen staff members rode out to see what was happening in the no-man's-land between the two armies. Jackson told no one in the front regiments what he was doing. It remains a mystery how Jackson's staff left their lines without anyone hearing them.

The adjutant of the Eighteenth North Carolina after the war wrote: "How Jackson and Hill and their staff and couriers got in front was never satisfactorily explained. They could not have ridden through any part of Lane's brigade that night without its being known. We were never more on alert, and wide awake that night, and I don't remember to have ever heard of a member of the brigade saying that he knew they had gone in our front."

Jackson rode forward beyond his lines for several hundred yards into the darkness until he heard the sounds of axes felling trees, the sounds of the Federals setting up defenses. Now was the time to relaunch the attack before giving more Federals time to regroup.

Jackson's staff wheeled and started back for Confederate lines. Jackson did not send a scout ahead to alert his units that his scouting party was returning. Jackson also turned down another road, not the same road on which he had left. That would bring him even closer to the Eighteenth North Carolina, which did not know that there were any Confederates in front of them.

As Jackson and his men rode through the moonlit night, a single musket rang out, then a ragged volley erupted from the south side of the road from the Seventh North Carolina Troops. That regiment apparently fired without any orders at the sound of riders coming from Union lines.

Joe Morrison, Jackson's brother-in-law, raced on foot toward the Eighteenth North Carolina after picking himself up off of the ground after his horse had been killed by the volley.

"Cease firing! You are firing into your own men!" Morrison shouted. It was the same thing that the clever Union scout had just shouted a few minutes earlier.

It was then that Barry gave his fateful order as the noise of horses crashing through the woods was now only twenty-five or thirty yards away.

"Who gave that order?" Barry shouted. "It's a lie! Pour it into them, boys!" The Eighteenth North Carolina, operating under direct orders, while the Seventh North Carolina had fired without orders, sent a sheet of flame into the darkness.

Three couriers and Jackson's civil engineer pitched over dead. Three others on Jackson's staff were wounded. Of nineteen men on horses, ten men and twelve horses were wounded or killed outright.

Jackson was hit three times, twice in the left arm and once in the right palm.

Remarkably, no one in any official capacity blamed Barry or the

Eighteenth North Carolina for shooting Jackson. In fact, it was not long after Chancellorsville that Barry was promoted from major to full colonel, skipping the intermediate rank of lieutenant colonel.

Lane wrote: "[Never] have I ever heard anyone else censure the Eighteenth regiment for firing under the circumstances; and those who knew the talented young Barry will always remember him as one of the most fearless, dashing officers who was especially cool under fire."

Barry continued to lead the Eighteenth through the Pettigrew-Pickett-Trimble assault on the third day of Gettysburg and through the heavy fighting of the Wilderness and Spotsylvania. At Cold Harbor he was given command of the entire brigade when Lane was wounded. On August 4, 1864, Barry was appointed a brigadier general and was due to formally take over the brigade, but he himself was wounded in the hand, requiring the amputation of several fingers. By the time Barry had healed and was ready to take command again, Lane himself had healed and had returned to combat duty. Since the brigade did not need two generals, Barry's brigadier appointment was rescinded.

Barry's apparent delicate health began to catch up to him and he returned to North Carolina early in 1865. He was not with his old brigade when it was surrendered at Appomattox. He died on March 24, 1867, of an unspecified illness at the age of twenty-seven.

Barry's obituary read, "Few of our young men enjoyed and none deserved a larger share of the esteem of this community and his death will cause a pang in the hearts of many of his friends who admired him for his goodness of heart, manly bearing and great personal worth."

On Barry's small tombstone in Oakdale Cemetery in Wilmington, North Carolina, is a strange but appropriate inscription, the same that is carved on the tombstone of a French general who had served Napoleon, "I met him a pygmy and left him a giant." The inscription apparently refers to the fact that Barry made the very rare transition from private to brigadier general in the course of four years.

Neither Barry's obituary nor his tombstone makes any mention of the greatest mistake Barry made in his life at Chancellorsville, one for which he took full responsibility.

Capt. James Keith Boswell

(1838–1863)

HALF OF THE SECRET BEHIND STONEWALL JACKSON

✴ BULL'S-EYE ✴

"JACKSON'S FOOT CAVALRY" IS A FABLED REFERENCE TO the seventeen thousand infantrymen Jackson marched up and down and across the Shenandoah and Allegheny Mountains and valleys in the spring of 1862.

Most casual historians give Jackson sole credit for confusing the three different Federal armies assigned to catch him and his little army. But Jackson depended heavily on two officers to win the Valley campaign.

One was Maj. Jed Hotchkiss, most famous as Jackson's mapmaker. The other lesser known man was Hotchkiss's friend, Capt. James Keith Boswell. Jackson's civil engineer, Boswell was the man who found the roads and bridges that Hotchkiss drew on his maps that Jackson would then use to plan his movements.

Had there been no Hotchkiss, Jackson would have had no maps showing him the locations of the bridges, fords, and mountain passes over and through which he could move his men.

Had there been no Boswell, Hotchkiss would not have known if the bridges could support the weight of artillery, or if the passes were wide enough for a marching column. Had there been no Boswell, Jackson would not have been able to surprise the Federals on all those occasions where Stonewall is given sole credit for being a military genius. Boswell was quite literally the eyes of Jackson's army. It was he who picked the routes of Jackson's foot cavalry. Boswell was Jackson's bull's-eye, the man who should share the credit for creating the legend of Stonewall Jackson.

Just twenty-two years old but already a skilled civil engineer when the war started, Boswell requested service with Jackson. The two men immediately liked each other. Boswell described Jackson in glowing terms as "one of the most pleasant men as commander who could be found in the Confederate army. He is very reserved, not particularly companionable, but extremely affable and polite."

Boswell may have been the only man in the army who found Jackson "pleasant" and "affable." Most who encountered Jackson found him cold, aloof, and demanding.

Jackson, rarely one to give praise to anyone other than God for victories, frequently mentioned Boswell in official reports as being instrumental in carrying out orders and finding roads.

Boswell probably helped Jackson plan to use the railroads to get his men to Manassas from Winchester in July 1861, the first time soldiers had ever been moved by train. The next spring Jackson again used rail to transfer his men from the east side of the Shenandoah Valley to Staunton. From there he marched them deep into the Allegheny Mountains to fight the battle of McDowell. When that battle opened, the Federals had a hard time believing they were fighting Jackson, as they had been told he was at least one hundred miles away. Boswell's scouting had once again contributed to the growing legend of Jackson.

After leaving McDowell, it was Boswell who scouted the roads from

McDowell to Front Royal on the east side of the Shenandoah Valley to confront another Union force.

Boswell proved to be an independent thinker, something Jackson normally did not tolerate in his command. Ordered to build a bridge outside of Bridgewater, Virginia, Boswell directly disobeyed when he realized it would take too long to build a proper bridge over the rushing river. Instead, he scrounged lumber to build boats and ferried men across the water. Jackson, who excoriated generals for not doing exactly what he told them to do, allowed his captain to get by with this disobedience.

Jackson did not always listen to Boswell. On the day before the battle of Port Republic in June 1862, a Union cavalry raid descended upon the village. Jackson barely escaped to the opposite shore of the river. While standing on the bank he noticed a cannon crew still in town. Thinking it was one of his crews, Jackson motioned for them to come over the river and join him. A persistent Boswell told a stubborn Jackson that he was motioning to a Union gun crew. It was not until the Federal cannon threw a shell Jackson's way that he realized that Boswell was correct and he was wrong.

It was finding the fastest, most secret way to get behind Union Gen. John Pope's army in late August 1862 that proved to be Boswell's most successful accomplishment. In Boswell's own official report on the campaign he casually mentions the towns through which his selected route passed, underplaying his role in making sure the roads and the stream bridges could support Jackson's men. Thanks to Boswell's selection of roads, Jackson was able to steal a flank march on Pope. Jackson had captured the Union supply base at Manassas Junction before Pope even knew he had moved from his front. That action would later lead to the complete Confederate victory at Second Manassas.

On the night of May 1, 1863, Jackson and Lee sent Boswell and Lee's chief engineer on a secret scouting mission to determine the Federal strength in front of them at Chancellorsville. Hours later, the engineers returned with the bad news that the Federal left and center were very strong and entrenched. At almost the same time Gen. J. E. B. Stuart arrived with news that the Federal right was "in the air," meaning that it was not anchored to anything such as a river or a rocky ravine. That open right flank invited attack the next day.

While others were confident about the coming attack, a suddenly moody Boswell remarked that he did not expect to survive the next day.

Before daylight on May 2, Boswell and a local scout led Jackson and twenty-eight thousand troops on a twelve-mile march down a country lane hidden from the Federals by thick woods. At the end of that march would be Jackson's famous flank attack.

That night Jackson and eighteen other staff members, including Boswell, would ride through Confederate lines toward the Federals, trying to determine what the enemy was doing to stem the Confederate attack. Returning to Confederate lines from the direction any Federal attack would come, they would be fired upon by two Confederate regiments nervously guarding the road.

Hotchkiss guessed the worst that night when he heard that Jackson had been severely wounded in both arms and Boswell did not return to their tent. The next morning Hotchkiss went looking for his friend and tent mate.

"I went to where the General was wounded and there I found him [Boswell], some twenty steps in advance, by the road-side, dead, pierced through the heart by two balls and wounded in the leg. I was completely overcome, although I had expected it from the state of his mind before, expecting him to be killed in this fight," Hotchkiss wrote.

Hotchkiss went on to write that Boswell looked "peaceful and as pleasant as in life." He took his friend's body and buried it beside Jackson's amputated arm in a nearby family cemetery.

"We buried him just as the moon rose, wrapped in his martial coat. I wept for him as a brother; he was kind and gentle and with as few faults as most men. Peace to his memory," wrote Hotchkiss. It was the last mention in his diary of Boswell.

At some later point Boswell's body was disinterred from the family cemetery and reburied in the Confederate Cemetery in Fredericksburg where he rests today

Capt. James Keith Boswell probably never shot anyone during the war; maybe never even drew his pistol. But Boswell played a major role in creating the image of Stonewall Jackson.

When Jackson needed to find a mountain pass that could accommodate his men, he asked Boswell to find it. When Jackson needed to know if his army could successfully ford a river before it rose from upstream rains, he asked Boswell if it was possible. When Jackson needed to know how many miles it was to his army's destination, he asked Boswell.

There was a final irony involving the death of Boswell. On the night he was shot, he was carrying a small map book in his breast pocket. Though not nearly the artist as his friend Hotchkiss, Boswell's own sketched maps were useful. The two Confederate balls passed through the thin map book and into his heart.

Comdr. John Mercer Brooke
(1826–1906)

THE SOUTH'S BEST INVENTOR

★ BULL'S-EYE ★

IT MUST HAVE BROKEN THE HEART OF U.S. ARMY MAJ. George Mercer Brooke when his son, John Mercer Brooke, born at the army fort named after his father, joined the United States Navy instead of following in his dad's footsteps.

The Confederacy was lucky that young Brooke did not follow his dad but chose instead a branch of the service that would whet his interest in developing the world's first ironclad proven in battle and the world's best rifled cannon.

Brooke had few peers in the prewar U.S. Navy or in the wartime C.S.A. Navy in pure thinking talent and ability to put into practical application the ideas he developed. Indeed, when judged against all of the talented men that the South depended upon to help it make war against an industrial giant, Brooke stands tall. Ironically, one of the few who could compete with Brooke on a thinking plane turned out to be a bitter rival who laid claim to the same invention Brooke considered his greatest triumph.

The South needed people like Brooke, men who could turn abstract thoughts into hard reality. His ability to quickly turn paper designs into war machines makes him a bull's-eye.

When young Brooke graduated from the United States Naval Academy in 1847 at the age of twenty-one, he quickly proved that he was meant to be a deep-water sailor. Among his interests was developing methods of deep-sea sounding, figuring the depth of water. That would come in handy in the future when he would design a ship that had a twenty-two-foot draft.

Brooke remained in the navy until April 21, 1861, resigning his commission in the U.S. Navy on the same day that Col. Robert E. Lee resigned his commission in the U.S. Army. Just as U.S. Army Gen. Winfield Scott expressed regret on losing Lee's services, future Union Adm. David Dixon Porter said of the 321 Southern officers who left the navy that Brooke would be missed most of all.

Brooke's commission as a lieutenant in the C.S.A. Navy did not mean much, because the Confederacy had few ships for any officer to command. What the South did have was men willing to think differently than the old, traditional, "blue-water" U.S. Navy that Brooke had just left. In June 1861 Brooke and Confederate Secretary of the Navy Stephen Mallory met to discuss what a shipless Confederacy could do in the face of the North's declaration that it would blockade Southern ports. Brooke brought up the idea that England and France were building "ironclad" ships that were virtually impervious to traditional cannonballs.

Mallory jumped at the idea, giving Brooke permission to design his own ironclad. Within a few days Brooke came back with a simple drawing showing a ship's hull in the water with iron mounted on sides sloped at a forty-five-degree angle to the surface of the water. Mallory then sent for newly appointed "naval constructor" John L. Porter, a man thirteen years older than Brooke who had experienced a much rougher time finding acceptance in the U.S. Navy.

Porter cringed when he saw Brooke's drawings. He had first tried to sell the U.S. Navy on the idea of an ironclad ship in 1847, the same year Brooke had graduated from Annapolis, but the navy's wooden-ship sailors had dismissed his idea. Now Brooke, once the U.S. Navy's golden boy and now assuming that same role in the Confederate Navy, had sold an enthusiastic Mallory on the very same idea. Though he agreed to work with Brooke, Porter would brood for the rest of his life about Brooke's taking credit for his idea of an ironclad.

Mallory, Brooke, Porter, and chief engineer William P. Williamson all agreed on the idea of building Brooke's ironclad on the hulk of the steam frigate USS *Merrimack*, burned to the waterline in Norfolk's Gosport Naval Yard but with a still serviceable hull. Brooke was assigned to the manufacture of the armor at Tredegar Iron Works. Porter handled the repair and outfitting of the *Merrimack* hull. Williamson tackled repairing the ship's engines.

Brooke set up a firing range on the James River not far from the first New World settlement of Jamestown where he kept firing naval cannon at various thickness of iron plating backed by wood until the plating did not crack. He found that the ideal plating was four inches thick. Since no foundry in the South could roll iron that thick, his final armor design settled on two layers of two-inch iron plating backed by twenty-four inches of wood.

At the same time Brooke was pursuing his experiments for plating the *Virginia*, he was also designing a cannon powerful enough to pierce Union armor. Brooke must have been aware of Union Capt. Robert Parrott's recent successful technique of placing iron bands around the breech of cannon then slowly cooling the bands until they constricted themselves around the breech. The now-strengthened breech could handle larger black powder charges, meaning heavier shells could be thrown longer distances without a nervous gun crew worrying about the breech exploding from the heavier force of the powder exploding.

Brooke figured if one band was good, two were better and three were best. Working with the Tredegar Iron Works in Richmond, Brooke developed rifled cannon ranging in caliber from the smallest at 6.4 inches in diameter up to 11 inches.

While similar in design, the Brooke and Parrott rifles went to two different branches of the service. Most of the 175 Brooke rifled cannon would go to naval vessels. Most of Parrott's rifles were smaller horse-drawn artillery pieces firing projectiles ranging in size up to twenty pounds.

What makes Brooke's wartime accomplishments remarkable is that he thought up the basic design of the *Virginia,* experimented with how thick its armor should be, supervised the development of that iron plating, and developed an entirely new type of cannon that would go into the ironclad—all within the course of nine months.

At some point Brooke began to ponder his place in history and what Porter was doing to claim it. To protect his future reputation, Brooke filed a patent for his ironclad with the Confederate Patent Office. Oddly, the patent application was filed barely a week before the *Virginia* was destroyed on May 11, 1862, when its crew determined that it could not go upriver out of reach of advancing Federals. The patent was not granted until late July, months after the ship itself had been blown to bits.

Once the *Virginia* was intentionally destroyed, Brooke seemed to lose interest in the development of better ironclads, ceding refinements to his rival Porter. At the same time Brooke never allowed Porter to claim any credit for the *Virginia.*

When Porter began to write articles after the war claiming he was the inventor of the *Virginia,* Brooke fired back with lengthy articles of his own backed by long-kept letters from Mallory giving him credit for the idea. Brooke's ace in the hole was the patent for the ship. Though Porter and his supporters never gave up their claims, most historians give Brooke credit for designing the *Virginia* and Porter credit for building it. Porter is then credited with improving on the *Virginia*'s design with lighter, smaller versions, such as the CSS *Albemarle.*

Brooke became head of the Confederate Ordnance Bureau in 1863, which allowed him to continue experimenting. Among his ideas were a cannon that could fire underwater and a magnetic mine that could protect Confederate harbors from ironclads.

Either the technology proved too complex or he was never able to recapture the sense of adventure and pressure that he felt while developing the *Virginia.* Neither idea proved immediately viable during the war.

Still, the ideas showed how far ahead of his time Brooke was. Both ideas would come into being in future wars, if the propeller-driven torpedo can be thought of as an underwater projectile fired by a compressed air cannon from a submarine's torpedo tubes. The magnetic mine dropped along shipping lanes and in harbors would be one of the most feared weapons of World War II shipping.

Brooke became a professor of astronomy, meteorology, and geography at Virginia Military Institute. He married the widow of Sandie Pendleton, one of Stonewall Jackson's aides who was killed in 1864. He spent thirty-four years on dry land teaching students, far longer than his combined service in the United States and the Confederate States navies.

Brooke died in 1906. According to his biography, the rain came down in torrents on the day this old sailor was buried.

First Lady Varina Howell Davis
(1826–1906)

A SHARP TONGUE SHE HAD

⭐ BULL'S-EYE ⭐

HE WAS TALL, GAUNT, SHAGGY-HAIRED, AND BLIND IN ONE
eye. Socially, he was an odd combination, a shy politician who felt so
uncomfortable in social settings that he did not like to do what politicians usually do best—shake hands.

She was short, dark, attractive, and seventeen years younger than he.
Socially, she was a bright, educated woman who openly spoke her mind
in an era when wives were routinely expected to be seen but not heard
on political matters.

He was Jefferson F. Davis, president of the Confederacy. She was
Varina Howell Davis, first lady of the Confederacy.

Their relationship was close, yet often strained; cooperative, yet often separate. It was a true romantic and political partnership bound by a love of each other and the Confederacy.

Just how much Davis depended upon his wife's advice in running the country will always be conjectural. It is clear that she provided him the personal and moral support he needed to remain on the job. Without Varina Davis, Jefferson Davis would not have become Confederate president. Without her, he might have slipped into inconsolable madness.

Mrs. Davis knew her husband's strengths and weaknesses and was able to use her own talents to help him during his budding political career right through his reluctant term as Confederate president. Even after his career was over and a vengeful Federal government imprisoned him, she recognized that he would always be a symbol of a Confederacy that no longer existed in reality but which would exist forever in spirit. Her ability to help create the image of the Confederacy while serving as a public figure and as a wife and mother makes her a bull's-eye.

When the seventeen-year-old Varina Howell first met the thirty-six-year-old widower Jefferson Davis in the winter of 1843, she wrote to her mother: "He impresses me as a remarkable kind of man, but of uncertain temper, and has a way of taking for granted that everyone agrees with him when he expresses an opinion, which offends me; yet he is most agreeable and has a peculiarly sweet voice and a winning manner of asserting himself."

Within two months after meeting, the two were engaged. Following a year-long engagement, they were married in February 1845.

Marriage to Varina made Davis bloom into public life, ending eight years of reclusion brought on by the death from fever of his first wife. A return to public life rekindled Davis's interest in politics. He was elected to the U.S. House of Representatives in the same year he was married.

Davis took a leave of absence from the Congress just one year later to lead a regiment of Mississippi volunteers in the Mexican War. He became a national hero, returning home with a painful foot wound that Varina said she enjoyed dressing for him to demonstrate her devotion.

The 1850s were a whirlwind for the Davis family. Jefferson moved from being a congressman to become secretary of war under President Franklin Pierce then to the U.S. Senate. All during this time Varina felt her love for her husband growing as their children were born. She realized there were two Jefferson Davises: the cold, aloof one in public who enjoyed debate but not personal contact with voters, and the warm family man who would not bother taking off his suit before crawling around on the floor with his children.

The Davises' greatest challenge as a couple would come when he was elected as president at a convention organizing the new Confederacy. He had intended to take the field as a general and had no desire to lead a nation. Reluctantly, he accepted, but only after Varina reluctantly approved.

Varina took to her new role as first lady. Before she made the move from the first Confederate capital in Montgomery, Alabama, to Richmond, some women started calling her "Queen Varina." The label was not fair. As the wife of a U.S. senator she was expected to be a socialite and now that her husband was president of the new nation, she had to play an even larger public role as his devoted wife.

What irritated Richmond's society women most of all was that Varina was so much younger than her husband—and them. When the Davises moved into the Confederate White House, they had a six-year-old daughter, a four-year-old son, a two-year-old son, and another baby on the way.

Pregnant society women in the 1860s often disappeared from the public scene, treating pregnancy like an illness that would be over in nine months. Varina ignored that custom and kept up her social duties as her belly grew larger. That shocked Richmond's blue bloods who already looked down their noses at this native of Mississippi, which was more populated by slaves than by whites.

It was on April 30, 1864, that Varina proved how valuable an asset she was to the Confederacy. Over the course of several days she kept the president from slipping into inconsolable grief, perhaps even madness.

Just as Varina was persuading her husband to eat a snack that she had brought to his office, a servant dashed in with terrible news. Five-year-old Joe had fallen off the balcony and had cracked his head. The child died soon afterwards.

"This child was Mr. Davis's hope and greatest joy in life," wrote Varina.

No matter how important the meeting, the little boy would always push his way through a crowd of officers and politicians to say his prayers at the knee of his father. Impatient adults stopped what they were saying to wait on the president who was paying rapt attention to his small son.

Davis was paralyzed in grief at losing his son. It was Varina who consoled him privately, encouraging him that they both would see Joe in heaven. She convinced the president that he had to remain strong for the country and for the couple's next child, who would arrive in two months.

As the Confederacy suffered more reverses on the battlefield for which Davis's political enemies blamed him more than the Federal armies, Varina seemed to wrap her arms around her husband. She became more publicly vocal in her support. When the Confederate Congress passed a law requiring Davis to name a general in chief of the Confederate armies, Varina considered it a slap at her husband who had always taken an active role in military affairs.

"I think I am the person to advise Mr. Davis; and if I were he, I would die or be hung before I would submit to the humiliation that Congress intended him," she spat into the face of a shocked Tennessee senator.

Varina's role as her husband's advisor is often debated, though she claimed that cabinet member Judah P. Benjamin often explained state affairs to her, perhaps knowing that she would carry his opinion on to the president as if it were her own. In one surviving letter, she counsels the president not to send Braxton Bragg to command the Trans-Mississippi Department. Of course, everyone in the Confederacy counseled Davis against giving any appointment to the always failing Bragg. Davis always ignored that advice, even when it came from his wife.

As the Federals encircled Richmond, Davis gave his wife a pistol, showed her how to fire it, and sent his family south. They reunited in South Carolina and she was with him when they were captured in south Georgia.

When Davis died in 1889, Varina moved on with her life. She became an accomplished journalist, though her book about her husband was not well received as she appeared to be too loving to write about him objectively. She remained a Confederate and never forgave her bitterest enemies, particularly Union generals Nelson Miles, who had been cruel in imprisoning Davis at Fort Monroe, and William T. Sherman, who destroyed much of Mississippi.

Neither did she forgive Confederate enemies. When she gave her Mississippi home, Beauvoir, to the United Confederate Veterans, she made it clear that Generals Joseph Johnston and P. G. T. Beauregard should not be honored with rooms named after them.

One journalist who knew Varina said that she "preferred the straight road to the tortuous bypath. She was naturally a frank though not a blunt woman, and her bent was to kindliness and charity. Sharp tongue she had, when set that way and the need came to use it; and her wide knowledge of people and things sometimes made that dangerous to offenders."

When Varina died in 1906, she was buried beside her husband in Hollywood Cemetery in Richmond. Her tombstone reads, "Beloved and faithful wife of Jefferson Davis and devoted mother to his children."

Gen. Nathan "Shanks" Evans
(1824–1868)

ALWAYS SUSPECTING A
COMANCHE AMBUSH

⋆ MISFIRE ⋆

NO ONE IN THE SOUTH SEEMED TO HOLD MORE PROMISE at the beginning of the war than Nathan "Shanks" Evans.

Though Evans's accomplishments in the war's first major engagement at Manassas, Virginia, would be overshadowed by another officer who would be dubbed with a famous nickname late in the battle, it was early intervention by Evans who kept the battle from becoming a quick Union victory. In his second engagement at Ball's Bluff, his command would wreck the Federal forces, creating a disaster that would lead to the creation of a congressional committee to investigate how the United States could fall to a Rebel rabble. Later in his career, forces under Evans would save Charleston, South Carolina, from capture at the battle of Secessionville, the only serious attempt ever made on the city.

Shanks Evans should have been an acclaimed hero throughout the South. He was—briefly. He could have become a legend like Stonewall Jackson, but Evans had a weakness that Jackson did not, a fondness for alcohol that was so debilitating it would wreck his career and forever label Evans a misfire in Southern history.

The son of affluent South Carolinians, Evans was also well educated. Although he had graduated low in his class at the Military Academy, he had been appointed to West Point by no less than former Vice President John C. Calhoun, and he had gained acclaim earlier by graduating from Randolph Macon College at age seventeen.

Evans had a distinguished career in the prewar U.S. Army. A West Pointer from the class of '48, he had served on the western frontier—first in the dragoons and then in the cavalry—and had earned a coveted captain's rank in the slow-promotion peacetime army. In 1858 he had even made the nation's newspapers by single-handedly killing two Comanche chiefs at the battle of Wichita Village.

He did generate controversy. In 1858 he tied several army deserters to a wagon and pushed them on a forced march across the prairie. One of them died, and the soldier's hometown newspaper pounded Evans as a hard-hearted and hard-headed villain—a charge that shadowed the officer's success.

Despite his peculiar nickname—bestowed as a youngster because of his skinny calves—Shanks Evans seemed destined for greatness at the beginning of the war. He resigned from the U.S. Army in 1861, served with South Carolina troops in the bombardment of Fort Sumter, and then was given a captain's command with a small brigade of Confederate cavalry at the battle of Manassas. The battle made him a hero in the South.

Posted to guard the Stone Bridge over Bull Run with one thousand one hundred troops and two artillery pieces, Evans was sent a message that the Federals were advancing north of his position. Their plan was to cross at Sudley Ford and sweep down on an unguarded flank. Leaving a detachment at the bridge, Evans rushed his small command to meet the threat. Rather than retreat, he aggressively attacked the Federal troops and stalled the Northern advance crossing Bull Run. Evans slowly retreated, giving the Confederates time to send more reinforcements his way. Eventually those reinforcements slowly pulled back to Henry House Hill where Gen. Thomas Jackson's troops were waiting. Jackson's late-in-the-battle defense of the hill would win him the nickname "Stonewall."

Had Evans not slowed the Federal assault at Sudley Ford early in the battle, Jackson might not have had time to place his forces on Henry House Hill. When Manassas ended in a Confederate victory, Shanks Evans received a large dose of praise from grateful Southerners and official recognition from his superiors. His actions at Manassas, according to Confederate battle reports, demonstrated "skill and unshrinkable courage" as well as "dauntless conduct and imperturbable coolness."

He was promptly promoted to colonel. Three months later he inflicted a humiliating defeat on Northern forces at the battle of Ball's Bluff. So one-sided was the Confederate victory—Evans inflicted five times more casualties on the enemy than he suffered—that the U.S. Congress created a committee to investigate the Ball's Bluff disaster. Shanks Evans received the official Confederate Thanks of Congress, a gold medal from his native state, and promotion to brigadier general.

Then events seemed to unravel for Gen. Evans. His fellow officers had always considered him a little odd. As noted by historian Douglas Southall Freeman, Evans looked "as if he always were suspecting a Comanche ambush." In his late thirties during the war, he was a thin, slightly balding man given to wearing a thick black mustache—and later a fully bushy beard—which made him appear "fierce" to some observers. With a restless or perhaps even a nervous disposition, he had a habit of giving darting glances left and right in a manner that some called a "quick, cunning and contentious" look.

Evans's most serious liability, however, was not his appearance; it was the rumor that he was too fond of the bottle. "Colonel Evans is as fierce as a pirate, a wild man with piercing, angry eyes," a contemporary observed. "But sometimes, when he smiles, a much happier and more likable person appears. He is mostly stern, however, and he likes whiskey even more than I do. He carries it around in what he calls a barrelista [a small keg]."

In fact, Evans had been seen at Manassas riding around with an aide following him with that barrelista. During lulls in the fighting, Evans was rumored to be taking shots of whiskey.

In late 1862 the rumors became official charges. Evans mishandled a retreat at the battle of Kinston in North Carolina, inadvertently abandoning many of his troops, then unknowingly shelling them with artillery fire. He was charged with drunkenness but was acquitted. Then he was tried for disobedience of orders, but those charges also failed to stick.

Officially, Shanks Evans was innocent, but despite his contributions to the Confederacy, his reputation was seriously tarnished. His superior, Gen. P. G. T. Beauregard, distrusted Evans and removed him from command.

Not until the spring of 1864 did he return to a post of authority. He was granted command of one of South Carolina's military districts, in which he was responsible mainly for garrison troops. It was during this period that luck shone once more on Evans when he was in overall command of the Confederate troops defending Charleston. Rushing reinforcements to a small fort southeast of Charleston near a community called Secessionville, Evans was able to beat back a Union attack. Had he lost the battle of Secessionville, the Union would have opened a backdoor land route that would have led to the capture of the city.

Evans's return to hero status in South Carolina ended disastrously not long after the battle, when he toppled off his horse for no apparent reason. No one formally accused him of drunkenness—he was painfully injured—but it surely appeared odd for a seasoned cavalry officer to take such a tumble when not even under fire. Shanks Evans, once a rising star among Confederate commanders, had a dark cloud attached to him for the rest of the war. A year later he managed to return to duty—just as the Confederacy collapsed. In Richmond at the time, he accompanied President Davis's party as the Southern leader retreated across the South.

The once-acclaimed general died in 1868 and is buried near his home in Cokesbury, South Carolina. Though a hero of First Manassas, Ball's Bluff, and Secessionville, his tombstone mentions only "Wichita, Kansas, 1858." Even in death, his contributions—and embarrassment— to the Confederacy is ignored in favor of a small Indian battle when Shanks Evans's reputation was still intact.

Gen. John Buchanan Floyd
(1806–1863)

WHY WAS HE EVER BORN?

✷ MISFIRE ✷

GEN. JOHN BUCHANAN FLOYD HAD A LONG, VARIED, exciting life and career. No other Confederate leader could match Floyd's life as grandson and son of Virginia governors, governor of Virginia himself, United States secretary of war, and Confederate general.

Built over decades, Floyd's sterling credentials ended with a disastrous one-year career as a Confederate general. Not only did his brief battlefield experience show him to be without any discernable military skills, it also proved him to be an inflexible egotist and finally a coward in the face of the enemy. Worst of all, Floyd's short career as a general helped to derail the early war career of another man who would eventually become the South's greatest hero—Robert E. Lee.

Being a poor general was not unique. Dozens of generals on both sides were spectacular failures. But almost destroying the career of the man who would become the Confederacy's greatest hero labels Floyd one of the South's misfires.

After failing as a farmer, Floyd found his early calling as a lawyer. Success there carried him into politics and the governor's chair in 1849, nineteen years after his father and thirty-three years after his grandfather had served.

After one two-year term, Floyd moved up to national politics, backing James Buchanan for president in 1856. Buchanan rewarded Floyd with the title of secretary of war though Floyd had no military experience. His appointment was also controversial. By 1856 it was clear that North and South were moving toward conflict so putting a Virginian in charge of the arsenals of the country set Northern politicians on edge.

Floyd actually did a good job in the post, completing a goal of modernizing the army started by his predecessor, Jefferson Davis. He had to endure false rumors that he was supplying the South with arms when evidence shows that he actually shortchanged the South of its share of modern arms replacement in its arsenals.

Floyd finally resigned from his post several days after Federal forces occupied Fort Sumter when President Buchanan refused to order the forces back to the mainland.

Confederate President Davis, eager to showcase such a prominent national figure, made Floyd a brigadier general. Floyd leaped to the task, recruiting a force of three thousand six hundred men he called the Army of the Kanawha to protect Confederate interests west of the Allegheny Mountains in western Virginia. Floyd was allowed to make his force an independent command, a mistake Davis would come to regret.

Also sent into western Virginia was Floyd's old political enemy Gen. Henry Wise, who had served as Virginia's governor through 1860. Floyd's commission was two weeks older than Wise's, making him senior officer. The two men, once allies, had split when new political parties replaced the old ones to which they formerly belonged.

Historians still question why Davis entrusted western Virginia, location of the state's vital lead, iron, salt, and other mineral mines, to two political generals who hated each other. By contrast, the Union sent trained West

Point graduates like William Rosecrans and George B. McClellan to attack Virginia through its lightly defended western "back door."

Floyd got his baptism of fire on August 26, 1861, at Kessler's Cross Keys, just thirty days after First Manassas and months before most other generals on either side would even see an enemy. Though Floyd won the little skirmish, the sloppiness of his performance should have told the Confederate high command something. His force outnumbered the Federals by several times but he allowed most of the enemy to escape.

Two weeks later a much stronger Federal force defeated Floyd at Carnifax Ferry, an embarrassing loss where he violated the first rule of defensive warfare: Never put your back to a river. Slightly wounded in the battle, Floyd abandoned his well-dug-in positions at nightfall, displaying a nervousness about facing the enemy that would constantly mark his short military career.

Floyd blamed Wise for his defeat, claiming Wise refused to speedily come to his aid. Wise countered that he had warned Floyd about poor placement of his troops. When Floyd ignored the advice, Wise ignored Floyd though it also meant Floyd's men were shot up in the process and the Confederacy suffered a defeat.

Both Floyd and Wise retreated toward Sewell Mountain. Coming to meet them was Gen. Robert E. Lee, sent west by President Davis to coordinate the two independent commands. Davis was trying to make up for his earlier mistake of trusting Floyd and Wise by sending a career soldier to guide these two inexperienced generals.

The plan did not work. Floyd and Wise hated each other so much that they refused to even camp on the same mountaintop. When Wise's men stopped to set up a defense on one mountain, Floyd's men kept marching to another mountain twelve miles away. Wise rarely referred to Floyd as "general," preferring after Floyd's wounding to call him "that bullet-hit son of a bitch."

Absolutely nothing Lee could do or say would get Floyd and Wise to cooperate with each other. Lee even tried riding back and forth between the two camps to try to act as a peacemaker to his generals. They absolutely refused to be in the same tent with each other.

Lee had spent a frustrating five days trying to deal with the two enemies when Wise received an order transferring his men to Floyd's command and bringing him back east as he was the junior officer. Davis had finally seen his mistake of throwing these two old hate-filled rattlesnakes into the same bag.

Though Lee's command problems had dropped 50 percent, it did not mean his troubles were over. The Federals, realizing the futility of attacking the dug-in Confederates with winter approaching, simply left the field without giving battle. Lee, anxious to make his own name on the battlefield, now had no enemy to face.

Lee returned to Richmond humbled and humiliated by two generals whose hate for each other had spoiled the Confederacy's chances to reclaim western Virginia. It would take another eight months before Lee could restore the damage to his reputation by winning the Seven Days' campaign.

The result of the failed 1861 western Virginia campaign went beyond damaging the reputations of Lee, Floyd, and Wise. The Federals would maintain control of more than thirty counties of western Virginia. Within a year and a half emboldened Unionists would take western Virginia out of the Confederacy and into the Union as West Virginia.

Had Floyd and Wise cooperated with each other—and with Lee—in planning a battle at Sewell Mountain, they might have driven the Federals from that part of the state. Unionist sentiment, though strong, would have had no military protection and the formation of the state of West Virginia might have been delayed or quashed.

Floyd would go on to deeply embarrass himself again just five months after Sewell Mountain. He and his command were transferred west where he was entrusted with the defense of Fort Donelson, Tennessee, a key position defending the Cumberland River, that became the object of Union Gen. U. S. Grant.

Floyd, the senior commander in the fort, missed at least two good chances for his forces to cut a way through the slowly encircling Federals. Finally, only after being completely surrounded, Floyd commandeered two river steamers and left with the Virginia brigade he had brought with him from Sewell Mountain. Left behind were fifteen thousand other Confederates who were taken captive by Grant.

Floyd had finally totally disgraced himself. Instead of using all of his forces to fight his way out of Fort Donelson, which would have freed all of the Confederates, Floyd personally fled the field. It was a breathtaking display of cowardice that forced Davis to relieve him of Confederate command.

Amazingly, Floyd still had many old friends left in the Virginia legislature. Bypassing the Confederate command structure, which had to be approved by Davis, they cooked up a state commission for Floyd. He was named major general of state troops and given command of protecting the salt works in southwestern Virginia. The irony was lost on them. Floyd had endangered the salt works when he performed poorly in western Virginia in the fall of 1861. Now his fellow Virginia politicians entrusted him with those same salt works again in the fall of 1862.

Floyd died at the age of fifty-seven, apparently from stomach cancer, in August 1863. One of the two Confederate generals who had almost destroyed the career of Robert E. Lee in September 1861 and a man who abandoned his command in the face of the enemy, now rests beneath a tombstone that compares his life to the trials of Job, a man tested by God with one disaster after another. The Bible verse on his tombstone asks, "Why was I ever born?"

Gen. Josiah Gorgas

(1818–1883)

THE MAN WHO FORGOT THE BOLTS

⋆ MISFIRE ⋆

GEN. JOSIAH GORGAS WAS FREQUENTLY CRANKY, USUALLY efficient, and always dedicated to making the best out of a bad situation. He had to be. As head of the Confederate Ordnance Department he faced a formidable task supplying the South's newly created army and navy with weapons.

Gorgas had his problems. Cannon would sometimes explode and artillery shells sometimes would not. Still, he did a remarkable job building new factories, monitoring the quality of munitions coming from those factories, and coordinating his own blockade-running fleet.

He seems to have made just one major mistake. In early March 1862 Gorgas may have been responsible for selecting the ammunition to load aboard the CSS *Virginia* when it was preparing to fight the wooden ships blockading Norfolk's harbor. He made the wrong choice. Had different ammunition been chosen, naval history and perhaps the course of the war would have changed.

While Gorgas's overall career could be normally classified as an unqualified bull's-eye, this one mistake is big enough that he has to accept the label of misfire. Had Gorgas only ordered the *Virginia's* ammunition lockers to be loaded a different way, the entire Union ironclad program would have been in a shambles.

Gorgas, a native of Pennsylvania, graduated sixth in the 1841 West Point class. Ranked so high that he could have gone into engineering as his specialty, Gorgas instead chose the relatively dull duty of ordnance officer. While his classmates were designing forts, Gorgas was making sure the black powder inside the forts was dry.

Anger at being demoted by a jealous U.S. Army superior in March 1861, plus the fact that his wife was from Alabama, helped Gorgas decide which side would get his services. Gorgas, a Pennsylvanian, was appointed to his Confederate Ordnance Department role while Virginians like Robert E. Lee, James Longstreet, and J. E. B. Stuart were still serving in the U.S. Army.

Gorgas's first problem was supplying the South with ammunition. After studying the battle of Manassas, he estimated most soldiers fired no more than twenty-six rounds. He worried that the South would run out of powder, which would be blamed on him.

Gorgas wrote, "I feel anxious to ascertain how long we can hold out before being thrown on our own resources, which are daily developing."

In July 1861 Gorgas and President Jefferson Davis selected George Washington Rains, a former iron foundry president, to develop the Confederacy's own gunpowder factory. Gorgas's deep thinking helped Rains solve his own supply problems. It was Gorgas who organized a bureau to collect the gunpowder ingredient niter by digging up the sinks in the South's outhouses and military latrines. Human urine is rich in niter.

After approving cannon contracts with Tredegar Iron Works in Richmond and seeing that Rains's gunpowder factory was under construction in Augusta, Georgia, Gorgas turned to organizing a fleet of blockade-runners. Wary that private blockade-runners would fill their ships with luxury goods, Gorgas supervised a half dozen ships owned by the Confederacy. Those ships eventually imported four hundred thousand rifles, three million pounds of lead (about one-third of the military's requirements), and two million pounds of saltpeter, another critical ingredient of black powder.

Gorgas sometimes had to quash foolish ideas such as that of Georgia's governor who wanted the Ordnance Department to manufacture long spears called pikes because the governor did not think all new soldiers were smart enough to operate rifles.

Writing with a sense of humor after the war, Gorgas remembered that "no excess of enthusiasm could induce our people to rush to the field armed with pikes."

It was in March 1862 that Gorgas made his most serious mistake.

For months spies had been keeping North and South informed on the two ironclads both were building. The South's CSS *Virginia* was clad in two layers of two-inch-thick armor over two feet of wood and armed with six smoothbore cannon and four rifled cannon. The North's USS *Monitor* had eight layers of inch-thick armor on its turret, which housed two smoothbore cannon.

The smoothbores of both ironclads could fire round cannonballs or explosive shells. Only the rifled cannon of the *Virginia* could fire "bolt shot," which were elongated solid pieces of wrought iron with knobs at each end designed to pierce iron plating.

When the *Virginia* was loaded with ammunition to attack the Union fleet of wooden ships blockading Norfolk Harbor, her ammunition chests were loaded only with explosive shells designed to pierce and start fires on wooden ships. She did just that on March 8 when the ironclad virtually destroyed three wooden Union ships.

When the *Virginia* returned on March 9 to finish off the Union blockaders, the armored *Monitor* was there to meet her. Neither ironclad seriously damaged the other during their hours-long battle. Solid shot and explosive shells bounced into the water.

"As we did not expect to encounter any ironclad, she was only provided with shells for all her guns, rifled and smoothbore," wrote John L.

Porter, the man who constructed the *Virginia*, answering a postwar letter from a curious Union naval officer who had been aboard a ship the ironclad had destroyed.

Later in the same letter, Porter wrote, "The action lasted several hours, the vessels at times touching each other, and with no seeming advantage to either, but in my opinion, had the *Merrimack* [original name of the ship] been provided with solid shot and slugs, steel pointed as she was afterwards, the result would have been different."

Who ordered only explosive shells to be placed in the *Virginia's* ammunition lockers?

It was not John Mercer Brooke, the man who designed both the ironclad and the rifled cannon she carried.

Brooke said: "The rifle guns were intended to throw bolts as well as shells, but owing to the fact that the enemy had no ironclad afloat at the time she first went out, and there being a great pressure upon the works [Tredegar Iron Works] for projectiles of other kinds proper to use against wooden vessels, she was not furnished with bolts. If she had been, the experiment made here with guns of the same caliber show that the turret of the *Monitor* would have been penetrated by them."

It was not Gen. Joseph Reid Anderson, head of Tredegar Iron Works, manufacturer of the ammunition. He was just a supplier. It was not his responsibility to select the type of ammunition going on board a ship he had never seen.

It probably was not Franklin Buchanan, the captain of the *Virginia*. He took command of the vessel only a few days prior to going into combat, so the ammunition was probably already onboard. His reports make no mention of his selecting ammunition or regretting the type of ammunition he had, though he believed he would be facing only wooden vessels.

If Porter, Brooke, Anderson, or Buchanan were all blameless for not loading the armor-piercing bolts onto the *Virginia*, who was to blame?

It may have been Gorgas, or at least one of his subordinates. While his diary never mentions arming the *Virginia*, the Ordnance Department supervised the production output of Tredegar. Manufacturing the *Virginia's* ammunition would have been a top priority Gorgas likely would have supervised.

What would have happened if armor-piercing bolts had been onboard the *Virginia?* Every direct hit from the four Brooke rifled cannon at least had the possibility of holing the eight layers of armor protecting the *Monitor's* turret. If the turret were not holed in one shot, repeated shots on the same weak points definitely would have pierced the turret, probably killing or injuring her gun crews, if not destroying her two cannon. The *Monitor's* deck was only one inch thick so even a glancing blow would have created a hole through which waves would pour. A hit below the water line would have sunk her within minutes.

The answer is clear. Had the *Monitor* been sunk or forced to surrender, the Union's wooden fleet at Norfolk on that day would have been doomed.

The aftermath would have been more interesting. With its prototype ironclad on the bottom, the Union probably would have shelved plans for the fleet of monitors later constructed based on the *Monitor* design. Their "plan B" would have likely been to rely on armoring existing wooden sailing ships (designs that did not prove conclusively effective in practice as exampled by the careers of the USS *New Ironsides* and *Galena*—two ironclad designs approved at the same time as the *Monitor*). While the *New Ironsides* had a reasonable career, the *Galena* was holed repeatedly by a Confederate fort at Drewry's Bluff on a mission up the James River to attack Richmond.

This presumed delay on the Union side on coming up with a new ironclad program would have given the Confederacy time to design and build more and better ironclads. One of the problems with the *Virginia* was she had a very deep draft, so she could not operate up rivers. She was also so heavy and large that she could not have survived ocean swells; consequently, she would not have been able to attack off-shore-lying Union vessels.

If the South had designed better ironclads with models operating on rivers and others that could go some distance into the open ocean, and if the North had been slowed in its response to those models, the effectiveness of the Northern blockade in closing Southern ports might have been in question.

The South tried its best to create such alternative history. After its battle with the *Monitor*, generally considered a draw since neither iron-clad seriously damaged the other, the *Virginia* returned to port and repaired its damage. Buchanan loaded his ammunition lockers with bolt shot and spent several days cruising back into Hampton Roads, daring the *Monitor* to come out and fight again.

The captain of the *Monitor* refused to do battle. He guessed from the *Virginia's* aggressive maneuvers that the ship was now properly armed and could probably sink him. He was right.

The North actually did not learn its lesson about bolt shot's effectiveness. Less than two years after the *Monitor* and *Virginia* battle, a fleet of Union monitors attacking Confederate-held Fort Sumter was crippled after being riddled with bolts fired from the fort.

After the war Gorgas became a college professor and later the president of the University of Alabama. When he suffered a stroke, he was given the job of university librarian. He died in 1883 and is buried in Tuscaloosa.

Gen. William J. Hardee

(1815–1873)

The Man Who Wrote the Book on Civil War Training

☆ MISFIRE ☆

GEN. WILLIAM J. HARDEE LITERALLY WROTE THE BOOK on Civil War infantry training. Both Union and Confederate officers carried his book in their haversacks so they could learn how to drill their men in camp and then march them forward into battle.

It would not be until after the war was over that surviving soldiers would realize the general whose nickname was "Old Reliable" played an unwitting but very specific role in the 620,000 deaths recorded in the war.

Hardee cannot be blamed directly for the battlefield deaths of the men who were trained using his book. After all, he did not personally order each side to march within a couple of hundred yards of the other's rifles. It is what Hardee failed to do that forces the label of misfire onto him.

Though his charge was to update the U.S. Army's training manuals, and though he specifically studied the new rifles that were changing warfare because they were increasing a soldier's ability to accurately hit his enemy, Hardee failed to realize that the very training methods he was teaching would put soldiers in greater danger. Hardee wrote the wrong book. He should have dumped his old training manual and written a book of tactics for modern warfare, compensating for the new rifles' accuracy. He did not and for that failure he can be called a misfire.

As early as 1830 while he was just fourteen, Hardee was applying to West Point, not an uncommon occurrence in an era when there were no formal high schools from which to draw college-age students. He tried every year for four years until he was accepted in 1834. A mediocre student, he placed twenty-sixth among forty-five graduates in 1838, something future readers of his required reading book must have missed.

After fighting the Seminoles tree to tree in Florida's swamps, Hardee was assigned to a French military school to study warfare on a grander scale. Coming back to the United States, he lectured other officers on the theories he had learned, before employing those tactics in Mexico in 1846. His theories did not always work. He was deeply embarrassed when he was captured by the Mexicans, indicating "avoiding the enemy" was not a lesson he learned well.

In November 1853 Lieutenant Hardee was ordered to report to Washington, D.C., where he met with Secretary of War Jefferson Davis who asked him to prepare a new manual of tactics for the U.S. Army.

It was needed, Davis reported to Congress, "in anticipation of an increased, if not exclusive use of rifle arms by the regular army, and because of the belief that the rifle or light infantry system of instruction is best adapted to the foot militia. With the recent improvements of small arms, it is probable that the distinction in the armament of heavy and light infantry, and riflemen, will nearly cease, especially in our service, where the whole force is liable to be employed as light troops."

The major reason it appears that the lowly lieutenant was picked to write the manual was that he had studied the tactics of the French army, then considered the finest military in the world. Though recognized for gallantry in Mexico, Hardee was no more skilled or brave than many higher ranking officers.

Before starting to write, Hardee visited the Harpers Ferry, Virginia (now West Virginia), Arsenal in December 1853. The arsenal was then manufacturing rifles to accept the minié ball, a conical-shaped rifle ball destined to replace the round musket ball still used in smoothbore muskets. The minié ball increased the effective range of a rifled musket to several hundred yards, compared to just one hundred yards for a smoothbore musket firing a round ball.

Hardee spent the next seven months writing *Hardee's Rifle and Light Infantry Tactics* using a French tactical manual as his guide. One critic claimed Hardee translated the French manual word for word into English.

Another critic made a valid point that could not be proved until war erupted again. Col. Ethan Allen Hitchcock, grandson of the famed Revolutionary War partisan soldier, complained to Davis that Hardee's draft did not address the advanced capabilities of the rifled musket, exactly what Davis had charged Hardee to do. Hitchcock complained the rifle had already changed tactics and his reading of early drafts of Hardee's manual showed it would be obsolete before it was published. Davis sided with Hardee and no major changes were made to the book. Not long afterwards, Hitchcock resigned his commission after being denied a leave of absence by Davis.

Hardee's *Tactics* did draw heavily on the French manual, but he merged the best of what the French were doing with a twenty-year-old manual developed by Gen. Winfield Scott. Hardee was savvy enough not to trash the official manual written by the general in chief of the army.

Hardee's manual simplified some troop movements and created other new movements, such as changing certain formations while on the march. In past manuals the marching column would have to be halted while complicated orders were given. While halted, the men might be under fire. Hardee's manual allowed the men to continue moving, shortening the time they might be under fire and making it more difficult for an enemy to hit them. If rigid compliance with old formations and methods was the hallmark of old manuals, flexibility to conditions was the hallmark of Hardee's *Tactics*.

Oddly enough Hardee ignored Davis's instructions about the modern rifle, describing how the soldiers were to fire their muskets by file or rank, by regiment, by battalion. Massed fire by hundreds of muskets was still considered the effective means of fighting. Hardee's *Tactics* even addressed the proper way to use an old weapon, the bayonet, which was virtually obsolete by 1861.

Hardee's book was not about tactics at all. It was a drill manual, describing in minute detail mundane things such as the number of inches a soldier should step in each stride, the *L*-shape in which a soldier should place his feet, and how much he should turn so as not to impede the view of the soldier behind him. A shift in the way the soldier should hold his musket, an arms movement that may take two seconds to perform, was described in excruciating detail.

Barely covered in the pocket version of Hardee's *Tactics* were true tactics. The book did not tell an officer what to do when he actually saw an enemy column approaching from the front, side, or rear. Not covered were instructions such as what to do at a range of one thousand yards when there is time to perform complex maneuvers, or at one hundred yards when the enemy is close enough to kill everyone he sees, and there is no time to perform the same maneuvers that work at one thousand yards.

What was covered was how important it is for each man to touch elbows with the man beside him, the same instructions given to soldiers in the American Revolution.

That the book was not what it was titled never bothered either the Union or the Confederacy. Both sides used the book, as well as one written by Gen. Silas Casey, a Northerner who included more battalion drill.

In perhaps a dozen major battles, Hardee lived up to his nickname of "Old Reliable." In his last battle at Bentonville, North Carolina, in March 1865, Hardee suffered a personal loss. His teenaged son Willie, who had secretly joined a Confederate cavalry regiment, was mortally wounded by one of those minié balls his father had never fully understood.

Was Hardee's *Tactics* responsible for the terrible battlefield carnage experienced by both sides? Not really. The book was really mistitled. It was always meant to be a drill manual to instill discipline in the men. Books teaching tactics—as opposed to drill—to the citizen-soldier officers in both armies were simply not widely distributed.

The book that Secretary of War Davis should have asked Hardee to write was how warfare should be immediately, radically overhauled because of the accuracy of the rifled musket. A few books published before the war touched on the issue, but they carried little weight with generals who had learned all about warfare of the previous thirty years at the U.S. Military Academy. It would take postwar analysis of facts, such as more than 90 percent of the deaths resulted from bullets, before the West Point-educated generals on both sides would realize that all of their training was obsolete.

After the war Hardee became a railroad president. He died of stomach cancer in 1873.

Gen. Henry Heth
(1825–1899)

THE MAN WHO
WOULD NOT LISTEN

⋆ MISFIRE ⋆

GEN. HENRY HETH HAD A HARD HEAD. THAT WAS PROVEN when a bullet cracked his skull but did not kill him on July 1, 1863.

Had it killed him, it might have been payback for what Heth had just done. He had started the battle of Gettysburg in violation of direct orders from Gen. Robert E. Lee.

Had Heth obeyed orders, Lee might have arrived on the field with an overwhelming force that would have swept everything before it. He might have taken the high ground of Culps Hill, Cemetery Hill, and Cemetery Ridge. It would have been the Confederates waiting for the Federals to attack over the next two days instead of the other way around.

Heth did not follow specific orders from a superior officer, did not trust the opinion of a subordinate officer who had thoroughly checked out the ground in front of him, and did not personally ride to that disputed ground to see for himself. Heth's sloppiness and casual attitude while deep in enemy territory should have resulted in his being replaced. Instead, Lee let his forgiving nature, one of his personal faults, get the better of him. Heth survived both Lee's brief wrath and the war, but he can be labeled a misfire.

Heth was a terrible West Point cadet, a foreshadowing of his career as a general.

"My thoughts ran to the channels of having fun. How to get to Benny Havens [local bar]occupied more of my time than calculus," Heth wrote in his memoirs.

He found fighting Indians in the 1850s appealing. He claimed to have been hit by six arrows in one battle, enough piercing that he was reported dead in the newspapers.

"It is a very pleasant thing to be killed if you live to read the nice things your friends wrote about you," Heth observed.

Heth was active in the early fighting of 1861, serving as a regimental commander under an incompetent general named John Floyd. Apparently following the old adage: It Takes One to Know One, Heth wrote of Floyd, "I soon discovered my chief [Floyd] was as incapacitated for the work he had undertaken as I would have been to lead an Italian opera."

Promoted to brigadier general in January 1862, Heth seemed on his way to making something of his career but he soon bungled his first independent battle at Lewisburg, Virginia.

A darker side to Heth emerged later that year when he blithely ordered some Unionists in western North Carolina to be dealt with. That resulted in the cold-blooded execution of thirteen men and boys at what became known as the Shelton Laurel Massacre.

Not long after the massacre, Heth was transferred to the Army of Northern Virginia. That is when the legend began that Henry or Harry Heth was the only general Robert E. Lee ever called by his first name. Heth hardly seems the type of person whom Lee would choose as a personal friend. Heth's attention to military detail was abysmal at best while Lee was a perfectionist. Heth was eighteen years younger than Lee. The only time Lee would have seen Heth previously during the war was at Sewell Mountain and that was only for two weeks. Finally, Lee was highly critical of the lack of military organization he saw in that campaign so it seems doubtful he would be impressed meeting Heth.

Circumstances more than skill contributed to Heth's rise in Lee's army. When General A. P. Hill was promoted to corps commander after the death of Stonewall Jackson, Heth was made a division commander in that corps, barely four months after his transfer into the Army of Northern Virginia. A man whose only major battlefield experience had been in a spectacular loss in a half-hour battle was now leading an entire division.

Heth had been a major general less than two months when Lee invaded Pennsylvania. As the lead division in Hill's corps, Heth headed one of the first units to arrive at Cashtown, a small village about eight miles west of Gettysburg. Somewhere along the way, perhaps from talking to civilians in Chambersburg, Heth got the idea that there was a storehouse of shoes in Gettysburg that was protected only by home guard.

Wanting those shoes for his men, he sent a brigade under Brig. Gen. Johnston Pettigrew to reconnoiter Gettysburg on June 30, 1863. The brigade returned with word that there were at least three thousand Union cavalrymen west of the town.

Heth did not believe Pettigrew, who had been a college professor and lawyer before the war. Heth looked at him and saw an educated egghead, not a general who could tell the difference between a home guard and a cavalryman.

Just as Pettigrew was giving his report, up rode Hill. Pettigrew repeated his report. An aide to Pettigrew, who also knew Hill, joined in the conversation. He confirmed Pettigrew's assessment that the force ahead was a brigade of three thousand cavalrymen. The distinction was important. If the men on the hill were home guard, then the Federal army was still miles and perhaps days away from the Confederates. If it was Federal cavalry, then the Union army was only hours away from a confrontation with Lee's army.

Hill listened to both reports. He too looked at Pettigrew and saw a nonprofessional soldier compared to him and Heth, who were both West Pointers.

Hill sided with Heth and decided that the troops were home guard. Neither general bothered to ride the four miles to see for himself.

A flabbergasted aide to Pettigrew later wrote, "Blindness in part seems to have come over our commanders, who, slow to believe in the presence of an organized army of the enemy, thought there must be a mistake in the report taken back by Gen. Pettigrew."

After dismissing Pettigrew, Heth turned to Hill and made a fate-filled comment, "If there is no objection, I will take my division tomorrow and go to Gettysburg to get those shoes."

Hill made an equally fate-filled reply, "None in the world."

The next morning Heth's division, accompanied by another division for a total of thirteen thousand men, started marching toward Gettysburg. At 7:30 A.M. on July 1, the advance units of Heth's division ran into the first pickets of Union Gen. John Buford's cavalry brigade of three thousand men. The last time Heth and Buford had seen each other they had been on the same side fighting Indians.

Instead of stopping in place, Heth pushed forward and started to deploy his division, in direct violation of Lee's orders not to bring on a general engagement until the army was "up" or concentrated in one place. Lee's tactics were to have been to roll over any opposition in front of him with his entire army, occupy some convenient high ground, and then have the Union army attack him. By allowing elements of the Confederate army to go into battle instead of the whole army, those elements would not only reveal the presence of the Confederates, but if they got bogged down in any early fighting, they could slow down any further advance coming along behind them.

When Lee arrived on the scene, he asked Heth if he somehow misunderstood the orders not to bring on a general engagement. Heth does not mention such an exchange in his memoirs. He does write that he kept asking Lee's permission to fully deploy his division.

Once the battle was on, thanks to Heth, Lee pressed it, hoping that he could bring enough men to bear on the thin Federal line to win before the rest of the Union army came up. The Confederates won the first day by pushing the Federals back through town, but as darkness fell, they lost the advantage and never were able to take the high ground east of the town.

Heth was shot in the head that first day and would have been killed except for his thick skull and some newspapers he had folded into the sweatband of his new, too-large hat. Heth had actually broken yet another Lee order by wearing the hat. When several shopkeepers in Chambersburg reported to Lee that his men were stealing from them, Lee ordered his men to return the stolen hats. Heth had kept his.

A bad headache kept Heth out of commission for the rest of Gettysburg. He turned over command of his brigade to Pettigrew, the general whose accurate report on Federal cavalry had been disbelieved on June 30.

Heth never admitted any blame for starting the battle of Gettysburg sooner than Lee wanted. He hinted in his memoirs that Lee could have won on the first day if he had given Heth permission to deploy all of his division sooner.

Heth lived to be seventy-three.

Maj. Jedediah Hotchkiss
(1828–1899)

THE SECOND HALF OF THE SECRET BEHIND STONEWALL JACKSON

★ BULL'S-EYE ★

WHEN STONEWALL JACKSON HEARD ABOUT JEDEDIAH Hotchkiss's hobby, the general gruffly ordered the mild-mannered civilian schoolteacher to do something that would change both their lives.

"Make me a map of the Valley, from Harpers Ferry to Lexington, showing all of the points of offense and defense in those places. Good morning, sir," Jackson told Hotchkiss within minutes of their first face-to-face meeting on March 26, 1862.

That sharp, short meeting began a two-year partnership that made Stonewall Jackson one of the most successful military leaders in the world. Using the maps Hotchkiss drew, Jackson defeated three different armies in the Shenandoah Valley, stole a march deep into the rear supply lines of the Union army at Second Manassas, and finally surprised another Union army by suddenly appearing on its right flank at Chancellorsville.

Jackson owed much of the success of those campaigns to a native New Yorker who carried colored pencils and a notepad more often than he carried a revolver.

Jackson needed Hotchkiss maybe more than he was willing to admit or what Hotchkiss was to realize at first. Though already famous as the general whose steadfastness had won the battle of Manassas in July 1861, Jackson had a flaw in his command abilities. He had no natural ability to look around him and understand how the terrain he could see had any military value as to placement of troops and artillery. He had even come close to failing basic drawing at West Point, a skill most other students easily mastered and which was essential in making basic maps.

Jackson was lucky when Hotchkiss came to him offering his services. Maps of the period, as Jackson would discover when he attacked at the Seven Days' battles, were often inaccurate as to road names, distances, and landmarks. Hotchkiss' personal makeup as a teacher with the professional demands on accuracy, caused him to be meticulous in preparing his maps for Jackson. Jackson knew he could trust that a Hotchkiss-drawn mile on a map would be a true marching mile for his men. This dedication to excellence in his work marks Hotchkiss as a bull's-eye.

Hotchkiss had not intended to move to Virginia from New York in the 1850s. He simply wandered there as he walked for a few years, marveling at the South's geography and geology. He finally settled in the Shenandoah Valley, eventually starting a private school that he closed when most of his students joined the Confederate army. As a civilian, Hotchkiss drew a map of western Virginia that drew the praise of Gen. Robert E. Lee, who passed on word of his talents to Jackson.

Unable to hold rank as an engineering officer since he did not have formal training in the profession, Hotchkiss was a civilian when he met Jackson. Still forming his staff and mindful of his limitations when it came to understanding terrain, Jackson readily accepted Hotchkiss onto his staff. Not until late September of 1862 did Hotchkiss apply for a commission. He would eventually rise to the rank of major, probably the most important major who served in the Confederate army.

Both men learned how to work together though Jackson complained about Hotchkiss, "He thought my great fault was talking too much." It likely helped that both were devout Presbyterians.

Hotchkiss and his map case became a familiar sight to Jackson's men. They would often see him poring over his notes, then drawing preliminary sketches that he would later turn into an official map. Jackson often had the only copy of the map, forcing his generals to get their directions from couriers stationed at points along the map.

Jackson treated Hotchkiss very well, even regularly granting him leaves, a privilege Jackson never took himself and which he rarely granted any other officer or soldier. Jackson may have suspected that Hotchkiss's health was delicate and drawing maps in a warm home would be more advisable than drawing in a drafty tent.

Normally a man who did not ask advice of anyone, Jackson readily called on Hotchkiss to explain some feature of the map he did not grasp. Jackson most appreciated Hotchkiss's use of different colored pencils to illustrate varying terrain, an important factor when an army might be forced to quickly march over a mountain range. The general frequently asked Hotchkiss and engineering lieutenant James Keith Boswell to scout ahead to draw some preliminary maps. While Jackson trusted this New York civilian and a twenty-two-year-old former surveyor to chart the direction of his army, he refused to tell his West Point-educated generals and colonels where they would be marching the next morning.

Jackson made one major mistake in his use of Hotchkiss. He left him at home in mid-June 1862 when Jackson's forces secretly left the Valley to reinforce Lee's defense of Richmond in what would be known as the Seven Days' campaign. Jackson ordered Hotchkiss to stay behind to finish drawing maps of the just-completed Valley campaign.

Jackson must have assumed both that such a long-established urban area as Richmond would have accurate maps and that Lee would provide them. In reality, the maps Lee and his generals used were often inaccurate as to distances and directions and sometimes mislabeled when identifying roads and communities. Had Hotchkiss been sent ahead to draw some preliminary maps of the area north of the Chickahominy River, he would have discovered the confusing neighboring communities of Cold Harbor and Old Cold Harbor. Had Jackson used those Hotchkiss-drawn maps, his reputation at the Seven Days' battles may today be better regarded.

After the death of his best friend Boswell in the same volley that mortally wounded Jackson, Hotchkiss transferred to the command of Gen. Richard Ewell, who was promoted to command Jackson's Second Corps. Hotchkiss continued doing what he did best—drawing maps.

Hotchkiss's crowning personal achievement in the war came in October 1864 when he planned the surprise predawn attack on the camped Federals at Belle Grove Plantation just north of Cedar Creek, Virginia. The previous evening he had climbed the northern slope of Massanutten Mountain, spotted an unguarded approach over Cedar Creek, and then drew maps showing the Federal disposition of troops. The Confederates completely surprised the Federals and drove them away from the battlefield, though they would rally later the same day and beat back the Confederate assault.

The end of the war found Hotchkiss at home rather than with Lee at Appomattox. Within days of the end of the war, a Federal officer showed up at his door demanding all of his precious maps. Hotchkiss, recognizing their historical value to the Confederacy, refused to give them up.

Hotchkiss took his right of ownership case all the way to the top: Gen. U. S. Grant. To the surprise of other Union officials, Grant sided with Hotchkiss and agreed that the Union had no right to his maps. The two men affably worked out an agreement where Hotchkiss made copies of maps that Grant decided were important.

Would there have been a Stonewall Jackson without a Jed Hotchkiss? Yes. Jackson's legendary stand at First Manassas occurred long before the two ever met. Would there have been Confederate victories in the Shenandoah Valley, at Second Manassas or Chancellorsville without a Hotchkiss? That point could be debated. The Virginia general likely could not have moved his men as well as he did without the maps supplied by the New York schoolteacher.

Gov. John Letcher

(1813–1884)

THE MAN WHO CHANGED
STONEWALL JACKSON'S MIND

★ BULL'S-EYE ★

GEN. THOMAS J. "STONEWALL" JACKSON RARELY LISTENED to anyone except his wife, Anna, and Gen. Robert E. Lee. Anyone else who tried to give Jackson advice, including his division and brigade commanders, was met with a cold, uncaring, unyielding stare.

But Jackson did listen to one man and after carefully considering the man's opinion, Jackson did something he almost never did. He changed his mind.

Had that man not approached Jackson with the right words, Jackson would have left the battlefield in February 1862. There never would have been Southern victories like Jackson's Valley campaign, successful defensive actions at Second Manassas, Sharpsburg, and Fredericksburg, or the famous flank march at Chancellorsville. Had Jackson not listened to this man and changed his mind, he would have spent the war being the same thing he was before the war: an eccentric college professor at a small military school in Lexington, Virginia.

The man who kept Stonewall Jackson on the battlefield was Virginia Governor John Letcher. While he performed rather well as a wartime governor, accomplishing thousands of tasks, Letcher's greatest accomplishment might have been writing one persuasive letter to his old prewar friend Jackson. Writing this letter outlining the reasons Jackson should stay in the Confederate cause puts Letcher in the ranks of the bull's-eyes of the war.

Letcher never quite fit the image of Virginia's previous governors, who usually came from the moneyed, educated, planter class. He was a common-born newspaper editor who came to enjoy politics. He was an innovator. One unique idea he offered in his 1861 inaugural address was to call a general convention of the states where delegates could talk about their differences on a stage different from the already hostile U.S. Congress. No state legislature acted on his suggestion.

A reluctant Secessionist, Letcher's ire was finally raised on April 15 when President Lincoln sent Letcher a letter demanding that Virginia provide several regiments to invade the seven states of the Confederacy.

Letcher's reply was simple and direct: "The militia of Virginia will not be furnished to the powers at Washington—your object is to subjugate the Southern states—and will not be complied with. You have chosen to inaugurate civil war, and having done so, we will meet you in a spirit as determined as the Administration has exhibited toward the South."

Letcher was somewhat slow in ordering state militias formed to capture the Federal property at Harpers Ferry and Gosport Naval Yard, a tardiness that resulted in Federal-set fires at both locations that destroyed valuable munitions, arms, and equipment.

He had better, quicker instincts when he ordered the teenaged cadets of Virginia Military Institute to Richmond. He recognized cadets already skilled in military drill would be useful in training the thousands of raw civilian recruits who were pouring into makeshift camps. Within a few days the cadets arrived under the command of an old acquaintance and Lexington neighbor, Professor Thomas J. Jackson.

When Letcher nominated Jackson for a field command as colonel, the suggestion met opposition from other prominent Lexington men. They thought Jackson eccentric and even a lawbreaker who had taught a Sunday school for black children in clear violation of Virginia statutes forbidding slaves to read.

Letcher ignored both Jackson's critics and the pious professor's flaunting of state law and rammed through his friend's appointment. The governor told another of his choices for high rank, Robert E. Lee, that Jackson would be a good person to put in charge of Harpers Ferry. Taking Letcher's word on Jackson's ability, Lee issued his first order as commander of Virginia's forces, sending Jackson to train the men rushing into Harpers Ferry.

On February 1, 1862, nearly ten months after the war started and five months after "Stonewall" had become a household name in the South, Letcher got the shock of his personal and political life. Alexander Boteler, another friend of Jackson, walked into the governor's office and showed Letcher a copy of a letter Jackson had just sent to Secretary of War Judah P. Benjamin.

Jackson was resigning from the army because Benjamin and President Davis had countermanded one of Jackson's orders keeping a brigade in Romney, Virginia, as a buffer against Union invasion from that direction.

Jackson wrote that Benjamin's order "was given without consulting me, and is abandoning to the enemy what has cost much preparation, expense and exposure to secure and is in direct conflict to my military plans."

Jackson went on to say that he was resigning from the army and he would be asking the governor to order him back to the Virginia Military Institute. Technically, an officer like Jackson could resign the army at any time, but he would need an appointment from the governor to take a post at a state institution like VMI.

Letcher stormed into Benjamin's office demanding that he do nothing about Jackson's resignation until he had a chance to talk to his old friend. Benjamin, already shaken by a shouting Boteler and already imagining the headlines describing how the South's Manassas hero had been forced to resign by the secretary of war, quickly agreed to Letcher's demand.

The governor was leaving when one of Benjamin's clerks muttered, "Jackson is a crazy fool."

Letcher lost it. "Crazy? Crazy? It's a damned pity that Jackson's character or insanity does not attack some in this department!"

Letcher, who soon received his own copy of Jackson's letter, did not immediately reply. Instead, he solicited letters to Jackson begging him to reconsider. Rather than confront him directly, Letcher sent Boteler to Winchester to deliver the governor's letter asking him to change his mind.

Boteler and Letcher's strategy was to convince Jackson that the South's citizens were for him even if the Confederacy's top two leaders were not. Boteler talked to the general for several minutes, trying to make the point that Jackson should not abandon those other men who were fighting for Virginia.

That was an error. An angry Jackson insisted that he had done his share of fighting.

Boteler must have bit his lip. Actually, over the past six months Jackson had only been in one minor skirmish at Falling Waters, one major battle at Manassas, and had planned two small campaigns to Dam Number Five and Romney. Of those four engagements, only Manassas had been a success. He had actually failed to shine in the other actions. He had not yet proved himself, but Boteler and Letcher were convinced he had the ability to win future battles.

Boteler steered the conversation back on track and kept Jackson talking until he could tell that the general was rethinking his resignation. Boteler finally ended the conversation by asking Jackson what message he should carry back to the governor. That was a master stroke of psychology, which Boteler and Letcher had likely planned together. Knowing that Jackson believed in duty above everything else, they knew Jackson thought of the governor as his superior and that superior was asking him to stay in the army. Jackson replied with a vague statement that the governor should do what was best for the state.

Letcher decided that doing nothing was best for the state. Two days after Boteler's visit and one week after the resignation letter had been written, Jackson contacted the governor and asked to withdraw his resignation. Letcher's plan of appealing to Jackson, but not begging him to stay, had worked.

Letcher and Boteler, two friends of prewar Professor Thomas J. Jackson, were the keys to convincing wartime Stonewall Jackson to remain in the army. While it was the face-to-face with Boteler that may have changed his mind, it was the letter from Letcher that made Jackson think through his decision.

Was Jackson serious in his resignation or was he using his friends in high places to put the secretary of war and the president back into their places? There is no evidence Jackson was bluffing but he rarely changed his mind once it had been made up. He offered no later apologies to either Benjamin or Davis. Nor did he dwell on the offense. Jackson tried to have the general he left in command at Romney court-martialed but was satisfied when he was transferred out of his command.

The last time Governor Letcher saw Jackson was May 12, 1863. Jackson lay in state in the governor's mansion after his death on May 10.

Governor Letcher went out of office in 1864 after serving the one term the Virginia constitution allowed. He tried for a seat in the Confederate Congress but was defeated by Virginians angry that he seemed to give in to the Confederacy over state matters. Letcher went home to the Valley as a private citizen. He died in 1884.

Letcher, who never embraced a religion during his life, is buried not far from his good Presbyterian friend Thomas J. Jackson, in the Stonewall Jackson Memorial Cemetery in Lexington, Virginia.

Gen. John Bankhead Magruder

(1807–1871)

THE ECCENTRIC WHO
TWICE SAVED RICHMOND

⋆ BULL'S-EYE ⋆

THE UNION MIGHT HAVE ROLLED UP THE VIRGINIA
Peninsula, capturing Richmond and ending the war in April 1862, had
it not been for the actions of a clever, pompous, overdressed, alcoholic
general who suffered anxiety attacks when under duress.

Nervous generals are rarely treated as heroes, so history is not kind to
Gen. John Bankhead Magruder, nicknamed "Prince John" for his gaudy
tailored uniforms.

Magruder is usually treated poorly by biographers who focus on his
career-long drinking bouts, his apparent nervous breakdown during the
Seven Days' battles, and his theatrical tendency to think much more of
himself than anyone else did. However disturbed Magruder was, the fact

remains that his ability to stage a show on the battlefield twice duped superior Federal forces into keeping their distance from him. Had the Federals tested Magruder's lines, they would have found them weak. Had they found them weak, they would have rolled over him. Had they rolled over him, the way to Richmond was clear and the Confederacy's capital would have been captured by summer 1862. For saving Richmond twice, Magruder deserves the title of bull's-eye.

After graduating from West Point in 1830, Magruder served in various posts during peacetime but came into his own during the Mexican War. His bravery with his artillery attracted a new West Point graduate lieutenant named Thomas J. Jackson, who asked to be transferred to his command.

For the next fifteen peacetime years Magruder cultivated a reputation for lavish entertainment and colorful uniforms that bordered on the ridiculous. A debate society once addressed the question if Magruder's pants were blue with red trim or red with blue trim.

April 1861 found Magruder in Washington, D.C., as commander of the defenses of the capital where he had the distinction of being the only Confederate general with whom United States President Abraham Lincoln had a personal meeting. While Virginia was still in the Union, Lincoln conferred with Magruder on defending Washington from Confederate attack. Magruder resigned once Virginia seceded.

Within two weeks of joining the Confederacy, Magruder was given an important command. He was ordered to Yorktown to protect the Virginia peninsula southeast of Richmond between the York and James Rivers. At the ocean tip of the Peninsula was Fort Monroe, long a key Federal installation that was still in Union hands. It was here that any attempt to capture Richmond would start.

Not everyone was impressed with Magruder.

"Colonel Magruder in command is always drunk and giving foolish and absurd orders. I think that in a few days the men will refuse to obey any order issued by him," wrote Col. Daniel Harvey Hill.

Magruder had been in command less than three weeks when on June 10, 1861, the first clash came. The battle of Big Bethel was not much of a battle, little more than Union regiments advancing to fire on the

Confederate positions before rushing back to the rear. Only one Confederate was killed compared to ten Federals, but the public relations value of the victory was impressive. The twenty-five hundred Federals had attacked twelve hundred Confederates but had been driven from the field with ten times the casualties. That led to an early belief that a single Confederate could whip many times his number in Yankees. It also led to the belief that the war would be short, as it was assumed all Yankee commanders would give up as easily as the ones at Big Bethel did.

Magruder took very little credit for himself in his official report but the Confederacy rewarded him with a promotion to brigadier general one week after the battle. He was promoted to major general in October.

Little happened to Magruder and his command over the next year as that first sting of defeat on the peninsula stuck with the Federals. Magruder continued harassing the enemy near Fort Monroe. He was particularly concerned that they would return to the peninsula after their defeat at Manassas. He kept begging Richmond for more men to help him build a defense of the peninsula for when the Federals returned.

By the first few months of 1862 Magruder was chronicling the arrival of thousands of Federals at Fort Monroe, but Richmond seemed unconcerned.

By the first of April, Union Gen. George McClellan had massed one hundred thousand men on the tip of the peninsula. He would move out with about half that number, but that was still more than five times the ten thousand men Magruder commanded at Yorktown. Because most of the Confederacy's troops were still in northern Virginia, Magruder's troops were the only ones facing McClellan.

For the next several weeks, Magruder did what he had always loved doing—putting on a show. In peacetime Magruder dressed in elaborate uniforms and put on fancy dinner parties. Now, for the benefit of McClellan, he put on another show on which the fate of the Confederate capital depended.

While details are strangely lacking in Magruder's own biography and in accounts of the action, Magruder decided that the best way to defend his men was to make them appear to be larger in number.

Magruder ordered regiments to march toward the front and into the trenches and encouraged the officers to shout out their regiment's numbered designation while giving orders. These same men would then quietly march out of the trenches under cover of darkness, march to the rear, and then return the next day with the officers shouting out the name of another nonexistent regiment. All the while Union spies were watching the arrival of more Confederate troops and dutifully recording the growing numbers.

At the same time the troops were moving, Magruder also ordered his artillery to move. At night the guns were quietly rolled to the rear from their positions in line. In the morning the artillerymen made a grand show of arriving as reinforcements in the same spots they had left the previous night.

Perhaps the most interesting joke played on the Federals was Magruder's placement of "Quaker guns" in his works. Quaker guns were tree trunks painted black. From a distance they looked like twenty-four-pound siege cannon that had the same—or more—range as Federal cannon. Union spies warned McClellan not to get his cannon too close to the Confederate trenches at Yorktown lest they be blown apart. The spies were warning the Yankees that trees could kill them.

All the time that Magruder was playing out his charade, the officials back in Richmond were questioning his abilities. President Davis eventually replaced Magruder with a more senior general, Joseph Johnston.

Recognizing that he could not stop McClellan at Yorktown, Johnston pulled all of the Confederate forces out just days before McClellan attacked. The Confederates made a stand at Williamsburg on May 5, but pulled back to defend Richmond.

Magruder started drinking again and taking a morphine-laced medicine. Lee went to see Magruder during one of these bouts and probably reported to Davis that the rumors of Magruder's heavy drinking were true. The hero of Big Bethel and the man who had stopped McClellan dead in his tracks had now been exposed as someone who was not steady under pressure.

Magruder, however, proved he could still deceive the Yankees, drunk or sober. As Lee moved fifty thousand men to concentrate on the Federal right wing north of the Chickahominy River, Magruder was ordered to harass the Federal left wing to keep it from attacking a now dangerously exposed Richmond.

With a force numbering only twenty-one thousand, Magruder pulled his old Yorktown tricks, parading his troops up and down the lines in front of seventy thousand Federals.

The ruse worked for a second time. As Lee was opening the Seven Days' campaign with the bulk of his army on McClellan's right flank, simple scouting on the Union left could have told McClellan how weak Magruder's side of the line really was. Prince John's showmanship had worked yet again, this time dissuading a superior Union force from walking right into Richmond.

Then in the middle of the battle for Savage Station that he was directing, Magruder finally cracked.

One of Magruder's own aides wrote: "He seemed to me to be under a nervous excitement that strangely affected him. He frequently interposed in minor matters, reversing previous arrangements and delaying the movements he was so anxious to hasten. I looked on with great sadness at what seemed to me to be a loss of equilibrium in a man whom I knew to be earnest and indefatigable in the discharge of duty."

Lee could not have a general on his staff who was that unsteady. Magruder was transferred to the Trans-Mississippi Department, where he actually performed well. He never returned to his home state of Virginia after the war, preferring to stay in Texas where his service was appreciated.

He was gaudy, alcohol and drug addicted, and given to mental instability when the chips were down, but had Prince John Magruder not been where he was in April and June 1862, Richmond likely would have been captured. The war would have lasted only one year.

Sec. of the Navy Stephen Mallory
(1813–1873)

THE LANDLUBBER WHO CREATED THE CONFEDERATE NAVY

✴ BULL'S-EYE ✴

WHEN YOU START WITH NOTHING, ANYTHING CAN MAKE a man look brilliant. Confederate Secretary of the Navy Stephen R. Mallory was not brilliant but he found such men who created amazing and formidable ships for the Confederate navy where not a single ship existed before secession.

While most men thrust into a critical position would likely revert to the tried and true, Mallory did the opposite. Instead of building a Confederate wooden fleet to match the Union wooden fleet, Mallory's thinking zeroed in on how to smash those wooden Union ships along the coast and how to outrun them on the high seas. Under Mallory the Confederate navy developed the nation's first fleet of high seas commerce raiders, the first ironclad, the first ironclad to sink an enemy ship, the first semisubmersible to attack an enemy ship, the first submarine to sink an enemy ship, and the first floating mine to sink an enemy ship.

All during his career as Confederate naval secretary, Mallory ignored his critics who questioned his commitment to what must have seemed like outlandish ship designs. He also ignored those moralistic critics who questioned what they considered his barbaric endorsement of torpedoes, or floating mines, which could sink Union ships and kill their sailors without a Confederate sailor ever firing a shot. Mallory's personal gift, first revealed to the nation while he was a U.S. senator, was a single-minded desire to do what was best for his constituents and his nation. He stuck to those principles if he was representing Florida, the United States, or the Confederate States of America. That is what makes him a bull's-eye.

Mallory, one of only two Confederate cabinet officers to keep his post for the entire war, was a natural as naval secretary because of his U.S. Senate career. Elected to the Senate from Florida in 1851, he was named chairman of the Naval Affairs Committee where he was appalled to learn that the U.S. Navy had deteriorated over the last several presidential administrations. In Mallory's view not a single ship was fit to do battle with any other nation's ships.

The Florida senator made it his personal mission to rebuild the U.S. Navy. Among his successes was pushing for adoption of new steamship designs to replace aging sailing vessels. Among his failures was not finishing an ironclad that had been barely funded by the Congress for nearly ten years. The Senate refused Mallory's appeals, but he never forgot the idea of building a ship of iron that could withstand cannonballs fired on it from wooden ships.

Mallory shifted his attention to urging further support of naval officer John Dahlgren, who was designing new cannon with longer range and punching power than the cannon currently onboard the navy ships.

Finally, Mallory championed a man who had designed a ship for the navy eight years earlier but who had never been paid because a cannon aboard the ship had burst, killing the secretary of the U.S. Navy. Mallory never could overcome the government's spite to get the man his due.

In 1861 Confederate Naval Secretary Mallory would be embarrassed.

All of the modern steam frigates forming the backbone of the U.S. naval blockade of the South and the Dahlgren cannon that armed them were positioned off the Southern shore thanks to former Florida senator and Naval Committee chairman Mallory.

Breaking the blockade became the obvious objective of the Southern navy, which meant most fighting would be in shallow coastal waters. That allowed Mallory to rekindle his idea of building coast-hugging ironclads that would be invincible to the Union wooden warships.

Ironclads had been under research and development for years in Europe but none had seen combat service. Mallory planned to bypass experimentation and go into full production of a design that did not even exist yet on paper. Just to cover his bets, Mallory also sent some representatives to Europe to look into buying any existing ironclads. At the same time those representatives would help the South carry out its secondary naval goal of disrupting private Northern commerce by acquiring fast wooden ships that could be used as high seas raiders.

Mallory moved quickly on his ironclad plan, approving the design for the CSS *Virginia* before he got the Confederate Congress to appropriate money to build it. By contrast, the Federal secretary of the navy called for the creation of a board to look into the idea of building ironclads. It wasn't until spies reported the *Virginia* was under construction that the Union navy began to develop its own ironclad. Its inventor was John Ericsson, the same ship designer whom Senator Mallory had unsuccessfully tried to get paid by the U.S. Congress.

Mallory's plan for constructing ironclads was perhaps his greatest contribution to the war. Besides the ten-gunned *Virginia*, the South built other large ironclads such as the *Arkansas* and the *Tennessee* that were loosely based on the design of the *Virginia*. Mallory added ambitious plans to build a variety of smaller ironclads such as the two-gunned *Albemarle* that would operate in shallower waters.

Because the South lacked the manufacturing capabilities to roll the armor plate, production of these planned smaller ironclads fell behind. To Mallory's irritation Southern newspapers began to question his abilities to build the promised ironclads. The newspaper editors acted as if the ironclads, which had not even been designed before secession, could be thrown together overnight by iron foundries that did not exist in most of the South.

Mallory did not neglect the other parts of his naval plan, purchasing commerce raiding ships for the Confederate navy and encouraging privateering.

Commerce raiding was a legitimate undertaking by both the Southern and Northern governments. Fast ships like the *Sumter, Florida, Shenandoah* and the most famous of all, the *Alabama,* were authorized by Mallory to stop, board, and capture Northern commerce and whaling ships. No place on the Atlantic and Pacific Oceans, even close to the Arctic Circle, was safe from Mallory's raiders, all of which were built in Europe.

The legality and morality of using privateers was a murkier question. While Mallory formally approved of privateering, the practice of government-authorized, civilian-owned ships attacking shipping interests made him uncomfortable. It smacked of piracy. Indeed President Lincoln tried to charge captured Confederate privateers with being pirates. Lincoln threatened to hang some privateers but he later backed down when threatened with retaliation against captured Union sailors.

Some who still believed "gentlemen" should fight wars found another aspect of warfare that Mallory championed even more distasteful. He authorized the creation of the Confederate Torpedo Bureau, which developed, manufactured, and placed various designs of naval torpedoes (now called floating mines) in the water to defend Southern harbors against Union wooden and ironclad ships. During the war Confederate torpedoes sank or heavily damaged seven Union ironclads and twenty-two wooden gunboats, killing hundreds of Union sailors.

Some of Mallory's ideas were not accepted by his peers but would be realized in modern times. One idea was the creation of a special service detachment that would row up to blockading Union monitors under cover of darkness and drop incendiary chemicals down their stacks. That sounds very much like today's navy SEALs.

Another rejected Mallory idea was to take the *Virginia* north to New York Harbor to destroy ships in port. The ship's captain finally persuaded the naval secretary that the ironclad was meant to operate only in deep bays and rivers and would never survive the shifting ocean swells. Actually, Mallory was just a little ahead of his time. His ocean-going ironclad idea would evolve into the steel-hulled destroyers, cruisers, and battleships that make the U.S. Navy the most powerful ocean-going force in the world.

If it was a bold idea, Mallory liked it. He championed the design of the Davids, semisubmersible ironclads manned by a handful of men that were called after the CSS *David,* an iron torpedo boat, and submarines like the *H. L. Hunley,* which was fully submersible. Both types of ships successfully attacked Union blockading vessels with the *Hunley* sinking its target.

Fleeing Richmond with Davis and the rest of the Confederate cabinet in April 1865, Mallory broke with Davis when the president suggested that the war could continue as guerrilla actions. Mallory told Davis that Southerners were tired of fighting and were willing to see what terms they could get from Lincoln. Arrested at the home of a friend in Georgia, Mallory spent nearly ten months in a prison in New York Harbor. During his imprisonment radical Republicans suggested that he be put on trial and then executed as a traitor to his country.

As United States constitutional scholars began to grow uneasy that former Confederates could successfully defend in court the South's right to secede, Mallory was released in March 1866.

In ill health resulting from his prison stay, Mallory moved to Pensacola, Florida, to rebuild his law practice. He died in 1873 at the age of sixty-two of an unspecified illness, perhaps tuberculosis, brought on by his ten months in the damp prison.

Gen. James Green Martin

(1819–1878)

NORTH CAROLINA'S ORGANIZATIONAL GENIUS

✯ BULL'S-EYE ✯

BRAVERY ONLY GETS A SOLDIER ONTO THE BATTLEFIELD. Once there, he has to be trained to fight and he has to have the equipment to fight. When the war started, the Confederacy had no standards for manufacturing equipment and uniforms or the infrastructure to deliver such supplies. Such details were left up to the states. Some, like North Carolina, handled logistical problems very well. Thanks to a well-established textile industry and its own blockade-runners, the state was able both to manufacture and import uniforms for its troops. North Carolina regularly resupplied its troops in the field and at the end of the war was rumored to have thousands of uniforms in storage waiting for the day they would be needed.

Training in North Carolina also met high standards. By the time regiments left their training camps for the battlefield, the Carolinians knew how to fire accurately and take care of their weapons, how to march in formation, and most important of all, how to move marching formations in complex maneuvers that would bring their muskets to target their enemies.

For that good training, North Carolina and the Confederacy owe only one man, Gen. James Green Martin, a middle-aged, one-armed Mexican War veteran affectionately known to his men as "Old One Wing."

It would not be Martin's fault but North Carolina would pay dearly for the distinction of fielding well-trained, well-equipped soldiers. The state contributed at least 120,000 soldiers to the war effort, more than the state's entire voting population in 1861, and more than any other Southern state. More than 40,000 of those soldiers did not return home. At 32 percent that is a higher percentage loss than suffered by any other state.

As each man marched off to battlefields as far north as Gettysburg and as far west as Georgia and Tennessee, he carried with him the training imparted by Martin. Known around his state as the man who organized its Tar Heels, Martin is remembered as a bull's-eye.

An 1840 graduate of West Point, Martin's arm was wounded during the Mexican War while working a section of cannon. He survived the amputation and returned to active duty.

Martin was a reluctant Secessionist, not resigning from the U.S. Army until June 1861, two months after the war officially began with the bombardment of Fort Sumter, and weeks after North Carolina had left the Union.

Governor Henry T. Clark recognized that Martin's twenty-year career in the U.S. Army made him one of North Carolina's greatest assets. Instead of rushing him into the field as a general as Martin expected, Clark asked him to organize and train the scores of regiments being raised around the state. Martin responded by setting up training camps where he was able to institute discipline and drill to make sure the men leaving those camps would be ready to face an equally well trained and much larger U.S. Army. By January 1862, forty-one Carolina troop regiments had been formed, armed, and equipped. Eventually seventy regiments would be sent into duty.

Martin's training brought the state troops a familiar nickname. After one battle Gen. Robert E. Lee was commenting on the bravery of a brigade of North Carolinians when he said the men stayed in battle lines as if their heels were coated in tar. The name literally stuck. "Tar Heels" became the nickname the proud Carolinians gave themselves. Later during the war, as a brigade of North Carolinians was marching past him, Lee took off his hat and called, "God bless my Tar Heels!"

Once the bulk of North Carolina's troops was raised, Martin considered his first job done and requested a field command. Reluctant to let him go to Virginia, the governor gave him command of all of the troops in his state. When increased fighting in Virginia demanded the presence of more experienced generals, Martin got his wish, a brigade. After one battle, Martin's men hoisted him on their shoulders and shouted, "Three cheers for Old One Wing!"

But field service began to tell on the forty-three-year-old Martin's delicate health. He complained that the stump of his arm caused him constant pain, almost as bad as when he had been wounded twenty years earlier. At his request he was relieved of field duty and transferred to western North Carolina to guard the mountain passes leading to Unionist East Tennessee. Martin thought his war was over.

But there would still be one more fight for Martin, perhaps the strangest of the war. The career military man who organized the state's first regiments was in command at the last engagement fought in North Carolina. Always a clever man, he maneuvered the Federals into doing things his way one more time.

On the night of May 6, 1865, nearly a month after Robert E. Lee had surrendered, a small Confederate force surprised a much larger Federal force in the little village of Waynesville, west of Asheville. Earlier that day the two sides had skirmished, and a Union soldier was killed, perhaps the last casualty of war east of the Mississippi.

Martin had a major problem. The war was over, but his men had surrounded a Federal force. If he continued to fight, more Union soldiers would soon arrive and his Confederates would then be surrounded. He worried about more bloodshed when the Federals would seek revenge for their dead soldier.

Thus Martin had to figure a way to surrender a small encircling Confederate force to a superior encircled Federal force. An idea began to form. Sure, the Confederates would surrender, but first they would have a little fun with the Yankees.

Most of the Confederates in the mountains were Cherokee Indians. The Cherokee wore Confederate uniforms but adorned their heads with traditional Indian turbans decorated with feathers. They had been "civilized" for decades, but early in the war they had gotten a little excited at one battle and scalped some dead Indiana soldiers. Embarrassed Confederate officers sent the scalps through Union lines promising the Federals that such lapses in Indian judgment would not happen again.

Martin knew that assurance had not done much to allay the fears of the Federals who recognized the surrounding Confederates as Cherokee. That night they set up bonfires on the hills around Waynesville where the Federals huddled. The Indians danced all night around the fires, shouting war cries that likely had not been heard by U.S. soldiers since Gen. Andrew Jackson had targeted the Cherokees for slaughter and removal.

The next morning the Federals sent a nervous man under a flag of truce asking for a meeting with Confederate commanders. Martin and the commander of the Cherokees, a colonel named William Thomas, agreed. To the Federals' surprise the officers arrived at the meeting accompanied by twenty huge, bare-chested, war-painted Cherokees. They even carried tomahawks, a weapon their grandfathers had used, but which they had not since the advent of the six-shot pistol and carbine.

As the Federal officers kept nervously glancing at the glaring Indians, they listened to Martin and Thomas inform them that they were surrounded. The Federals carefully responded that the war was over and any further fighting would no doubt be dealt with swift retaliation. The Confederates politely listened, knowing they had come there to surrender themselves. After some negotiations, the Confederates agreed that they, the surrounding force, would surrender to the surrounded force of Federals.

After his surrender, Martin decided that he liked the mountains. He took up the study of law in Asheville until his death at the age of fifty-nine.

Marion Myers
(1838–1893)

THE BRASH WOMAN WHO KILLED HER HUSBAND'S PROMOTION

✫ MISFIRE ✫

COL. ABRAHAM MYERS KNEW THAT HIS WIFE, MARION, talked too much. What he didn't know until too late was that she would talk enough to ruin his career and his chances to become the first Jewish general on either side.

Can a civilian who never saw a battle or even heard a gunshot influence American history? Mrs. Myers did. She forever ruined the chance of the Confederacy to be the first to cast aside the white-Anglo-Saxon-Protestant criterion that had been required for anyone advanced to army general in the antebellum United States. Worse, she deprived the Confederacy of her husband's formidable skills as quartermaster. Because she could not resist the urge to blab a catty remark, Mrs. Myers is a misfire.

Marion Myers was born Marion Twiggs, daughter of Gen. David Twiggs, one of four brigadier generals serving in the U.S. Army when the war started.

While commanding U.S. troops in Florida in the 1850s, Twiggs renewed a professional relationship with a young Jewish officer he had met in the Mexican War, Abraham C. Myers. Myers came from an impressive background. He was a third generation American and South Carolinian whose grandfather had served as first rabbi of the temple in Charleston. Graduated from West Point in 1833, he had served in the First Seminole Indian War during 1836–38 and had won brevet promotions in the Mexican War ten years later. Apparently he was very good at the distribution of equipment as he was made chief quartermaster for the army in Mexico.

Twiggs liked Myers so much that he named a new army post for him, what is today the city of Fort Myers, Florida. The general also liked Myers so much that he allowed the forty-two-year-old Myers to romance his fifteen-year-old daughter Marion.

When Louisiana and then Texas left the Union early in 1861, both Twiggs and Myers turned over millions of dollars' worth of army equipment to the Secessionists. The haul included everything from rifles to uniforms to horses, more than one-fourth of the supplies of the entire U.S. Army. An appreciative Confederacy soon named Myers acting quartermaster general, the same post he had occupied on a smaller scale while stationed at the U.S. Arsenal in New Orleans. By February 1862 he was given the rank of colonel, the designated rank of the office.

Being named quartermaster general of an instant army by an instant nation that by definition was against centralization of power and authority was an impossible task. Myers tried his best. He tried to set up purchasing departments and methods of transportation around the South but met resistance at every step.

Among Myers's problems was convincing the Southern state governors to supply the Confederate government rather than just their own state troops. Governors of states like Georgia and North Carolina insisted that their first duty was to equip their own men. Such partisanship hampered

Myers's ability to make sure that all of the armies in the field, made up of men from many states, had equipment.

Despite occasional complaints from the field about lack of supplies, Myers had the unquestioned support of the Confederate Congress. In 1863 Congress decided to reward him by changing the law so his position would require the rank of brigadier general. Besides passing the law, Congress sent President Davis a letter saying, "We think he [Myers] has shown himself able, honest, and diligent in the discharge of his responsible and laborious duties and [we] take pleasure in bearing our testimony to his services and his merits."

Davis, who had appointed generals such as John Floyd, Henry Wise, Leonidas Polk, and Braxton Bragg and watched them become spectacular failures on the battlefield, refused to consider the simple request to promote Myers to brigadier general from colonel. Though presented with facts and personal endorsements that Myers was growing ever more successful in supplying the Confederacy, Davis refused to give him the honor of being the first Jewish general in either army.

Why would Davis refuse to reward a man who was doing a good job in a difficult position? It did not seem that Davis had a problem with Jews in power as he had appointed Judah P. Benjamin to his cabinet. Still, some Confederate congressmen accused Davis of being anti-Semitic.

The problem of Colonel Myers's appointment to a generalship had nothing to do with his being Jewish and everything to do with the earlier actions of Myers's wife, Marion Twiggs Myers.

The few published descriptions of Marion Myers's life in Richmond show her to be a social butterfly, a woman interested in going to and planning parties for the social elite of which she was a member. The war might have been swirling around her husband and the rest of the South, but she did not notice.

At a party in 1861 Mrs. Myers sealed the fate of her husband. The April 1861 party was to welcome President Jefferson Davis and his wife, Varina, to Richmond, after the Confederate capital was moved from Montgomery.

Varina Davis had a dark complexion and was pregnant at the time she attended her first social function. It was the custom for most society-conscious women in the 1860s to remain secluded until their distorted figures had returned to shape after the births of their children. Varina ignored the custom and played her role as first lady to the new president.

At that welcoming party, or a similar one soon after the Davis family arrived in Richmond, Mrs. Myers remarked to her friends that Varina, with her dark complexion and pregnant figure looked like a "squaw."

Such an insult was too juicy to be kept a secret. Soon Mrs. Myers's nasty comment was flying around Richmond. If she ever tried to stop the rumor with a personal apology to Mrs. Davis, the account does not show up in Mary Chesnut's famous diary of the social and political occurrences of the day. Strangely, Chesnut's detailed diary does not mention the party or the insult, but she must have been present at such an important social event. Mrs. Chesnut only cryptically mentions Mrs. Myers as the source of discomfort for the Davis family. Her lack of mention of the insult may be because she was friends with both women, though Mrs. Myers is mentioned in only a few accounts and Mrs. Davis in many.

At some point President Davis was told of the insult, but it is not clear if Mrs. Davis or a cabinet member told him. By 1863 Davis had a choice: promote the man who had been doing a good job over the previous two years or take the opportunity to stick it to the man whose wife had insulted his wife.

Davis stuck by his wife and blackballed Myers's appointment to general.

What Davis actually did was use the new law requiring the quartermaster general to be a general as a means to fire Myers. As a colonel, Myers now could not be quartermaster general.

All Davis had to do to comply with the law was promote Myers, as the Confederate Congress intended. Instead he fired Myers and spent two months looking for a new quartermaster general. In August 1863 Davis appointed Gen. Alexander Lawton to the post vacated by Myers. Lawton had been a fighting general who had no experience at being a quartermaster, a tedious job that Myers had held for thirty years in the U.S. and Confederate armies.

Davis stood alone in his firing of Myers. Congress was livid. Other Confederate officials such as Ordnance Department head Josiah Gorgas complained, though privately to their diaries, that Myers had "fulfilled his duties very well."

The Confederate Senate passed a resolution recognizing Myers as the legitimate quartermaster general, but Davis still sent Lawton's name before them for confirmation. Not wishing to beat the issue into the ground once the president had made up his mind, the Senate reluctantly approved Lawton.

Myers could have served under Lawton to teach him the ropes, but he refused to suffer that insult. He resigned from the army and had no further role in the war. Myers died at age seventy-eight in 1889, followed in 1893 by his wife at age fifty-five. Both are buried in an Episcopal cemetery.

The lesson of the story of Col. Abraham C. Myers, so close to being named the first Jewish general, seems clear and simple. When your spouse has a big mouth, tell her or him to keep it shut when attending parties where the spouse of your boss is the guest of honor.

Gen. William Nelson Pendleton
(1809–1883)

THE LEE LOOK-ALIKE WHO
FAILED AT GETTYSBURG

⋆ MISFIRE ⋆

GEN. ROBERT E. LEE POINTED TOWARD GETTYSBURG'S Cemetery Ridge and said, "The enemy is there. We must attack him." Then he ordered the Pettigrew-Pickett-Trimble assault on July 3, 1863.

Gen. William Nelson Pendleton, Lee's close friend who also looked remarkably like the commanding general, may have doomed that same attack, more commonly known as Pickett's Charge.

It was not so much what Pendleton did that sealed the fate of the twelve thousand men who started the mile-long march across that open field from Seminary Ridge to Cemetery Ridge, it was what he failed to do. He did not carry out his very basic job as artillery chief of the Army of Northern Virginia. He did not make sure that all of his cannon were properly placed to support that infantry attack. Because he did little to support the men walking across that open field and may have even doomed the attack to failure with the one active order he did give, Pendleton deserves the role of misfire.

Never much of a soldier, Pendleton resigned his officer's commission just three years after graduating from West Point in 1830, choosing to become an Episcopal rector.

When Virginia seceded, Pendleton felt compelled to again put on a uniform, which he had not worn in more than twenty-five years. Pendleton captained the Rockbridge Artillery of Lexington, Virginia. It consisted of four six-pounder smoothbore cannon nicknamed Matthew, Mark, Luke, and John. He wrote to other Episcopalians a long defense of his decision to fight, which concluded that a "defensive war on gospel grounds cannot be condemned."

Pendleton's early performance with his little cannon so impressed Gen. Joseph Johnston he appointed him chief of his army's artillery. When Johnston was wounded and Lee took over the Army of Northern Virginia, Lee kept Pendleton.

Lee was blinded by his friendship with Pendleton, who had graduated from West Point one year behind him. Pendleton never did well in his job. He failed to mass his guns at Malvern Hill in July 1862 and then again at Sharpsburg in September 1862. He lost four cannon on the retreat back from Sharpsburg when he failed to monitor the Potomac River crossings, allowing Federal regiments to cross undetected.

While Lee never demoted his old friend, he did pass many of Pendleton's field responsibilities to other officers. Pendleton shifted his attention to devising new ways of assigning artillery battalions to infantry divisions, a logistical change that resulted in faster deployment. That demonstrated his ability to think in a headquarters tent. Kept off the battlefield, Pendleton could contribute. On the battlefield, he made mistakes.

At Gettysburg on July 3, 1863, Pendleton once again meddled on the field. Perhaps what he did and didn't do made no difference in the overall defeat. Perhaps what he did and didn't do contributed directly to the defeat.

As chief of artillery, Pendleton was the only commander on the field other than Lee who had the direct authority to place all of the army's cannon. A key component of the third day attack plan was a blanketing artillery barrage along the stone wall lining Cemetery Ridge. To blow away the guns and men behind that wall, Lee needed the cannon of all three of his corps facing the ridge in a semicircle. That placement created enfilading fire, meaning aiming down the enemy's line so fired rounds would do continuous damage down the line beyond the round's initial impact point.

In his Gettysburg report Pendleton blithely claims that all artillery commanders were given "proper directions." Other accounts of Pendleton's actions do not show him spending much time placing the artillery where it would do the most good. Postwar accounts claim that more than sixty Confederate cannon were not even fired on the third day. Many of those were rifled pieces that could have contributed greatly to the bombardment.

The man who was in nominal charge of the Confederate bombardment was the First Corps artillery commander, Col. Edward Porter Alexander. Alexander did not have much respect for Pendleton. After the war he wrote that Pendleton was "too old and had been too long out of army life to be thoroughly up to all of the opportunities of his position."

At some point during an inspection ride, Pendleton mentioned to Alexander that an officer of the Third Corps had nine twelve-pounder howitzers that could not be used in the cannonade because their range was too short. Did Alexander want them? Alexander wrote that he "jumped" at the offer. He intended to hide the howitzers in a hollow, then send them out with the infantry assault as close-in support for the soldiers.

The Confederate cannonade before the assault did not have much effect in driving the Federals from the crest of Cemetery Ridge because most of the cannon were firing straight into the Federal line. What shells did not hit the stone wall flew over the ridge to explode far beyond the defending Union infantry. For all its noise and spectacle the cannonade failed to seriously damage the Union line.

At 1:25 P.M. Alexander sent a handwritten note to Pickett saying, "If you are to advance at all you must come at once." At almost the same time an aide told Alexander that the nine howitzers were missing from the hollow.

Alexander later discovered that Pendleton had personally moved several of the guns for some unknown reason, and the howitzers' commander had moved the rest once scattered Federal shells started landing in the hollow. Neither Pendleton nor the guns' commander reported to Alexander where the guns had been moved. Alexander never again saw the guns and never learned where they had been moved.

One scenario that never happened that Alexander likely envisioned would have taken place called for the howitzers, already limbered to full teams of horses, to race from their hiding place onto the field. Running at full tilt, the howitzer crews may have surprised the distant Federal gunners who would have stayed focused for a while on the line of guns that had just finished the cannonade.

Once in front of Pickett's advancing men, the howitzers would have encountered a major obstacle to the infantry, two stout wooden fences bordering the Emmitsburg Road. The gunners' job would have been obvious to them, to blow down or at least shatter those fences using canister, tin cans full of minié balls that when fired from ranges of six hundred yards or less made each cannon a giant shotgun. Therefore, the infantry could have easily pushed over the remaining fragments, hardly slowing down as they made their way toward the Federal lines.

Pendleton seems to have made two mistakes at Gettysburg. Because he did not place the guns of all three corps in a semicircle, there was not enough enfilading fire on Cemetery Ridge. Because he moved those howitzers and those guns never knocked down those fences, each Confederate had to stop in his tracks, put down his rifle and climb over or through the fences, becoming an easy target.

Pendleton remained unreconstructed. He was once arrested for refusing to pray for President Andrew Johnson. He speculated that the South lost the war because "the Savior and apostles lived under foreign domination as did the martyrs." The Federals noticed his defiance. When Pendleton visited the grave of his son Sandie, he found his tombstone marked with obscenities.

Chief Constructor John Porter

(1813–1893)

THE DISGRUNTLED, SUCCESSFUL BUILDER OF THE *VIRGINIA*

✯ BULL'S-EYE ✯

JOHN L. PORTER NEVER SERVED AS A NAVAL OFFICER FOR either the United States or the Confederate States. While his ship constructor skills defined how the navies fought, his name is little known because he lost the public relations battle over who designed the CSS *Virginia.*

Porter was a man who felt every slight, every sidelong glance, every minor insult. He stored those up and let them eat at him for most of his life.

While allowing pettiness to rule his life might be the mark of a misfire, Porter's career-long accomplishments in sharing his ship designs with constructors far removed from his personal control make him a bull's-eye.

Had the South been better equipped with iron rolling mills, had it developed more of a prewar manufacturing base around its major river and seaport cities, and had it more time, a Porter-led effort to build dozens of ironclads could conceivably have stymied the eventual success of the Union. Porter's ironclad-based ideas to wreck the blockade and disrupt the broadly successful joint operations of the U.S. Army and Navy, seem to have been workable. Had all of Porter's dreams and plans been accomplished, the South never would have relinquished control of its sounds, ports, and rivers.

Born to a Portsmouth, Virginia, shipbuilder who died young, Porter inherited his father's skills and his sense of curiosity. While working in a U.S. Navy shipyard on an experimental iron-hulled ship, Porter pondered how much more shock resistance iron had than wood. He reasoned that rolled iron plating mounted on the side of a ship at a sharp angle would make it invulnerable to cannon fire.

Porter's 1846 design was for a ship to be covered by three inches of iron plating sloping at 45 degrees. He estimated a warship of significant size would need a draft of nineteen feet. The navy acknowledged receipt of Porter's design but never acted on it. The plans have never been found in government archives. That could indicate that the admirals running the navy in the 1840s never worried about iron replacing wood as a shipbuilding material. Perhaps they just tossed Porter's ironclad plans in the trash.

Porter kept his copy of the plans but focused on establishing a respectable career as a wooden shipbuilder in the 1850s.

Porter never had much faith in the Confederacy.

"I did not think from the beginning of the war that the Confederacy could succeed if the Federal government chose to prosecute the war," Porter wrote. "We had a great many incompetent men placed in positions of trust and responsibility. We had no navy to keep our ports open and no money but paper to carry on the war. It was almost hoping against hope that we would ever gain our liberty."

Once Virginia left the Union, Porter volunteered his services as a ship constructor, the same post he had occupied while working as a civilian for the United States. He was posted in Norfolk just across the river from his hometown of Portsmouth.

On June 21, 1861, Porter met with Secretary of the Navy Stephen Mallory and Lt. John Mercer Brooke for the first time. Brooke had been a rising golden boy in the U.S. Navy and something of an inventor in his own right, but he had not spent any time designing ships, which had been Porter's lifework.

The idea for the CSS *Virginia* was hatched at this meeting, but the stories about how the idea came about differ sharply among the participants. Porter said he brought a modified model of his 1846 ironclad to the meeting, and everyone agreed that would be the prototype for the Confederate ironclad. Brooke claimed he had already sold Mallory on the idea of creating an ironclad at an earlier meeting when Porter showed up with drawings—not a model—that closely matched Brooke's idea.

If Mallory sensed the immediate conflict between Brooke and Porter he did not acknowledge it. He assigned Brooke the job of designing and procuring the armor plate, Porter the job of repairing the hull of the sunken USS *Merrimack* which would become the platform for the *Virginia*, and another engineer named Williamson the job of repairing the *Merrimack*'s engines.

To their credit, Brooke and Porter did not allow their competitive juices to get in the way of building the *Virginia*. Both men stuck to their jobs and did not interfere with the other. As built, the *Virginia* looked much like Porter's 1846 plans. Its draft was just three feet more than he had envisioned fifteen years earlier.

But once the *Virginia*'s two-day battle, first with the wooden ships of the U.S. Navy and then with the USS *Monitor* ironclad, was over on March 8 and 9, 1862, Brooke and Porter opened their own broadsides on each other. Brooke struck the first blow within two weeks after the battle by claiming credit in Richmond newspapers for inventing the *Virginia*. He then filed a patent on the ship. His claim revolved around attending that first meeting with Mallory, pointing out that Porter and Williamson were invited on another day after Mallory had approved the basic ironclad design.

Porter answered a few days later with his own newspaper article, ridiculing the idea that Brooke could have developed any ironclad without himself and Williamson, who had been shifted to support status in Brooke's article.

"I would ask any one at all acquainted with the circumstances, how Lieutenant Brooke could have had anything to do with this report further [than] signing his name to it; what did he know about the condition of the *Merrimack* or her engines, or whether there was enough of her left to make a floating battery or not, or anything about her, what it would cost, or anything else about her, for he had not even seen her, and knew nothing of her condition really," wrote Porter. "Engineer Williamson told me of his [Brooke's] aptness to appropriate other people's plans for his own, and warned me against letting him see my plan before I had shown it to the secretary of the navy."

Porter and Brooke broke whatever frosty working relations they had with each other. After their personal break, Porter continued to design ironclads while Brooke dropped his interest in shipbuilding completely and shifted his attention to perfecting rifled cannon of his own design.

While no doubt bitter when Mallory supported Brooke, Porter did not let hard feelings stand in his way of helping the South. He did his best design work after the controversy was over.

Porter treated the *Virginia,* a giant ship 262 feet long and 51 feet wide with a draft of 22 feet as a rough draft for designing smaller, more manageable ironclads that could operate in much shallower waters. Within two months of the *Virginia's* battle with the *Monitor,* the CSS *Richmond,* a 150-foot-long, four-gun ironclad was in the water and its plans were delivered to other ironclad constructors scattered around the South.

One design prototype of Porter's that was captured by the Federals before it could go into production was a flat-bottomed, two-cannon ironclad designed to fit in the small, shallow Dismal Swamp canals running from Portsmouth to the North Carolina sounds. Porter envisioned this small ironclad being mass-produced throughout the South to do night battle with blockading ships. The "Dismal Swamp ironclad" sounds much like what would become World War II patrol torpedo boats—the famous PT boat.

Porter's most successful design would be the 152-foot, twin-screw

CSS *Albemarle*, armed with two 6.4-inch rifled cannon designed by his enemy, Brooke. Each gun backed up to the other and would be run out to fire through one of three gun ports, one facing straight ahead and one on either side. Like the *Virginia*, she had four inches of armor. Her draft was only eight feet, allowing her to operate in shallow rivers.

Porter's *Albemarle* was an amazing success. It smashed through the four Union ships holding Plymouth, North Carolina, in April 1864 and later fought and almost defeated an entire Union squadron of seven wooden ships. She would later be sunk at her berth by a daring Union raid, the only Porter ironclad to be lost to enemy action. All of his other ship designs would be surrendered or captured, but none was ever sunk in direct combat with a Union ship.

Another famous, if larger, Porter design was the CSS *Tennessee*, a 209-foot long ironclad armed again with six rifled Brooke cannon. Manufactured from Porter's design in Selma, Alabama, the *Tennessee* would go against the entire Union fleet trying to enter Mobile Harbor in August 1864. Outnumbered and surrounded, she surrendered.

Porter returned to his home at Portsmouth after the war, eventually returning to his first trade as ship's carpenter. He died in 1893 at the age of eighty.

Though to his dying day he remained angry about being denied credit for the *Virginia*, Porter remained proud of his accomplishments. By the end of the war, the South had built twenty-one ironclads, all of them based on Porter designs that he had freely turned over to shipyards far removed from his direct control.

The final irony about Porter's career as an ironclad constructor was that his idea of four inches of iron plating mounted at a 45-degree angle made his ships impervious to enemy fire, but it was the rifled cannon designed by his old enemy John Mercer Brooke that made Porter's ironclads the terror of Southern waters.

Gen. Gabriel Rains
(1803–1881)

THE GENERAL WHOM LEE BELIEVED COULD STOP THEM

✬ BULL'S-EYE ✬

THE CIVIL WAR WAS THE LAST POLITE WAR WHERE IT WAS politically correct to attack your enemy where he could see how many men you had and what weapons you were using. It was also the first modern war where any advantage over your enemy was fair game no matter how sneaky it seemed before the war started.

Gen. Gabriel James Rains was the bridge between those bygone days of chivalric warfare and a new warfare when soldiers could be blown to bits without an enemy in sight.

While it is doubtful that the Federal forces ever feared Rains by name as they did men like Jackson and Forrest, they definitely were afraid of his invention—the torpedo. Today's equivalent, which still frightens soldiers, is the land mine. The sailor is afraid of the floating mine. Rains developed both variations. What frightened the men was not only the enemies they could see in front of them, but what they couldn't see buried just beneath the ground or bobbing just below the surface of the river or bay. Thanks to Rains, Federal soldiers often were tentative in attacking Confederate forts, and Federal sailors were often reluctant to run up Southern waters. Rains was a bull's-eye.

A native of New Bern, North Carolina, Rains and his brother George Washington Rains (page 240) both went to West Point, with Gabriel graduating in 1827.

Gabriel Rains began experimenting with the destructive force of black powder during the Second Seminole War in Florida. In 1840 Rains, avenging the death of one of his patrolling soldiers, set a booby trap using the dead man's uniform. Hidden beneath the lifelike dummy was a gunpowder bomb triggered when a wire attached to the uniform snapped down on a percussion cap. The percussion cap, the newest technology for firing muskets, had just replaced the old flint-lock method.

When Rains heard a loud explosion where he had left the dummy he led a patrol to the site. Waiting Indians ambushed the patrol, wounding Rains. He never learned if his bomb had killed any Seminoles, but Rains assumed the ambush was in retaliation. He believed he had discovered a new way to fight.

Recovering from his wound, he continued his career. By 1860 he was a lieutenant colonel, the same rank held by Robert E. Lee. Rains's ranking in the small peacetime army proved that his commanders had faith in his abilities.

Rains must have been torn about his loyalties because most accounts say he did not resign from the U.S. Army until July 31,1861, three months after Fort Sumter, and weeks after the battles of Bethel, Rich Mountain, and Manassas.

The two Rains brothers, separated by fourteen years in age, probably spent little time with each other during the war, as George left Richmond on July 10 to look for a site for what would become the Confederacy's major gunpowder factory.

While George was busy manufacturing gunpowder in Augusta, Georgia, Gabriel was honing his skills as a field officer. Promoted to general within weeks after joining the Confederacy, as suited his high ranking in the regular army, Rains was given command of a brigade near Yorktown on what would be the front lines on the Virginia Peninsula between the York and James Rivers. The peninsula formed a natural land bridge with water on either side that invited the Union army to march northwest toward Richmond with supporting naval ships in both rivers.

While waiting for the Federals to attack, Rains renewed his experiments with the bombs he now called torpedoes. Working with standard artillery shells, Rains developed the "Rains Patent," a fuse covered by a thin brass cap and sealed with beeswax against water intrusion. A man or horse walking on top of the cap exploded the shell. It is essentially the same technology used today in land mines.

The first practical use of Rains's subterra explosive shell came in May 1862 when Union Gen. George McClellan's Army of the Potomac was slowly working its way up the peninsula. Realizing that the Confederate army under Gen. Joseph E. Johnston was outmanned and outgunned, Rains, perhaps without any clear orders from anyone, buried some of his torpedoes along a road leading toward Richmond.

An advancing Federal cavalry column stepped on and blew up some of the shells, killing men and horses. The entire Union advance halted, confirming Rains's theory that the hidden shells would surprise, slow, and maim the enemy.

Remarkably, Union generals, who had no qualms ordering their men to march forward shoulder to shoulder directly into massed Confederate cannon, considered torpedoes barbaric. Nevertheless, they ordered Confederate prisoners forward to stamp their feet and act as human mine detectors.

Even more remarkably, Rains's Confederate superiors thought just like their Union counterparts. Maj. Gen. James Longstreet, Brigadier Gen. Rains's superior officer, issued specific orders that the torpedoes be banned as they were "not a proper or effective method of war."

Rains, apparently hardheaded if not insubordinate, appealed

directly to Secretary of War George Randolph for a ruling on the use of the torpedoes.

Randolph wrote back:

Whether shells planted in roads or parapets are contrary to the usage of war depends upon the purpose with which they are used. It is not admissible in civilized warfare to take life with no other object than the destruction of life. Hence it is inadmissible to shoot sentinels and pickets, because nothing is attained but the destruction of life. It would be admissible, however, to shoot a general, because you not only take life but deprive an army of its head. It is admissible to plant shells in a parapet to repel an assault or in a road to check pursuit, because the object is to save the work in one case and the army in the other. It is not admissible to plant shells merely to destroy life and without other design than that of depriving the enemy of a few men, without materially injuring him. It is admissible to plant torpedoes in a river or harbor, because they drive off blockading or attacking fleets. As Generals Rains and Longstreet differ in this matter, the inferior in rank should give way, or if he prefers it, he may be assigned to the river defenses, where such things are clearly admissible.

The judging of his morality angered Rains. Though the North was already experimenting with the policy of total war against civilians in some sections of the South by looting and then burning entire towns, the South's leaders were debating killing enemy soldiers while still being officers and gentlemen.

Irritated that he had not won a complete victory concerning how to use his invention, Rains still came away pleased. He never abandoned his belief that the South would adopt his weapon.

A corps of sappers, each having two ten-inch shells, two primers, and a mule to carry them, could stop an army. "No soldier will march over mined land," Gabriel wrote.

As the war dragged on and the South began to experience more Northern deprivations against its civilians, Confederate officials began to relax their feelings about using torpedoes. In June 1864 Rains was made the official head of the Torpedo Bureau. Once rebuffed, now he was encouraged to manufacture and plant as many torpedoes as possible. He spent much of the war traveling all over the South instructing others in how to manufacture the devices.

Rains followed Randolph's guidelines to plant torpedoes only around the approaches to Southern forts. The fear of stepping on these mines so frightened Union forces that undermanned Confederate forts often held out against much larger attacking forces. The best example came in December 1864 when 1,600 soldiers under Union Gen. William T. Sherman attacked Fort McAllister, a dirt fort south of Savannah, manned by just 150 Confederates. The Federals suffered about 10 percent casualties killed or wounded with most losses coming from stepping on mines.

Rains's torpedoes, sometimes heavily modified and improved upon by others using his designs, were most successful when adapted for water use. By the end of the war, Southern torpedoes had sunk seven Union ironclads and twenty-two wooden ships with the loss of hundreds of sailors.

At one point, Gen. Robert E. Lee, concerned that Union warships would come up the James River to shell Richmond, ordered that the river be mined and said of Rains: "If there is a man in the whole Southern Confederacy that can stop them you are the man."

Modern day Civil War travelers can thank Rains for a remarkable artifact.

Capt. Thomas Selfridge, commanding the ironclad USS *Cairo*, ignored warnings in December 1862 that glass jugs converted into torpedoes had been seen in the Yazoo River near Vicksburg. According to one derisive report, Selfridge found two torpedoes and disposed of them by placing his ship over them. The *Cairo* sank in a few minutes with no loss of life. Found and raised in the 1960s, it is now on display in the Vicksburg National Military Park, the only complete example of a Civil War–era ironclad ever recovered.

Perhaps the most famous sea battle where torpedoes could have made a difference but did not was at the battle of Mobile Bay in August 1864. During this attack, the Union fleet led by Adm. David Farragut ran through a field of torpedoes that were supposed to protect Forts Morgan and Gaines, two brick forts guarding the relatively narrow approach to Mobile's inner harbor.

When warned that his fleet was nearing the danger, Farragut made his famous statement, "Damn the torpedoes! Full speed ahead!" Luck was with the fleet. The torpedoes had been in the water so long that their connections had been corroded by seawater. Nervous Union sailors below decks could hear the snaps of the primers against their wooden hulls. Had the mines been regularly maintained or replaced, as Rains always preached they should be, all of the Union ships would have been sunk. The ironclad USS *Tecumseh* did hit a live mine. It turned over and sank, taking ninety-nine sailors to the bottom.

The North's best success with Rains's invention came when a Union raiding party shoved a small torpedo under the hull of the Confederate ironclad CSS *Albemarle* at Plymouth, North Carolina, in October 1864. It was the only Confederate ironclad sunk by Union forces.

While the North decried the use of torpedoes during the war, there apparently was no consideration of trying Rains as a war criminal after the war. He ended his career working as a clerk in the U.S. Army's Quartermaster Department.

Col. George Rains

(1817–1898)

HE BUILT THE BEST POWDER MILL IN THE WORLD

⭐ BULL'S-EYE ⭐

THE SOUTH CAN THANK—AND THE NORTH CAN BLAME—
one man for the manufacture of nearly 3 million pounds of black powder during the war. Without the innate chemical knowledge and acquired sense of construction and business developed by Col. George Washington Rains, the South would have run out of black powder within the first year of the war.

The contributions of Rains came not on the battlefield, but from behind the desk. His business skills were much like those of Gen. Joseph Reid Anderson, manager of Tredegar Iron Works, the South's major supplier of iron and cannon. Rains, however, actually accomplished more than Anderson, who took over a large, working, prewar iron foundry and

240

expanded its wartime capacity. Rains started with nothing more than the knowledge that the South needed to build a gunpowder factory. He had no building plans for a factory, not even a sheet of paper with the formula for gunpowder. From absolutely nothing, Rains created what must have been the most remarkable factory ever built by either side during the war. He was a bull's-eye.

The son of a cabinetmaker and homemaker from New Bern, North Carolina, Rains graduated third out of fifty-six in the 1842 West Point class. A brilliant student, he was so proficient in chemistry that one of his first army assignments was as a West Point instructor of chemistry, geology, and mineralolology.

After the Mexican War Rains married Frances Ramsdell, daughter of a Newburgh, New York, iron foundry owner. Leaving the army in 1856 to join his father-in-law's business, he proved to be the perfect son-in-law partner and was soon named president of two different companies. He was also innovative and was awarded patents for several devices used in the ironworks.

Rains remained president of the iron works until 1861 when the sectional ties that so many Northerners and Southerners felt finally pulled him back to the South to defend his native region. Rains must have thought about sitting out the war up North as he was not commissioned a major in the Confederate artillery until July 1861. That was two months after his home state had seceded and several weeks after some of the early engagements in the war.

Within days of his arrival in Richmond, Rains had a meeting with Confederate President Jefferson Davis and the Ordnance Bureau chief, Col. Josiah Gorgas. The apparent purpose of the meeting was to put Rains's rare combination of knowledge about chemistry and business to work behind the lines rather than put him onto the battlefield.

Rains impressed Davis and Gorgas. Almost immediately he was transferred from the artillery to the Ordnance Bureau and was promoted to lieutenant colonel, the standard rank of chief ordnance officers in the field.

Most importantly, he was given one single—if gigantic—charge: to develop the South's ability to manufacture its own gunpowder.

It did not matter to the Confederacy that Rains's experience with gunpowder had been shooting shells out of cannon and that he had manufactured iron. Men of Rains's manufacturing talents were lacking in the South, whose society was based on agriculture rather than industry. He knew chemistry and he had been a factory president. He was as close as the South could get to a gunpowder expert.

"Manufactories existed on a very limited scale [in the South], and none for war purposes, hence their speedy erection was of extreme importance, and had to be accomplished under the most unfavorable conditions. The entire supply of gunpowder in the Confederacy at the beginning of the conflict, was scarcely sufficient for one month of action," wrote Rains in an address he gave in 1882 before the Confederate Survivors Association.

Rains was irritated that saber-rattling Southern politicians had failed to prepare for war. At the start of the war there were only two small gunpowder factories in the South serving local markets. No one had thought to expand these factories or even to stockpile their small outputs.

"To enter upon a great war without a supply of this essential material [gunpowder] and without effective means of procuring it from abroad, or of manufacturing it at home, was appalling," he wrote.

Luckily for the South, Virginia's militia captured about sixty thousand pounds of powder at Gosport Naval Yard in April. When added to the rolled cartridges and barrels of powder stored at other captured U.S. arsenals, the South could wage war for a while before its on-hand supplies would be expended. It would be up to Rains to get his factory into production before the North started to exert its manufacturing might.

Rains seemed to enjoy the impossible assignment. Using his knowledge of chemistry and geology, he sat down with a map to determine where he could build a central gunpowder manufacturing facility.

"Without plans, without machine shops, without powder makers, without mechanics, I was required to erect somewhere a giant works. I was thrown upon my resources to supply these deficiencies," he wrote.

After a quick tour of the South by rail and horse, Rains settled on Augusta, Georgia, a small town on the Savannah River. Augusta was centrally located, accessible by both water and rail, and was far from any potential attack by Union forces. It was also surrounded by cottonwood trees that were well suited for the production of charcoal, an ingredient of gunpowder.

Now that he had the site, Rains had to build the powder factory. He had no experience in construction and did not have a single drawing of how it should look or what types of equipment it should have. He found a former gunpowder worker from England who had a pamphlet describing how to manufacture gunpowder. With that man in tow, Rains then found one of the South's rare combination architects and civil engineers.

The three of them then drew plans for a gunpowder factory based on nothing more than details gleaned from the English "how-to" pamphlet.

The factory was remarkable in its scope. Had it survived the wrecking balls in the 1870s, the building complex would still be amazing compared to modern factories. The complex stretched for two miles along the Savannah River with the main refinery building being 300 feet long on each side. The chimney, the only part of the building to survive today, was 175 feet tall. Surrounding the main refinery were twelve other buildings with walls 4 to 10 feet thick to keep accidental explosions contained.

In an age when mass manufacturing was still in its infancy, the gunpowder factory was a model of efficiency. Raw materials of niter (saltpeter or potassium nitrate), charcoal, and sulfur were unloaded into one side of the factory and the finished, ready-to-use gunpowder barrels were loaded onto wagons or barges on the other. This efficient "flow through" practice has only been fully adopted by companies over the last decade as part of "just-in-time manufacturing."

No detail concerning efficiency or safety escaped Rains. Rubber-soled shoes were made for his workers instead of leather so scuffed shoes would not create sparks. The separated buildings were buffered by earth and timbers so explosions in one building would not spread to others.

Rains, however, could not protect his building from human nature. In August 1864 more than three tons of gunpowder exploded, killing nine men. Rains speculated that a worker, though strictly forbidden from smoking, had dropped a match.

Actually, human nature was essential to the success of the powder works. Niter, an essential ingredient of gunpowder primarily brought in by blockade-runners, is also found in human waste. Rains set up a broad network of niter collectors who made the rounds of outhouses in towns surrounding the South.

The Augusta factory produced powder for three years, ironically starting production just two days before the one-year anniversary of the Confederate shelling of Fort Sumter. After ramping up to full production, the plant made about seven thousand pounds a day, operating only during daylight hours to avoid the danger of open-flame lanterns.

Augusta residents were proud of their gunpowder factory and even a little insulted when Union Gen. William T. Sherman bypassed their town on his march into South Carolina.

Hearing after the war that some Augusta residents claimed he had spared the city and its powder works because of personal friendships, Sherman wrote a letter to the newspaper editor. He explained he had bypassed Augusta in order to keep its garrison in place and out of action instead of rushing to the front to fight him.

Sherman could not resist needling the Southerners in his letter.

"If they think I made a mistake in this strategy, let them say so, and with the president's consent I think I can send a detachment of a hundred thousand or so of Sherman's Bummers and their descendants who will finish up the job without charging Uncle Sam a cent," Sherman wrote.

Rains's gunpowder works never fell behind in production and operated right to the end. When the Federals occupied Augusta, they found a stockpile of seventy thousand pounds. Rains later wrote how proud he was upon hearing that the Federals tested the powder by firing it from large naval cannon at Fort Monroe, Virginia. The Federal artillerymen pronounced his powder the best they had ever used.

Rains remained in Augusta immediately after the war. He found a job as professor of chemistry at the Medical College of Georgia and became dean in 1877 where he served through 1883. He retired from the faculty in 1894 and moved back to Newburgh, apparently at the request of his wife so she could be near her family.

Rains was proud of his contributions to the Confederacy to the day he died in 1898 in Newburgh. His will specified that a folded Confederate flag in his desk drawer be buried at the foot of the Powder Works chimney in Augusta as a memorial to his contributions.

Gen. William Booth Taliaferro
(1822–1898)

THE MAN JACKSON BOTH HATED AND NEEDED

✦ MISFIRE ✦

WILLIAM BOOTH TALIAFERRO (PRONOUNCED TAL' IVER) was a brilliant man. His undergraduate degree came from the College of William and Mary and his law degree from Harvard. He was a man dedicated to his country, even leaving his law practice to volunteer in the Mexican War. His militia skills were so respected that Virginia's governor rushed him to Harpers Ferry to help put down the John Brown raid in 1859.

How could such an experienced citizen–soldier make the mistake of signing a letter implying Confederate national hero Stonewall Jackson was incompetent to command? Perhaps the larger question is what would have happened to the South if the letter had driven Jackson from the battlefield?

Taliaferro is another Southern figure whose career should not be judged solely on his one major mistake. The remainder of his military service was long and heroic. In fact, he likely served longer than any other Confederate officer. But Taliaferro's one lapse in judgment, trying to get the Confederate president and the secretary of war to countermand the orders of Jackson, was so egregious that he has to be held accountable.

At the time Taliaferro undoubtedly felt he was doing the right thing for his men, trying to get them back to the safety of a warm, hospitable town instead of the cold pigpen of a place where Jackson had ordered them. Taliaferro's only real mistake was in crossing Jackson, a man who was not quite the living legend he would become in just a few months. Ironically, Jackson's legend would be cemented during the still-to-come Shenandoah Valley campaign. That legend would only be created through the help of Taliaferro. For criticizing a man who would become a legend, Taliaferro is a misfire.

Taliaferro participated in some of the first fighting of the war in June 1861 in the Allegheny Mountains of western Virginia. As a colonel, he soon was put under the command of Gen. William Wing Loring, a one-armed Mexican War veteran.

Nearly two hundred miles away in the Shenandoah Valley Stonewall Jackson was putting into motion an idea that would bring him, Loring, Taliaferro, and other regimental commanders onto a collision course.

Jackson had been given the responsibility of protecting the Shenandoah Valley but he had few troops with which to accomplish his mission. Aware of Loring's command to his southwest, Jackson asked Richmond for Loring's brigade to be assigned to help him capture several nearby towns under Union control.

Loring reluctantly agreed to "cooperate" with Jackson though he protested his men had been in the field for months.

Jackson's plan to capture the towns was militarily sound. The most distant, Romney, was only fifty miles away, a march of just four days. It was now the dead of winter, usually a time of military inactivity. That would give Jackson the element of surprise. The weather was mild, meaning the men would not have to battle the elements as well as any encountered Federals.

What was outrageous was Jackson's timing. His own brigade had been lounging around Winchester for weeks, having enjoyed the company of the people of Winchester. Loring's men were exhausted from mountain marching. Now that they were in a town again, they needed time to recuperate.

The condition of Loring's men did not concern Jackson. They were soldiers and would do their duty.

On December 27, 1861, the last of Loring's men trudged into Winchester. At 3:00 A.M. on January 1, 1862, Jackson began his march toward Romney. The day began with mild temperatures. Loring's men, making up two thirds of Jackson's command, piled their blankets and overcoats in wagons that would be following along behind the column.

While the day started with temperatures in the sixties, the day ended with temperatures below freezing. Snow and sleet began to fly. That night the men who had left behind their overcoats and blankets were forced to rest on frozen ground. It would take three days before the wagons with the overcoats and food would catch up with the column.

Three days after leaving warm, comfortable Winchester, the temperature still had not risen above 18 degrees. On January 5 Jackson captured Bath, Virginia. That night Jackson committed an almost unpardonable sin among military men. He quartered his old Stonewall Brigade in the buildings of Bath while Loring's men were forced to make do in the open land south of the town. Jackson openly favored his old unit over the unfamiliar men in Loring's brigade.

Finally, on January 14, two weeks after he had started, Jackson marched into Romney. He captured some stores but not any Federals. They had fled when they heard Jackson was approaching. The mission of capturing the towns had been accomplished, but it was a hollow victory as very few Federals had been killed or captured. The threat from the Union troops had not been eliminated.

From his temporary headquarters in Romney, Jackson first suggested pressing still farther westward in search of a fight, but Loring convinced him that more than half of his men were sick and ready to collapse. He virtually refused to follow Jackson's orders.

At that point, Jackson abandoned plans for any more attacks and announced his forces would go into winter quarters. He ordered Loring's men to stay in tiny, cold, crude Romney while his own Stonewall Brigade would be quartered back in warm, hospitable Winchester.

One of Loring's men wrote of Romney: "Of all the miserable holes in creation, Romney takes the lead. It is nothing more than a hog pen."

Loring's officers considered Romney to be in an exposed position, just one day's march from the closest Federals and several days' march from the closest Confederates in Winchester. They were not thrilled when Jackson promised that he would string a telegraph line between Romney and Winchester so they could get regular orders from him.

Jackson and the Stonewall Brigade marched away on January 23, just a week after they had arrived. The Stonewall Brigade, on their way "home" to Winchester, taunted Loring's men who were being left behind in the "hog pen." If Jackson noticed Loring's men's open contempt for him and his Stonewall Brigade, he did not acknowledge it.

Almost before Jackson was out of sight, Loring's officers began to figure a way out of Romney. One of them, Col. Samuel Fulkerson, wrote a letter to two Confederate congressmen complaining that he didn't think he could convince a single man to reenlist if they had to remain in Romney. Taliaferro added a note of his own: "It is ridiculous to hold this place. For Heaven's sake use the withdrawal of the troops, or we will not have a man in this army for the spring campaign."

Apparently without Jackson's knowledge, Taliaferro traveled to Richmond to plead his cause. His political connections got him audiences with both President Davis and Vice President Alexander Stephens.

Taliaferro reported back to Loring: "Jackson's prestige is gone, public sentiment is against him. The leading men of the N.W. [northwest Virginia] have asked me if he was not deficient in the mind."

On January 31, 1862, Jackson received a telegram from Secretary of War Judah P. Benjamin ordering Loring's men out of Romney. In a return note Jackson replied that he would follow the order, but he was also immediately resigning from the Confederate army because "with such interference in my command I cannot expect to be of much service in the field."

Jackson's friends in the Confederate capital mobilized, embarrassing both Benjamin and Davis into begging Jackson to reconsider his resignation. Jackson finally agreed.

The day after he withdrew his resignation, Jackson preferred insubordination charges against Loring. Rather than try him, Confederate officials transferred Loring out of Jackson's sight.

Within a couple of months Loring's Virginia regiments, including those under Fulkerson and Taliaferro, were given to Jackson, a great surprise to both Jackson and the two mutinous officers.

Jackson complained to Richmond officials that he didn't want Taliaferro in his command as he had been part of the plot against him. He was ignored. Apparently Benjamin and Davis were trying to impress upon Jackson that he could not always get everything he wanted. If he wanted men for his command, he would have to take Taliaferro.

Apparently to control Jackson a little more, Taliaferro was promoted to brigadier general rank just before he was assigned back to Jackson. Jackson complained about the Confederacy appointing "political generals," conveniently ignoring that Taliaferro had served as a major in the Mexican War when Jackson himself had been just a lieutenant.

Taliaferro performed very well under Jackson. It was Taliaferro and Gen. Edward Johnson who led the Confederates on the field at the battle of McDowell, Virginia, on May 8, 1862. Jackson, figuring the Federals would not attack at night, had gone back to his headquarters and did not arrive on the battlefield until the fighting was almost over. Once the battle was finished he sent a simple message to Richmond, "God blessed our arms with victory at McDowell yesterday." There was no mention in the report of Taliaferro's contributions.

Taliaferro probably fought the longest of any officer of the war, from two weeks before First Manassas to two weeks after Lee surrendered at Appomattox. He was wounded three times. After the war he reopened his law practice and won election to the Virginia legislature. He died at age seventy-six.

Capt. Sally Tompkins

(1833–1916)

NO ONE LOVED THOSE BOYS MORE

☆ BULL'S-EYE ☆

THE CAPTAIN, A COMMISSIONED OFFICER IN THE CONFEDERATE States Army cavalry, did not own a saber or a revolver. In fact, the captain had never even held a pistol.

The captain was a lady, Capt. Sally Tompkins, probably the first woman to hold an active duty military commission from any army in the world.

In a war where most nurses were males and in a time when the woman's place was in the home making bandages rather than in hospitals applying those bandages, Tompkins was a rarity. Overshadowed by Northern-generated tales of civilian nurses like Clara Barton and Mary Ann "Mother" Bickerdyke, Confederate "Captain Sally," as the wounded commonly called her, quietly went about her volunteer role of saving young men from death.

Captain Sally never became famous, never married, and spent her family fortune and her youth in her hospital. That is not very unusual, but what Captain Sally did that marks her a bull's-eye was break a huge military barrier for all time. Until she came along, the military-medical establishment in both North and South never allowed women to join the military, much less hold rank or any measure of power. Now, nearly a century after her death, subordinate military men salute ranking military women without thinking twice about it. Women are generals and admirals. It all started with Captain Sally of the Confederate army.

Tompkins was twenty-seven years old in July 1861 and living in Richmond when the Confederate government called on the public to care for the wounded flooding Richmond from the battle of Manassas. Tompkins boldly walked up to Judge John Robertson and asked him to donate the use of a house he owned at the corner of Third and Main Streets. Her plan was simple if audacious. Without any medical training and using her own inherited money she would convert that house into a hospital. The skeptical judge gave in to her wishes. It would be the first but certainly not the last time that a Southern male, used to women being in their places, would give in to Tompkins.

Tompkins's hospital opened ten days after Manassas, not soon enough to help the desperately wounded, but she was able to help the slightly wounded. As her hospital was just a small house holding no more than twenty-five beds, she could not treat many patients at once, but the ones who were assigned to the Robertson Hospital thanked their lucky stars. In the four years Tompkins operated the hospital, only 73 of her 1,333 patients died, a death rate of only 5 percent.

There are few detailed records that account for the high survival rate, other than Tompkins provided the men with plenty of personal space, fresh air, regular changes of linens, and good cooking. This seemingly simple formula for good health care was actually groundbreaking in 1861 when doctors barely bothered to wipe off their saws before amputating the next man's limb.

The medical men in Richmond did have some thoughts about

Tompkins's civilian hospital. They wanted to close it. It did not matter that the wounded men survived at a higher rate than the official government-run hospitals. In the eyes of the military-medical bureaucracy, a decentralized hospital system was too difficult to maintain with a limited supply of medicine and bandages. Besides, men were needed at the front lines and good-hearted civilian nurses might be too willing to let them lie about in bed rather than get them back on their feet. Finally, a woman ran the hospital. Having women in power did not sit well with the male government bureaucrats. Eventually, the establishment convinced President Davis to sign an order calling for all hospitals to be run by military personnel.

Irritated, but undaunted, Tompkins demanded of Davis that he make an exception, since she had such a high survival rate. Someone, Davis or Tompkins, hit on a unique solution. Davis did not want to break his own regulations. Instead, he commissioned Tompkins as an officer in the cavalry. Technically, as of September 9, 1861, she was a member of the Confederate army and her hospital was in compliance with the new regulations. Robertson Hospital was now a military hospital under a military officer. Her circumstance was so unusual that the paper issued for her cavalry commission calls her "sir." No one thought to make up a commission identifying her as a woman.

Tompkins treated Union soldiers with the same care as Confederates. Mary Chesnut, the famed diarist in Richmond, described the Robertson Hospital: "We saw among the wounded at the Federal hospital a Negro soldier. He was with the others, on equal terms—and a sister was nursing him." Mrs. Chesnut wrote of visiting one of the larger military hospitals: "Horrors upon horrors again—want of organization. Long rows of them dead, dying. Awful smells, awful sights." Later, she wrote of looking in on some South Carolinians from her home state who were "at Miss Sally Tompkins's. They were nice and clean and merry as grigs." Later Chesnut described Tompkins as "our Florence Nightingale."

Incredibly, even after President Davis granted Tompkins her commission and officially endorsed her hospital, the male doctors continued their efforts to shut her down. On October 24, 1862, the surgeon and inspector of hospitals praised Robertson Hospital for its "order and neatness in every part of the hospital" and commented, "The food is of a better material than in large hospitals being prepared and under the supervision of experienced ladies who consider the patients their guests."

Despite his praise the hospital inspector recommended that "the patients now in these hospitals be removed" and that "the support in rations and medical supplies be withdrawn" and that "the managers who deserve honor and commendation as among the heroines of the war be requested to [join one of] our many wards where their ministrations may be productive of greater usefulness."

Captain Sally apparently ran a tight ship. One soldier who was in Robertson Hospital said, "She would not say much, but before those rebuking eyes the bravest soldier of the Confederacy would quake. Miss Sally trusted to the honor of her patients, and it was laughable to see some half-tight six-footer blush and stammer his excuses before the reproving four feet ten inches of femininity."

Tompkins kept her hospital open for the entire war, ignoring attempts to shut her down and sometimes throwing inspectors out. Though she was eligible to receive a captain's salary she never drew any money, saying the government needed it more than she did.

After the war, her prewar fortune gone, Tompkins lived in the Home for Confederate Women. Alone, but never lonely, she was often visited by soldiers whose lives she had saved. She died on July 25, 1916, in the home. Her body was taken to her hometown of Matthews, Virginia, where she was buried in the front yard of a church her sister had dedicated her life to building.

The inscription on her tombstone comes from the Bible, Matthew 25: 35–36: " I was hungry and ye gave me meat. I was thirsty and ye gave me drink. I was sick and ye visited me."

Sally Tompkins saved fewer than 2,000 soldiers from death during the war, a number that is hardly significant in a war in which 620,000 died. But if Tompkins had been put in charge of all hospital operations instead of having to constantly fight to keep her little hospital open, she may have saved many more. Her other accomplishment was that Tompkins forced a government to give her respect and a commission. She paved the way for all of the future women officers in the United States Armed Forces.

Gen. Henry Wise

(1806–1876)

A GOOD SOUTHERNER BUT A MEDIOCRE GENERAL

✷ MISFIRE ✷

THE LIFE OF GEN. HENRY WISE OF VIRGINIA HAD ALL OF the elements that make a good story. He was an orphan who found a loving home. He was successful at almost everything he tried. Then, after nearly thirty years of a prominent public life, he made a gigantic mistake. Wise contributed to the early sabotaging of the career of Gen. Robert E. Lee, the man who would be the South's best hope for victory.

It is easy to label Wise a misfire. After all, ignoring a superior officer's orders to combine forces with another subordinate general is almost a firing squad offense. Still, Wise did his best to make up for his early war mistake. He has to be given credit for improving his command skills in each campaign in which he was involved. But when the war was over and the accounting was done, the fact remains that because Wise refused to cooperate with Lee on Sewell Mountain, Virginia (now West Virginia), in the fall of 1861, the South was almost deprived of the general it needed the most in the spring of 1862.

Orphaned at an early age, Wise drove himself hard, excelling in college and teaching himself law. He seemed addicted to politics, serving in the U.S. Congress and as minister to Brazil before stepping back to the Virginia legislature and then the governor's seat from 1855 through 1859.

Wise privately leaned toward gradual abolition of slaves, a moderate stance that took him to the jail cell of condemned John Brown to learn what inspired the fiery abolitionist to undertake his dangerous Harpers Ferry raid.

By 1860 Wise had enough of a national standing to consider a run for the presidency as a Southern moderate but he never got into the race. When Lincoln won, Wise advocated "fighting in the Union," meaning he believed Virginia could best serve the other Southern states by not seceding and by speaking out against any war against the South. When Lincoln demanded several Virginia regiments to invade the Deep South, Wise finally voted in the secession convention to take Virginia out of the Union.

It was common at the start of the war for both presidents to appoint prominent political leaders to brigadier general status. When Wise heard his political foe John B. Floyd, the immediate past U.S. secretary of war, had been appointed a general, he demanded the same honor. Neither man had ever served in the military but they both figured their political prominence garnered them special rights to be generals.

The reason for the animosity between Floyd and Wise is murky. Wise was a party switcher between Whigs and Democrats while Floyd stayed a Democrat, but they shared some common beliefs, such as fighting the anti-Catholic movement championed by the American Party (commonly called the "Know Nothings") in 1852. Perhaps the mutual hatred was based on nothing more than rivalry between politicians.

Wise was assigned an area he had little knowledge of, Virginia west of the Allegheny Mountains (now West Virginia). He started organizing Wise's Legion, a type of force used early in the war that combined infantry, cavalry, and artillery into one fighting unit.

One Richmond newspaper ad for Wise's Legion read: "We predict for Wise's Legion a reputation equal to that of Lee's Legion of the Revolutionary War. Arms of all kinds: rifles, double-barreled shotguns, sabers, and revolvers, private arms of every description will be used by the Legion. Long range guns will not be needed, though not rejected by the Legion. Governor Wise is not a man to stand at long range."

The newspaper was overly enthusiastic. Wise's Legion never lived up to Lee's Legion, commanded by "Lighthorse Harry" Lee, the father of Robert E. Lee.

Wise actually retreated after his first victory at the battle at Scary Creek, Virginia, after he learned the Confederates had lost another battle at Rich Mountain, Virginia. With a strong Federal force to his northeast, Wise thought his position in the southwest to be exposed. He moved his men to the east where he reluctantly formed an alliance with Floyd. To Floyd's delight and Wise's irritation, Floyd was the senior officer since his general's commission predated Wise's by two weeks.

When Floyd was attacked at Carnifax Ferry, Virginia, on September 10, 1861, Wise was so slow in sending reinforcements that Floyd accused Wise of intentionally withholding troops.

Whatever smidgen of good will might have existed between the two governors/generals before Carnifax Ferry disappeared after the battle. The two now literally hated each other. They even refused to combine their two separate forces into one and camp on the same mountaintop. Floyd's camp was twelve miles from Wise's.

Into the dispute rode Lee, sent to western Virginia by Davis to unite Wise and Floyd and stop the slowly advancing Federals. Lee, trained as a military engineer, believed that Wise had the more defensible position, but he could not persuade Floyd to march those twelve miles to unite with Wise.

An exasperated Lee spent several days negotiating peace between Floyd and Wise, time better spent setting a trap for the wary Federals under Gen. William Rosecrans, who were starting to advance on the Confederates.

Finally, Davis, overwhelmed with letters from political leaders telling him that Floyd and Wise's hatred for each other was hampering the military effort, recalled Wise to Richmond. The recall came too late.

Rosecrans decided not to attack and no battle took place. Lee was thoroughly humiliated by the Richmond press as a general who could not even get the Yankees to attack him.

Davis actually recalled the wrong man. Starting with the recognition that Floyd put himself in a trap with his back to the Gauley River at Carnifax Ferry, Wise would steadily develop into a better commander during the war. Less than six months later, Floyd would be forced to resign from the army after still more poor decisions made at Fort Donelson, Tennessee.

Wise was transferred to coastal North Carolina, taking over the defenses on Roanoke Island. He immediately saw the island's forts were poorly placed and he had too few men. He pleaded for more men and arms but his superiors were more concerned about defending northern Virginia than eastern North Carolina. No reinforcements were sent and Wise literally worried himself sick about the vulnerability of his new command. He was sick in bed when the Federals attacked Roanoke Island on February 8, 1862.

Just as Wise predicted, the Federals launched an amphibious assault on the unprotected southern end of the island and just as he predicted, two of the island's forts never even fired a shot as the Union transports landed out of their range. Wise avoided capture but one of his sons was mortally wounded.

Wise continually grew in his role as a general, even receiving some praise for his handling of troops in the Seven Days' battles in June 1862. Commanding the Army of Northern Virginia for the first time during those battles was Lee, the general Wise had refused to cooperate with just nine months earlier.

Lee tried to avoid the irascible former governor who had ruined his early war career. After the Seven Days' battles, Wise was shipped off to other commands. Over the next two years he served under other generals until deteriorating circumstances around Petersburg finally forced Lee to recall Wise to help out in the trenches.

After the battle of Sayler's Creek, Virginia, on April 2, 1865, Wise forced himself on Lee at Farmville, Virginia, to complain about the performance of another general.

"General, are you aware that you are liable to court-martial and execution for insubordination and disrespect toward your commanding officer?" Lee asked of Wise.

Wise, ignoring Lee's status as commanding general, replied: "Shot? You can't afford to shoot the men who fight for cursing those who run away. I wish you would shoot me. If you don't, some Yankee probably will within the next twenty-four hours."

Wise then launched into an entirely inappropriate conversation considering his rank as a brigadier and Lee's rank as commanding general.

"What do you think of the situation?" Lee asked Wise.

"There is no situation. Nothing remains, Gen. Lee, but to put your poor men on your poor mules and send them home in time for spring ploughing. This army is hopelessly whipped. They have already endured more than I thought flesh and blood could stand. The blood of every man who is killed from this time is on your head, General Lee," Wise said.

Lee then asked, "Oh, General. Don't talk so wildly. My burdens are heavy enough. What would the country think of me, if I did what you suggest?"

"Country, be damned!" Wise replied. "There is no country. There has been no country, General, for a year or more. You're the country to these men. They have fought for you, without pay or clothes or care of any sort. There are still thousands of us who will die for you."

Wise would march all the way to Appomattox Court House and would surrender along with the rest of Lee's army. He was nearly sixty years old.

After the war the Reconstructionists figured that forcing former high ranking Confederates to appeal to get back their civil rights was one way to keep them under control. Wise refused to even ask for a pardon, maintaining that he had done nothing wrong. He often signed letters "prisoner of war," but it was as much a joke as it was a political statement.

Wise continued to be unpredictable. In 1872 he supported U. S. Grant for president. He died in 1876 at the age of sixty-nine from tuberculosis.

BIBLIOGRAPHY

"A Hero Gone to His Rest." *The New York Times* (Oct. 21, 1878).

Adams, George Worthington. *Doctors in Blue – The Medical History of the Union Army in the Civil War*. New York: Henry Schumann, 1952.

Alexander, Edward Porter. *Fighting for the Confederacy – The Personal Reflections of General Edward Porter Alexander*. Chapel Hill, N.C.: University of North Carolina Press, 1988.

Alvord, Reed. "Captain Sally" [online]. *Civil War Times Illustrated*. October 1998 [cited 1 May 2002]. Available from: <http://www.thehistorynet.com/civilwartimes/articles/1988/10983>.

Bampfield, Jim. *How To Capture A Rebel Warship* [online]. Washington, D.C.: U.S. Naval Institute, U.S. Naval Institute Proceedings, February 2001 [cited February 1, 2002]. Available from: <http://usni.org/Proceedings/Articles01/PRObamfield2.htm>.

Barrett, Kevin. *George Washington Rains* [online]. Newburgh, N.Y.: Newburgh City Web site, 2001 [cited 15 February 2002]. Available from: <http://www.newburgh-ny.com/historian>.

Bean, W.G. "James Keith Boswell-Jackson's Civil Engineer." *Virginia Cavalcade* 19, no. 3 (winter 1970): 30–34.

Bennett, Joseph E. "Behind the Guns" [online]. *General Rufus Ingalls* 19, no. 9. Spring 1999 [cited 1 February 2002]. Available from: <http://members.aol.com/PUSHEE/RAMM259.html>.

Bergeron Jr., Arthur W. "James Wolfe Ripley." *American National Biography*. New York City: Oxford University Press, 1999.

Bielakoswki, Andrew Paul. "Battle of Port Royal Sound/Hilton Head." In *Encyclopedia of American Civil War*. Santa Barbara, Calif.: ABC-CLIO, 2000.

Bilby, Joe. "The Henry Rifle-Then" [online]. *Civil War News,* July 1991 [cited 1, May 2002]. Available from: <http://www.civilwarguns.com/9107b.html>.

Blue, Frederick J. *Salmon P. Chase–A Life In Politics*. Kent, Ohio: Kent State University Press, 1987.

Bonney, F. N. "John Letcher." In *American National Biography*. New York City: Oxford University Press, 1999.

Bragg, C. L. "The Augusta Powder Works: The Confederacy's Manufacturing Triumph." *Confederate Veteran* [online]. Vol 1, 1997 [cited 15, February 2002]. Available from: <http://www.rose.net/%7Eclbragg/apw.htm>.

Brooke, Jr. George. *John Mercer Brooke, Naval Scientist and Educator.* Charlottesville, Va.: University Press of Virginia, 1980.

Brooke, John M. "The Plan and Construction of the Merrimac." *Battles & Leaders of the Civil War* 1 (1887): 715–716.

Brown, Russell K. "Twiggs Family Roots Run Deep" [online]. *Augusta Chronicle,* 14 October 1999 [cited February 1, 2002]. Available from: <http://celebrate2000.cjonline.com/stories/101499/his_twiggs.shtml>.

Bushong, Millard K. *General Turner Ashby and Stonewall's Valley Campaign.* Verona, Va.: McClure Publishing Company, 1980.

Calkins, Chris. "William Farrar Smith." In *American National Biography.* New York: Oxford University Press, 1999.

Canney, Donald L. *Lincoln's Navy: The Ships, Men and Organization, 1861–65.* Annapolis: Naval Institute Press, 1998.

Capers, Ellison. "Brig General Nathan George Evans." In *The Civil War In South Carolina* 5, *Confederate Military History.* Atlanta, Ga.: Confederate Publishing Company, 1899.

Carroll, Anna Ella. *Petition To Congress for Compensation For Suggesting Certain Plans of Operation for the Armies of the United States During The Late War* [online]. 41st Congress. 31 March 1870 [cited 15, February 2002]. Available from: http://www.usd.edu/~acjones/index.html

Casdorph, Paul D. *Prince John Magruder-His Life and Campaigns.* New York: John Wiley & Sons, Inc., 1996.

Cashin, Joan "Varina Howell Davis." In *American National Biography.* New York: Oxford University Press, 1999.

Chesson, Michael B. "Henry Alexander Wise." In *American National Biography.* New York: Oxford University Press, 1999.

Churchill, Ed. "Fitz John Porter: Wrong Friends In High Places" [online]. *Civil War Web,* 2001, 2002 [cited 1, May 2002]. Available from: <http://civilwarweb.com/articles/05-99/porter.htm>.

Cohen, Stan. *The Civil War In West Virginia: A Pictorial History.* Charleston, W.V.: Pictorial Histories Publishing Corporation, 1976.

Coryell, Janet L. *Neither Heroine Nor Fool: Anna Ella Carroll.* Kent, Ohio: Kent State University Press, 1990.

Crow, Vernon H. *Storm In The Mountains: Thomas' Confederate Legion of Confederate Indians and Mountaineers.* Cherokee, N.C.: Press of the Museum of the Cherokee Indian, 1982.

Current, Richard N., ed. *Encyclopedia of the Confederacy.* 4 vols. New York: Simon & Schuster, 1993.

Curry, J. L. M. "Southern Justification for Secession." Appendix in *Confederate Military History.* Vol. 1. Atlanta: Confederate Publishing Company, 1899.

Daniel Larry J. *Shiloh: The Battle That Changed The Civil War.* New York: Simon & Schuster, 1997.

Davis, Burke. *To Appomattox – Nine April Days, 1865*. New York: Rinehart & Company, Inc., 1959.

Davis, William C. *Battle at Bull Run: A History of the First Major Campaign of The Civil War*. New York: Doubleday, 1977.

Davis, Michael. "Gustavus Vasa Fox." In *Encyclopedia of the American Civil War*. Santa Barbara: ABC-CLIO, 2000.

DeKay, James T. *Monitor-The Story of the Legendary Civil War Ironclad And the Man Whose Invention Changed The Course of History*. New York: Walker & Company, 1997.

Dew, Charles. *Ironmaker To The Confederacy-Joseph R. Anderson and the Tredegar Iron Works*. Cambridge: Yale University Press, 1966.

Dobyns, Kenneth. "History of the United States Patent Office" [online]. 1994 [cited 15, Feb., 2002]. Available from: <http://www.myoutbox.net/popstart.htm>.

Durkins, Joseph T. *Stephen R. Mallory, Confederate Naval Chief*. Chapel Hill, N.C.: The University of North Carolina Press, 1954.

Edelstein, Tilden. "Thomas Wentworth Higginson." In *American National Biography*. New York: Oxford University Press, 1999.

Eldridge, David P. "Reduction of Fort Pulaski." In *Encyclopedia of American Civil War*. Santa Barbara, Calif.: ABC-CLIO, 2000.

Evans, Clement. "General Nathan Evans." In *Confederate Military History*. Vol. 5. Atlanta: Confederate Publishing Company, 1899.

Evans, Clement. "Major General William Booth Taliaferro." Pages 670–672 in *Confederate Military History*. Vol. III. Atlanta: Confederate Publishing Company, 1899.

Faust, Patricia. "Gustavus Vasa Fox." Page 283 in *Historical Times Illustrated Encyclopedia of the Civil War*. New York: Harper & Row Publishers, 1986.

Fishel, Edwin C. *The Secret War For the Union – The Untold Story of Military Intelligence in the Civil War*. Boston: Houghton Mifflin Company, 1996.

Flanders, Alan B. *John L. Porter – Naval Constructor of Destiny*. White Stone, Va.: Brandylane Publishers, 2000.

"Florida Expedition" [online]. *E-History*. [Cited 1 May 2002]. Available from: <http://www.ehistory.com/uscw/features/battles/campaigns/blockade/0004.cfm>.

Foote, Shelby. *The Civil War – A Narrative*. 3 vols. New York: Random House, 1958.

Freeman, Douglas Southall. *R. E. Lee*. 4 vols. New York: Charles Scribner's & Sons, 1935.

Gorman, Michael D. "Captain Sally Tompkins" [online]. *Civil War Richmond*. [Cited 2 May 2002]. Available from: <http://www.mdgorman.com/robertson_hospital.htm>.

Gorman, Michael D. "Elizabeth Van Lew" [online]. *Civil War Richmond*. [Cited 1 January 2002]. Available from: <http://www.mdgorman.com/>.

Grant, Ulysses Simpson. *Personal Memoirs of U. S. Grant*. New York: Dover Publications, 1995.

Guelzo, Allen C. "John Ellis Wool." In *American National Biography*. New York: Oxford University Press, 1999.

Hagerman, Edward. "Gabriel James Rains." In *American National Biography*. New York: Oxford University Press, 1999.

Hagerman, Edward. "George Washington Rains." In *American National Biography*. New York: Oxford University Press, 1999.

Haskew, Mike. "The Account of the Battle of Chickamauga, Sept. 19–20, 1863" [online]. *Main Street*. [Cited 1, May 2002] Available from: <http://www.geocities.com/Heartland/Prairie/3274/chicka.html>.

Hattaway, Henry. "Nathan George Evans." In *American National Biography*. New York: Oxford University Press, 1999.

Hennessy, John J. *Return to Bull Run – The Campaign and Battle of Second Manassas*. New York: Simon & Schuster, 1993.

Hess, Earl J. *Pickett's Charge – The Last Act at Gettysburg*. Chapel Hill, N.C.: University of North Carolina Press, 2001.

Higginson, Thomas Wentworth. *Army Life in a Black Regiment*. New York: W. W. Norton & Company, 1869.

Hoehling, A. A. *Thunder At Hampton Roads – The USS* Monitor: *Its Battle with the* Merrimack *and Its Recent Recovery*. Englewood Cliffs, N.J.: Prentice-Hall, Inc., 1976.

Hogue, James K. "Thomas John Wood." In *American National Biography*. New York: Oxford University Press, 1999.

Hoogenboom, Ari. "Gustavus Fox." In *American National Biography*. New York: Oxford University Press, 1999.

Hotchkiss, Jedediah. *Make Me A Map of the Valley – The Civil War Journal of Stonewall Jackson's Topographer*. Dallas, Texas: Southern Methodist University Press, 1973.

Hoyt, Edwin. *James Buchanan*. Chicago, Ill.: Reilly & Lee Company, 1966.

Hughes Jr., Nathaniel Cheairs. *General William J. Hardee: Old Reliable*. Baton Rouge La.: Louisiana State University Press, 1992.

Hunt, Henry J. "The Third Day at Gettysburg" [online]. *The Gettysburg Discussion Group*. [Cited 1, May 2002]. Available from: <http://www.gdg.org/blhunt.html>.

Johnson, Clint. *Touring Virginia's and West Virginia's Civil War Sites*. Winston-Salem, N.C.: John F. Blair Publisher, 1999.

Keckley, Elizabeth. *Behind The Scenes – Thirty Years A Slave And Four Years in The White House*. New York: G. W. Carlton & Company, 1868.

Klein, Philip S. *President James Buchanan – A Biography*. University Park, Penn.: Pennsylvania State University Press, 1962.

Latner, Richard B. "Crisis At Fort Sumter" [online]. New Orleans: historical simulation program. [Cited 1 May 2002] Available from: <http://www.tulane.edu/~latner/>.

Lee, Susan P. *Memoirs of William Nelson Pendleton*. New York: J. P. Lippincott Company, 1893.

Legan, Marshall Scott. "Men and Arms and The Civil War" [online]. Lecture at University of Louisiana at Monroe. [Cited 1 May 2002]. Available from: <http://www.ulm.edu/~legan/300PL3.htm>.

Longacre, Edward G. *The Man Behind The Guns: A Biography of Gen. Henry Jackson Hunt, Chief of Artillery, Army of the Potomac*. Cransbury, N.J.: A. S. Barnes & Company, 1977.

Mallory, Stephen R. "Who Planned The Merrimack?" Testimony before Confederate House of Representatives, March 29, 1862. Transcribed from *The Rebellion Record: A Diary of American Events*. Vol. 4. 1862.

Meade, Rebecca Paulding. *Notes From The Life Of Hiram Paulding*. New York: Baker & Taylor Company, 1910.

Miller Jr., Edward A. *Gullah Statesman-Robert Smalls from Slavery to Congress, 1839–1915*. Columbia, S.C.: University of South Carolina Press, 1995.

Morris Jr., Roy. "A Welsh Journalist's Unfiled Story Saved the Career of the Civil War's Greatest General" [online]. *America's Civil War*. [cited 1 May 2002]. Available from: <http://www.thehistorynet.com/americascivilwar/editorials/2000/0500.htm>.

Morrison Jr., James L., ed. *Memoirs of Henry Heath*. Westport, Conn.: Greenwood Press, 1974.

Mulicant, Ivan. *Divided Waters – The Naval History of the Civil War*. New York: HarperCollins, 1995.

Niven, John. *Salmon P. Chase – A Biography*. New York: Oxford University Press, 1995.

Nulty, William H. *Confederate Florida – The Road to Olustee*. Tuscaloosa: University of Alabama Press, 1990.

Patterson, Gerard A. *Rebels From West Point*. New York: Doubleday, 1987.

People and Events: The Secret Six" [online]. Washington, D.C: PBS. [Cited 1 May 2002]. Available from: <http://www.pbs.org/wgbh/amex/brown/peopleevents/pande06.html>.

Pelzer, John D. "Mission to Relieve Fort Sumter" [online]. *America's Civil War*, September 1997 [cited 1 February 2002]. Available from: <http://columbiad.com/americascivilwar/articles/1997/0997.html>.

Perry, Milton. *Infernal Machines: The Story of Confederate Submarine and Mine Warfare*. Baton Rouge: Louisiana State University Press, 1985.

Pranz, Harry W. *Gettysburg – The First Day*. Chapel Hill, N.C.: University of North Carolina Press, 2001.

Proctor, David A. "Quincy Adams Gillmore." In *Encyclopedia of American Civil War*. Santa Barbara, Calif.: ABC-CLIO, 2000.

Rains, George W. "History of the Confederate Powder Works." Address given by the Confederate Survivors Association, April 26, 1862. Wendell, N.C.: Avera Press reprint, 1979.

Renehan Jr., Edward J. *The Secret Six – The True Tale of the Men Who Conspired with John Brown*. New York: Crown Publishers, Inc., 1995.

Rhodes, James Ford. *History of the Civil War 1861–1865*. New York: The Macmillan Company, 1917.

Robert Smalls' Experiences in the United States House of Representatives [online – cited 1 January 2002]. Available from: <http://www.usbol.com/ctjournal/RSmallsbio.html>.

Robertson Jr., James I. *Stonewall Jackson – The Man, The Soldier, The Legend*. New York: Macmillan Publishing, 1997.

Rosen, Robert N. *The Jewish Confederates*. Columbia, S.C.: University of South Carolina Press, 2000.

Ross, Ishbel. *The General's Wife – The Life of Mrs. Ulysses S. Grant*. New York: Dodd, Mead & Company, 1959.

Ross, Ishbel. *The President's Wife – Mary Todd Lincoln*. New York: G. P. Putnam's Sons, 1973.

Ryan, David D., ed. *A Yankee Spy in Richmond – the Civil War Diary of "Crazy Bet" Van Lew*. Mechanicsburg, Penn.: Stackpole Books, 1996.

Scott, Candace. *Ulysses S. Grant Home Page* [online – cited 1 May 2002]. Available from: <http://mscomm.com/~ulysses/>.

Sears, Stephen W. *To The Gates of Richmond – The Peninsula Campaign*. New York: Ticknor & Fields, 1992.

Shade, William G. "John Buchanan Floyd." In *American National Biography*. New York: Oxford University Press, 1999.

Sifakis, Stewart. *Who Was Who In The Civil War*. New York: Facts on File Publications, 1988.

Simon, John, ed. *The Personal Memoirs of Julia Dent Grant*. New York: G. P. Putnam's Sons, 1975.

Simonhoff, Harry. *Jewish Participants in the Civil War*. New York: Arco Publishing Company, 1963.

Sloan, Edward William. *Benjamin Isherwood – Naval Engineer*. Annapolis, Md.: United States Naval Institute, 1965.

Smart, Jeffrey. "History of Chemical and Biological Warfare: An American Perspective" [online]. *Medical Aspects in Chemical and Biological Warfare*. [Cited 1 May 2002]. Available from: <http://www.nbc-med.org/SiteContent/HomePage/WhatsNew/MedAspects/contents.html>.

Smith, Herbert. "Lew Wallace." In *American National Biography*. New York: Oxford University Press, 1999.

Smith, Michael Thomas. "John Ellis Wool." In *Encyclopedia of the American Civil War*. Santa Barbara, Calif.: ABC-CLIO, 2000.

Sokoloff, Alice. *Kate Chase For the Defense*. New York: Dodd Meade, 1971

Sommers, Richard J. *Richmond Redeemed – The Siege At Petersburg*. New York: Doubleday & Company, 1981.

Stackpole, Edward J. *The Fredericksburg Campaign*. Harrisburg, Penn.: Stackpole Books, 1957.

Sterling, Dorothy. *Captain of the Planter – The Story of Robert Smalls*. New York: Doubleday & Company, 1958.

Still Jr., William N., ed. *The Confederate Navy – The Ships, Men and Organization, 1861–65*. Annapolis, Md.: Naval Institute Press, 1997.

Symonds, Craig L. *Confederate Admiral – The Life and Wars of Franklin Buchanan*. Annapolis, Md.: Naval Institute Press, 1999.

Tagg, Larry. "Generals at Gettysburg – General Alexander Hays" [online – cited 1 May 2002]. Available from: <http://www.rocemabra.com/~roger/tagg/generals/general12.html>.

The Story of July 3, 1863: I Will Strike Him There [online]. Gettysburg National Military Park [cited May 1, 2002]. Available from: <http://www.nps.gov/gett/getttour/day3-det.htm>.

The Civil War Book of Lists. Compiled by editors of Combined Books, Conshohocken, Penn.: Combined Books, Inc., 1993.

Tucker, Spencer. "John Mercer Brooke." In *Encyclopedia of the American Civil War*. Santa Barbara, Calif.: ABC-CLIO, 2000.

Trudeau, Noah Andre. *Like Men of War – Black Troops in the Civil War*. New York: Little, Brown & Company, 1998.

Turner, Justin G. and Linda Levitt Turner. *Mary Todd Lincoln – Her Life and Letters*. New York: Alfred A. Knopf, 1972.

Vandiver, Frank E. *Poughshares Into Swords, Josiah Gorgas and Confederate Ordnance*. Austin, Texas: University of Texas Press, 1952.

Victory and Defeat: The 1862 Battle of Harpers Ferry [online]. Harpers Ferry National Military Park, [cited 1 May 1 2002]. Available from: <http://www.nps.gov/hafe/new/siege.htm>.

Warner, Ezra. *Generals in Blue*. Baton Rouge, La.: Louisiana State University Press, 1964.

Warner, Ezra. *Generals in Gray*. Baton Rouge, La.: Louisiana State University Press, 1959.

Kane, Harnett. "Crazy Bet" [online]. *Shotgun's Home Of The American Civil War*. [Cited 1 May 2002]. Available from: <http://www.civilwarhome.com/vanlewbio.htm>.

Welsh, Jack D., M.D. *Medical Histories of Confederate Generals*. Kent, Ohio: Kent State University Press, 1996.

Welsh, Jack D., M.D. *Medical Histories of Union Generals*. Kent, Ohio: Kent State University Press, 1996.

Wert, Jeffrey D. *Gettysburg – Day Three*. New York: Simon & Schuster, 2000.

West Jr., Richard. *Mr. Lincoln's Navy*. New York: Longmans, Green, and Company, 1957.

Wheeler, Richard. *On Fields of Fury – From the Wilderness to the Crater – An Eyewitness History*. New York: HarperCollins, 1991.

Wiley, Bell Irvin. *Confederate Women*. Westport, Conn.: Greenwood Press, 1975.

Williams, Seth. "General Orders No. 147." [online]. *Official Records of the War of the Rebellion*. [Cited 1 May 2002]. Available from: <http://www.civilwarhome.com/ambulanceor.htm>.

Woodward, C. Vann, ed. *Mary Chesnut's Civil War*. New Haven, Conn.: Yale University Press, 1981.

Zinnen Jr., Captain Robert O. "City Point: The Tool that Gave General Grant Victory" [online]. *Quartermaster Professional Bulletin, Spring, 1991*. [Cited 1 May 2002]. Available from: <http://www.qmfound.com/citypt.htm>.

INDEX

ABOUT THE AUTHOR

CLINT JOHNSON, 49, IS A NATIVE OF THE UNMAPPED FARMING community of Fish Branch, Florida, in Hardee County. He majored in journalism at the University of Florida and started studying the War as a fourth grader in Arcadia, Florida, after his teacher told an exciting story about how the young boys and old men around Tallahassee banded together in a militia to defeat the Federals at the Battle of Natural Bridge.

The young boys (14 to 18-year-olds) were students at West Florida Seminary (later Florida State University). Clint identified with the boys and has been studying the War ever since. He is still fascinated with the Federal commander (Gen. John Newton) of that little battle. Newton was blackballed by the Federal high command after complaining about Burnside at Fredericksburg. (Clint is convinced he attacked at Natural Bridge to win back some prestige.)

A Civil War reenactor for 25 years, Clint serves as a color corporal with the Twenty-sixth Regiment of North Carolina Troops, which goes as the Twenty-fourth Michigan when serving as Federal. He is a descendant of Confederates from Florida, Alabama, and Georgia, including one soldier whose pension application says he was "addle-brained by the war."

Other books by Clint Johnson include: *Touring The Carolinas Civil War Sites* (1996), *Civil War Blunders* (1997), *Touring Virginia's and West Virginia's Civil War Sites* (1999), *In The Footsteps of Robert E. Lee* (2001), and *In The Footsteps of Stonewall Jackson* (2002).

Clint is a freelance business writer currently living in Winston-Salem, North Carolina.